A Comparative Analysis of Cicero and Aquinas

Also available from Bloomsbury

Aristotle and Natural Law, Tony Burns
Cicero, Kathryn Tempest
Plotinus the Platonist, David J. Yount

A Comparative Analysis of Cicero and Aquinas

Nature and the Natural Law

Charles P. Nemeth

Bloomsbury Academic
An imprint of Bloomsbury Publishing Plc

B L O O M S B U R Y
LONDON • OXFORD • NEW YORK • NEW DELHI • SYDNEY

Bloomsbury Academic
An imprint of Bloomsbury Publishing Plc

50 Bedford Square
London
WC1B 3DP
UK

1385 Broadway
New York
NY 10018
USA

www.bloomsbury.com

BLOOMSBURY and the Diana logo are trademarks of Bloomsbury Publishing Plc

First published 2017

British Library Cataloguing-in-Publication Data
A catalogue record for this book is available from the British Library.

ISBN: HB: 978-1-3500-0946-2
ePDF: 978-1-3500-0948-6
ePub: 978-1-3500-0947-9

Library of Congress Cataloging-in-Publication Data
A catalog record for this book is available from the Library of Congress.

Series: Bloomsbury Studies in Ancient Philosophy

Typeset by Newgen Knowledge Works Pvt Ltd., Chennai, India
Printed and bound in Great Britain

To Michael Augustine Nemeth—my youngest of seven splendid children—now all adults and all making a difference in a world in dire need of virtue.

For in Michael Augustine, there is that classical spark—that desire to connect to what has been and shall always be true.

To the Vincentians, the Benedictines, and the Sulpicians—priest teachers who instilled my unquenchable yearning for St. Thomas Aquinas.

Contents

Preface

The question of whether St. Thomas Aquinas and Cicero are philosophically, morally, and ethically compatible at any level has been considered in various settings throughout the history of the West. Each figure brings his own, exceedingly rich background and intellectual preparation to the forefront in a wave, almost a horde of publications and texts. Both are extraordinarily prolific writers on a wide range of topical considerations. Both are considered major intellectual forces in their own lifetimes—held to account for their often provocative viewpoints and critiques. In many ways, while their occupations were vastly different from one another, Cicero, the lawyer-philosopher, and Aquinas, the theologian, philosopher, Dominican priest— their intellectual interests met at many a compatible crossroad and each thinker thought about similar subjects in curiously similar ways. This uncanny complementariness provided the initial impetus for this undertaking, asking how two figures so vastly far apart in time and space, in culture and occupation, and in station and position, could be on the same page so to speak. Despite all the anecdotal evidence of these similarities, no text of any substantial coverage had ever been written on this comparison. In short, what of Cicero and Aquinas—at least in a comparative sense?

Chapter 1 introduces the reader to this comparative reality of Cicero and St. Thomas and prods the reader to stress their obvious differences but more importantly to discover the compatibility of their approaches. Aligned to this general purpose are a host of rationales for this scholarship: what if a pagan and Roman Catholicism's Angelic Doctor agree on moral questions; what does this agreement say about how truth may be discovered in moral and ethical dilemmas; and, finally, if agreement seems apparent in some corners of this analysis, how can any philosopher or moral agent argue that universality in moral reasoning is an impossibility? In this way, the text forces a variety of questions that challenge the traditional caricatures of natural law reasoning, it being the stuff of prelates and ecclesiastical types rather than the conclusions of reason, which examines nature, the scientific world, and the natural order of the universe itself. The chapter delivers a full background of each thinker and outlines the many works they authored during their powerful lifetimes.

In Chapter 2, the comparison commences with a stress on nature, the natural order, natural design, and natural use as providing a rationale for moral measure. In this narrower way, both thinkers tend to the biological and the biogenic nature of things—how things work and what functions, purposes, or ends each being seeks. Nature, at its base, is a highly scientific way of looking at ethical parameters, and Cicero does just that. Cicero's cosmology is often mistaken for a sort of global pantheism that subsumes a vision of the gods or God into an operational whole. Certainly, Cicero's language can lead in that direction. This interpretation tends to be more caricature than reality for Cicero gazes at how things are and work not simply to prove the natural order for its own sake but because he resides in the natural order, and as he learns how things work and play out, these observations lead to instructions for proper behavior and moral propriety. Indeed, the natural order of an easily discoverable universe makes clear what is good and what is bad behavior. For example, excessive drinking or eating undercuts our natural health and operational efficiency and therefore cannot be good, correct, or just behavior. Another illustration might be promiscuity, which nature has a great deal to edify concerning its consequences, a sexual frenzy that has triggered the wave of STD's that plague the physical body. And in a more functional sense, our eyes, our hands, our appendages have express purposes and express usages, not because we imagine it but because we can deduce those usages with our overall well-being. St. Thomas fully concurs on this examination but fleshes it out with a stronger and more cogent theological analysis especially since God could only create a nature and natural order that would tend to its preservation rather than its destruction. In essence, the observable world operates as the natural law dictates or commands. God makes only a natural order that makes perfect sense. Thomas becomes much particularized about human action, whether sexual or familial, isolated or communal, and applies what occurs in the natural world. Hence for both thinkers, nature and the natural order is a series of instructions that contribute to a comprehensive view of what the natural law is. In many respects, it is a vision of the natural law on autopilot because nature does not choose this or that but rather, nature simply is. Finally, nature and the natural order for both Cicero and Aquinas, mirror the creative process and the Creator who would not likely shape and author a universe or a function that operates in chaos or disorder.

Chapter 3 takes us to the next level of natural law consideration in both Cicero and Aquinas, each of whom placed reason and rationality in the natural context. Reason, for Cicero and Aquinas, was a component piece in the makeup of the human person—a part of the larger composite of Homo sapiens. Reason, since it is part of our natural makeup, is bound to nature and the natural order just as eyes and teeth carry out specific functions for the human player. To be sure, reason cannot be equated with an eye or a ear, and admittedly the comparison is one of extreme degree, although valid. Every human person possesses reason as part of their makeup and constitution. Cicero and Aquinas would hold that thinking, reasoning, judging, and critically examining are as natural to the human person as hunger itself. So at its base, reason is a natural functionality and a piece of a larger puzzle, while at the same time a uniquely human characteristic.

While much of natural order analysis requires more observation than thinking, the application of reason, aside from being a further building block in the natural order, reflects Cicero's and Aquinas's preference that reason serves as the intellectual center for natural law reasoning and that in reason itself we can discover the content, sum, and substance of what the natural law means and is. Natural law is more than a series of mindless commands and proscriptions and instead, a dynamic series of rational conclusions and judgments about how the human person lives in accordance with its content. Natural law is gauged and evaluated intellectually, not emotionally or by willful deliberation and given this rock hard conclusion. Cicero and Aquinas have no reservations finding universality and consistency in natural law precepts. They tether their natural law philosophy to a rational and thinking being, first, in the human person, each of whom possess reason, and, second, in God, the only other being that possesses reason. In this sense, reason reflects God and gives rise to the long-standing Christian view that the human person is made in the image

Chapter 4 assesses the overall compatibility of Cicero and Aquinas to the content, theory, and application of the natural law. As already noted, each thinker gravitates to natural thinking, to a naturalistic method by which the universe and the beings within it operate and exist. Both parties emphasize the role of reason in the discovery of natural law principles and tenets and, as a result, conclude that natural law concepts are not relative but universal and global in application. In addition, Cicero and Aquinas posit a natural law theory that depends upon a higher, theological order for its full discovery and understanding. In the final analysis, while Aquinas is more precise, both he and Cicero put forth an ad seriatim list of human conducts that comport or disagree with their natural law reasoning. That is the chief aim of Chapter 4—to determine or decipher the commonality and difference in specific natural law precepts.

At first reading, Cicero's template for the natural law lacks the systematic precision of St. Thomas and in places, the emphasis differs markedly. What can be concluded is that both figures hold similarly:

1. A natural law emanates from a Creator
2. A natural law imprint or reflection is impressed on every human being
3. Natural law precepts, inclinations, and dispositions are identifiable
4. The natural law is universal and unchangeable
5. The natural law is rooted in reason and not in will, passions, or appetites
6. The natural law is the same for every person
7. The natural law is superior to every human law, though subservient and dependent upon a higher eternal or divine law

While some disagreement exists, it may be explained as more stylistic and cultural than substantive. In other words, the natural law theory of Cicero is really in its infancy stage when compared with the life and times of St. Thomas. Argued from another slant, Cicero is advancing a natural law theory—its most developed version to date—in a theoretical sense, still anticipating its application in particular situations. For example, while St. Thomas looks at suicide as being contrary to natural law, Cicero never touches the subject matter—due to ignorance, cultural tolerance of the "noble" suicide, or other reasons. The same could be said of adultery, fornication, and other cultural practices now so certainly in opposition to the natural law of the thirteenth century, although Cicero was silent on these dilemmas. Hence, there is a gap between the theory of the natural law and its practical application to specific moral settings. In other words, Cicero lacks actual experience testing the natural law consequences of one form of behavior or another. The morality of pagan Rome was strikingly different from that of Christian Europe in AD 1275.

In addition, the styles and methods of each figure are just as radically different. While St. Thomas continues his scientific approach to posing queries with the subsequent didactic and debate, Cicero continues to walk along his endless river trying to cajole and dialogue with his many peers to discover the ultimate truth of things. Cicero always has a harder time pinning the information down than Aquinas. But in the final analysis, they both arrive at a remarkably similar station with even more remarkably similar results.

Chapter 5 weighs the compatibility of these major philosophical players in the history of the West. At its heart, the analysis delves into whether their respective theories of nature, reason, the natural order, and the natural law easily blend and rest comfortably with one another. In more particular terms, does the natural law theory of Cicero and Aquinas reflect a compatible vision or a horizon of contrast and difference? Will Cicero and Aquinas invoke the divine element so often aligned with natural law reasoning and often critiqued for its overly theological nature? With that divine perspective in mind, how does it impact the propriety and correctness of human law and its various promulgations? In conjunction with this examination, Chapter 5 demonstrates the interplay and interweaving that is utterly predictable when using terms such as the law of nature and the natural law – a distinction with multiple meanings. In the case of Cicero, it seems to manifest his biological edge when compared to Aquinas. That each advocates a natural law is undeniable and that the natural law is fully discoverable in reason itself and the rational makeup of the human person is just as obvious. Cicero and Aquinas, at first glance, appear to agree on the elementary elements of a natural law system. The concurrence is evident on some sides of the argument such as universality, immutability, and exchangeability. However, as the analysis descends into more particularized moral questions, such as promiscuity, abortion, homosexuality, and other issues, that agreement appears less certain. While stoical visions of nature, the cosmos, and the natural order are part of the Ciceronian dialogue, in addition to debate about how positive law can never be an adequate system for discovering the right and just, the overall systematic treatment of natural law is almost infantile when compared to St. Thomas. Cicero does not offer an encyclopedic vision of the natural law, but rather imparts pieces of something that Thomas will microscopically scrutinize. What Thomas offers comprises a comprehensive scrutiny of every facet of the natural law—from its biogenic connectivity to nature, to its rules and commands fully discoverable in reason, and with extraordinary clarity and specificity as to those applications, to its ultimate tie to the divine mind of God Himself. In the end, the question of whether Cicero and Aquinas are closer than most realize represents the most powerful conclusion of this humble analysis.

Acknowledgments

It is difficult to imagine a work of this sort coming about due to the efforts of the pen and writer alone. Of course, anything authored by St. Thomas has an unrivaled originality yet still owes its creation to other forces. Where would St. Thomas be without Aristotle—or Cicero for that matter? And the same can be said of Cicero whose works, even though largely tied to experience and his lawyerly profession, display a metaphysical depth that only comes about because of Plato, Aristotle, and his progeny. Indeed, nothing arises in a vacuum.

In this text, the debts to others are many and numerous. First, to the City University of New York and the PSC Enhanced Award program for scholars looking to examine something in great depth, my thanks for the funding and environment to accomplish the task. Second, to the John Jay Research Foundation staff, who are always encouraging, always helpful, and forever positive about the projects we submit. This is particularly true of Susy Mendes; the college is lucky to have her on staff. Third, my appreciation extends to John Jay's provost, Dr. Jane Bowers, who really creates the setting for scholarship for faculty—despite the lean budgets and economic pressures faced by CUNY. In granting release for this project, she provided the impetus for getting the job done.

At the research level, the project was greatly aided by the sophisticated skills of my research assistant Ina Wanca, who delivered exceptional updates and the latest findings on a subject matter, namely, the blend of Cicero and Aquinas, that no one had yet tackled. I was always confident that the topic had been scoured at every imaginable level and Ina provided that assurance. To the staff and librarians of St. Michael's College at the University of Toronto where the holdings of the Pontifical College of Medieval Studies is housed, my highest plaudits. The collection at St. Michael's is a rich Thomistic treasure that is accessible, current, and unrivaled in breadth and depth. Next, pulling the text together from an editorial perspective is a massive undertaking that calls for precision, attention to detail, and an ability to give cohesion to material that can be difficult. Hope Coddington does this without much effort and is a first-rate editor. Editorial suggestions and critiques from Professor Kevin Govern of Ave Maria Law School and Professor Ronald J. Rychlak of the University of Mississippi were not only incorporated but deeply appreciated. Their reputations for scholarship and ethical rigor are richly deserved.

Finally, heartfelt thanks to Andrew Wardell and Bloomsbury Publishing for taking on this project. In an age when academic presses are buffeted by many forces, both economic and political, and when most presses have difficulty engaging anything previous to the twentieth century, Bloomsbury takes on ancient and medieval subject matter with an unrivaled passion.

Charles P. Nemeth JD, PhD, LLM
Chair and Professor
John Jay College of Criminal Justice
New York
December 2016

1

Background and Context: Cicero and Aquinas

Introduction

The fact that philosophers, theologians, and ethicists have been on a continuous mission to discover principles that constitute proper moral action has been obvious for most of recorded history. Exactly how we are to live in society, and under what measurable standards of moral and ethical scrutiny, encompasses a large part of the debate. For some, the search remains impossible, a pipe dream and an overall exercise in futility for such questions cannot be answered in a universe so utterly chaotic or relative. For others, the question of good or proper behavior is strictly a reflection of cultural relativity, socialization, and formation that is dependent on personal experience. In this setting, decisions on standards for human life can never really be discerned—at least in a universal sense. Some would argue that this drift toward an incapacity to formalize and finalize moral standards is a trend best described as "ominous."[1]

In other schools of inquiry, the conclusion on proper moral action is based on what is of use or utility;[2] whether the act is pleasurable or not; how power and status compel the answer; how the Sacred Scriptures dictate a particular recipe for life. Other select proponents present rationality, custom and use, tradition, cosmology, and history as the basis for their analysis. For more than 4,000 years, since the earliest Greek philosophers penned their wisdom on ancient documents, commentators have mightily yearned for an ad seriatim listing of what makes action right or wrong.

While it is surely certain that explanations undoubtedly vary throughout the course of history, there are identifiable threads of explanation that never evaporate from the discourse. For example, within this long-term analysis, it cannot be disputed that the role of the gods or God has been proffered as a meaningful force in this discernment. Neither would it be sensible to deny our observations based on experience and the objective reality we encounter, nor on the subjective reality that we hope to be true. In another vein, matters on morals and ethics often find significant meaning and explanation in particular religious traditions and authority such as in the case of the Decalogue, the Magisterium, the Torah's rabbinical instructions, and the Koran's express directives for a productive and adherent life. All of these concepts appear and reappear continuously in the analysis of moral and ethical explanation.

In a larger context, this quest can be reduced to two fundamental trends. First, those that define human nature based on needs, wants, and desires—and thusly the moral and ethical rules need to mirror these criteria. Second, those that argue that an ethic built on the individual horizon is destined to collapse on its faulty and unpredictable foundations, and, as a result, some type of "teleology" is necessary for this determination.[3] In other words, there cannot be, the latter school claims, any moral or ethical system without a dependency on something higher than or external to the human player. Alasdair MacIntyre's *After Virtue*[4] appears to have identified the lack of teleology as guaranteed "failure."[5]

> On the one hand the individual moral agent, freed from hierarchy and teleology, conceives of himself and is conceived by moral philosophers as sovereign in his moral authority. On the other hand, the inherited, if partially transformed rules of morality have to be found some new status, deprived as they have been of their older teleological character and their even more ancient categorical character as an ultimately divine law.[6]

MacIntyre, among many others, appreciates this extraordinary chasm in those that crave the personal over the teleological. In the former instance, man is essentially a moral agent with little or no boundaries, while in the latter case, he or she may grasp something more perennial or permanent. In an individual world, what is of use to you may be of no use to me, and therein lays the vacuum. Platitudes about doing the right thing, being kind to others, and showing respect to your neighbor mean nothing to some and everything to others. MacIntyre further dissects the inevitable futility of an ethical system devoid of some sort of higher authority when he refers to these individualized arguments as nothing more than "moral fictions" because this sort of rationale fails to provide "objective and impersonal criterion" resulting in a "gap" that cannot be bridged.[7] Schools of individual preference, whether utilitarian, consequential, or functionalist by design, favor the one by one ethical construct without much appeal to higher authority. Getting your hands wrapped around this approach, for the purposes of delineating some formula for proper human action is simply, and very practically, impossible. Individualism means what it says—it is "my" determination not yours and I shall be damned if we need go any further than my present considerations. Jeremy Bentham's entire ethical edifice is built on this conceptual framework since his pleasures sought and pain avoided undergirding could never be universalized.[8] Each person unto his own tastes cannot lead to a precise conclusion about what works and what does not for the human species. Jean Porter's insights illustrate the dilemma by declaring the Bentham approach a form of "rational egotism" emanating from isolated individuals.[9]

What alternative evolution could there be when an ethical system is built on personal preference and desire? Nothing, and to be plain and unequivocal, nothing can be safe in a system where one's desire is construed as just as good as any other. While it is accepted that Bentham and his adherents looked further toward the majoritarian count—the greatest benefits to the greatest number of people counted—this too cannot be depended upon, though advocates of utility theory wander the halls of academia with majoritarian numbers.[10] Heinrich Rommen's philosophical masterpiece *The Natural Law: A Study in Legal and Social History*, written during the terror years of Hitler's Third Reich, captures the futility of the utility argument:

> The moral law is far from being intrinsic and objective; even the utility of our actions is not an objective quality. It is consequently but a sum of societary conventions that are adapted to serve human needs and urges according to our experiences, which, however, may be superseded by different experiences at some future time.[11]

A moral or ethical system built on collective preference is just as faulty as the individual version. Rommen witnessed the contagion and fervor of an adoring German population over one of the worst moral agents in history, a man capable of morally justifying the death of millions because it was his preference and choice, while his infatuated supporters swooned in either direct praise or abject silence. Rommen decries a moral formula that depends on the "*Volkgeist* or spirit of the people."[12]

Something more dependable and more meaningful than the whim and fancy of the one or the many is crucial in this analysis. While the array of possible alternatives is legion, the scope and ultimate aim of this text is to weigh and assess two major variables in the world of ethical theory; first, the role "Nature" might play in elucidating the correct recipe for a productive, happy, and moral life, for being a sort of measuring stick for behavior sanctioned and behavior condemned, and second, to determine whether "Nature" equates with or is part of that jurisprudential school known as the "Natural Law." Argued from another vantage, do theories of regarding the natural order of things, the rational order of the cosmos or universe, and just as critically the unique operational qualities of each, distinct and differing sort of being, offer any lessons about the acceptability of human behavior? Can the teleology be nature and the natural order or is this simply insufficient?

More keenly and attentively, would a comparative commentary on the Roman philosopher, orator, and lawyer Cicero and Dominican preacher and professor St. Thomas Aquinas, the Western world's most influential natural law advocate, provide clarity to these queries? Why Cicero and Aquinas? No one would dispute the significance of either thinker in the unfolding of our history and tradition. In Cicero's case, the Roman Empire's most famous legal advocate and philosopher developed a body of work that touched a host of topical concerns from oratory and rhetoric, to old age and friendship; from legal defense pleas and petitions, to comprehensive discourses on the nature of the gods, and on ends and duty.[13] Cicero, when coupled with Aquinas, anticipates a host of predictable critiques often hurled at the Angelic Doctor of Catholicism, for example, the mouthpiece for the clerics and Curia, theologian rather than philosopher, rigid doctrinaire rather than philosophical, inquisitive, and open, to name just a few. Often victimized by caricature, St. Thomas provides an extraordinary, if not incomparable body of work on the law, virtues, justice, and the paths to a happy and ethical life. As Anton Hermann Chroust indicates, only St. Thomas was capable of "this complete and harmonious integration."[14]

With nearly fourteen centuries of separation, one could readily conclude that the eras of these two figures make a compatible vision an unlikely event. Indeed, Cicero's paganism in relation to the Christian philosophy of Thomas Aquinas would, on the surface, make the comparison seem a series of bridges too far. At what conceptual, intellectual, and philosophical point do these two figures mesh? How could such starkly different eras and corresponding worldviews find aligned thoughts and ideas worthy of examination? How is it possible that Cicero's philosophical outlook may have foretold or projected perennial ideas that Thomas takes for granted or that he even adopted, then refined, and built upon? In the matter of ethics, morality, and the good and productive life, how plausible is it that each figure intersects more often than it diverts to an alternative road? In Cicero we find a renowned secular figure, a republican humanist, a procedural advocate for criminal defendants, a politician, and a man capable of disregarding the unjust law and even calling for the death of emperors engaged in tyranny.[15] S. Adam Seagrave urges readers to appreciate the depth and breadth of Cicero's philosophical works:

> Although Cicero has always been esteemed for his achievements in the field of rhetoric, it is only in recent years that he has begun to regain the scholarly appreciation which he received in the Middle Ages for his achievements in political philosophy.[16]

Cicero's philosophical works come later in life—in between his loss of station and politically imposed exiles—most of which display a sort of melancholy about the state of human and moral affairs.[17] Cicero is a statesman in search of something more dependable than promulgations of the Senate or the sweeping eradication of those same issuances by divinely titled Caesars.[18]

By contrast, the life and times of St. Thomas Aquinas were radically oceans apart. Though born of nobility, Aquinas decided the intellectual and religious life tugged harder than any other force. Joining the Dominicans signified his intense intellectual curiosity and was bolstered for nearly three decades as a Friar, and professor of philosophy and theology at the Universities of Paris, Cologne, and Naples. During this time he amassed a prolific body of scholarly works culminating in his comprehensive *Summa Theologica*.[19] Throughout his unrivaled scholarly production, St. Thomas considered a bevy of subjects—some of which weave their way into the same intellectual pool as Cicero—namely, justice and injustice in human action and human nature, nature and the cosmos, natural law, virtue theory, ends and the good of the human person, order in the universe, and a host of other concepts. Controversy always swirled around Thomas for his obvious affection and need for the Hellenic and Roman philosophical traditions that are commonly cited in his major works. In this sense, the pagan Cicero appears closer to the Christian, penultimate Catholic philosophy of Aquinas, due to the nexus of their intellectual interests, even by contemporary standards. At no place is this more obvious than in their measures of good and bad behavior, right and wrong thinking, natural versus unnatural conduct—for in these express contexts, both thinkers seek a formula to measure by. Both speak of nature and the natural law. Both analyze and assess the role of virtue and vice in this continuum of human conduct while trying to meaningfully define the nature of being and the laws that can be discerned from said definitions. Finally, both thinkers scoff at relativity and offer a systematic approach to determining when human action stays on track or crosses the line and deviates from its natural norms. Rommen appreciates this reality when he observes:

> Good is that which corresponds to the essential nature. The being of a thing also reveals its purpose in the order of creation, and in its perfect fulfillment it is likewise the end or goal of its growth and development. The essential nature is thus the measure.[20]

Cicero and Aquinas, regardless of their differences, may be either the oddest of pairs or the most compatible brothers in ideas ever conceived—at least on some of these issues. That is what this study is all about—finding a common thread or theme between these two traditions—from the classical to the medieval and determining whether or not there exists common ground where ethical debates and dilemmas might be evaluated with dependability and reasoned respect. Instead of a polemical diatribe, Cicero and Aquinas may edify a method of compromise whereby the bulk of the parties leave satisfied. Thusly, the urbane apologist for libertarian pursuits such as same sex equality and marriage; early termination of life without extraordinary medical necessity and intervention; and claims of natural method and methodology in child rearing, discipline, and family size, to name just a few, might find Cicero a more sympathetic ear, while Aquinas, on the other hand, may or may not have the same techniques of measurement, using the same barometers. Here we have to wait and see and discover how their express language in a host of works and titles might afford a more or less restrictive series of judgments about ethical quandaries. Somewhere along the way, Aquinas had to have made some accommodations—not out of utility or moral compromise but a larger understanding of things. Otherwise, his frequent descriptor, as the man who Christianized the philosophy of Aristotle, would yield scant fruit. It is no secret that Aquinas loved Aristotle, designating him "The Philosopher" much to the consternation of prelates and churchmen. His affection for Hellenic and Roman philosophy did not end with the Aristotelian project but extended to and caringly include Cicero whom he quoted substantially in his works. In this way, Thomas, not Cicero, took all the risks, risks that related to his possible apostasy and heresy.[21] This type of intellectual courage should not be discounted for it signifies an intense passion for the Ciceronian ideal—an unbridled compliment concerning both its foundational elements and its well-developed ideas. Thomas unequivocally loved the major tenets of Cicero's philosophy, namely, human nature and natural order, law as a reflection of nature, law as a rational exercise, nature and reason joined, and the obligation of a citizen to rise up against injustices. This analysis connects the dots to see where unity reigns supreme or where differences make impossible a perfect cohesion.

Finally, given all of these comparisons, will Cicero and Aquinas offer a new pathway for moral measure, based on specifically defined and developed principles? Will their philosophical approaches encompass the degree of compatibility upon which agreement or possible disagreement could be discovered? Do Cicero and Thomas deliver certain moral and ethical principles for human life that each agree to be true and binding? To arrive at any worthwhile answer will require in-depth and incisive coverage of the following problems:

1. The idea and definition of nature and the natural order
2. Cicero and Aquinas on nature and the natural order
3. Cicero and Aquinas on nature and reason
4. Cicero and Aquinas on the natural law
5. Nature and natural law: principles for human action
6. The Compatibility of Cicero and Aquinas

Identified here are the currents of thought and expression witnessed in the works of Cicero and Aquinas.[22] Uncannily, these categories appear with significant regularity in most of their works—a clear and undeniable concern for the rules and law of nature, especially how to live in accordance with its tenets and its proper human activity. In both worlds, we encounter the preeminence of reason and rationality and how reason and nature are inexorably and undeniably bound together in the moral enterprise. At both junctures of philosophical ideas, we discover that a higher law, a teleology exhorting a divine guidance, a providence, and a Creator issuing a natural law that each being, particularly the rational being, is bound to without exception. Within these parameters, this analysis discovers whether the worlds of Cicero and Aquinas merge in such a way to more inclusively and convincingly bequeath a moral recipe for human life that is undeniable. Given the current choices of fixed dogmatism and unshackled relativity, it is a chance worth taking.

The comparative setting

With more than 1,350 years of separation, the question of whether or not Cicero and Aquinas could compatibly agree on certain aspects of their philosophy is a challenging one. Aside from the obvious differences in religious upbringing, occupational directions, worldly interaction, and contrasting cultural experiences, each thinker manifested a level of creativity that generated a large body of work that simultaneously challenged the status quo on many issues of the day. For example, Cicero's intense republicanism, his unwavering "denunciation of the aims and methods of all so-called popular leaders, warning of promises from these falsely styled friends of the people whose only goal was self-aggrandizement and whose chief hope of success lay in dissension and civil order"[23] can only be described as politically and socially risky, although most admittedly courageous. Whether Caesar was elevated to the role of dictator and divine ruler, regardless of senatorial preferences, was a pressing question during this era. On another front, Cicero the lawyer-advocate takes on criminal defenses that most fear as too great a risk and again displays the type of courageous personality that never loses sight of the dominant role that law plays in any society hoping for longevity. As Thomas Mitchell deduces, Cicero considered law "the only master that a free people can endure and no group or individual whatever their position, can be allowed to become more powerful than the law."[24] Cicero develops a reputation for fierce and creative advocacy that works in both the courtroom and between the pages he pens. Biographer Anthony Everitt shares this vision regarding a courageous spirit since from his childhood: "He was determined to be the best and the bravest, to join the ranks of the Republic's greatest heroes. He planned to excel, however, not on the battlefield, but in Rome's sacred center, the Forum."[25]

In a similar way, St. Thomas, despite the caricatures, carries on his very remarkable life during a time of differing challenges. At issue are the emerging critiques of once staid Catholic doctrines, to the politics of the papacy and the world, from the development of an intellectual class distinct from the clerical orders, to the increasing dissemination of ideas. As Chesterton so poetically puts it:

> It will not be possible to conceal much longer from anybody the fact that St. Thomas Aquinas was one of the great liberators of the human intellect. The sectarians of the seventeenth and eighteenth centuries were essentially obscurantists, and they guarded an obscurantist legend that the Schoolman was an obscurantist. This was wearing thin even in the nineteenth century; it will be impossible in the twentieth.[26]

Rather than the view that St. Thomas is merely a dogmatist and errand boy for the papacy, most who encounter his work and evaluate it honestly are left with a clarity of purpose and a conceptual comprehensiveness that the typical intellectual simply cannot cover nor master. His productivity as scholar-author is more than legendary as he has bequeathed to generations of Catholic intellectuals treasures that marvel even the most seasoned philosopher. Living in dogmatic times did not dull or thwart the mind of Aquinas but instead seems to have provided even greater stimulation by covering topics once forbidden for reading and incorporating Hellenic and Roman principles directly into his texts. Thomas displayed an unwavering affection for Aristotle—whom he labeled "The Philosopher"—when the mainstream Church hierarchy vociferously condemned pagan insights by Greeks or Romans. Here Thomas displays an intellectual courage, suffering condemnations for his journey into the world of Aristotle, even to the point of episcopal discipline and challenge.[27] At the heart of these charges was the fundamental motive, by clerics, to remove Aristotelian theory from consideration in Catholic theological inquiry or philosophical conclusions. Comfortable with the Platonism of St. Augustine, those who chided and condemned St. Thomas reminded him that St. Augustine had more influence than any pagan philosopher; that the will is predominant in human action over reason; that creation is fixed in Platonic forms more than a scientific unfolding. For St. Thomas to reject outright a challenge to the status quo would be and was intellectually vacuous, for Thomas "appears to have read almost everything that seemed significant or interesting to the universities of his time. Much of this was quite new, deriving as it did from Arabian and Jewish sources."[28] Holding fast to these novel theories signifies an assured yet respectful bravery in the face of a wide array of negative consequences. Chesterton remarks,

> Anathema after anathema was thundered from high places; and under the shadow of the persecution, as so often happens, it seemed for a moment that barely one or two figures stood alone in the storm-swept area. They were both in the black and white of the Dominicans; for Albertus and Aquinas stood firm.[29]

The implications of this intellectual mettle are far-reaching and still felt in our contemporary period. Aquinas provides, according to Alisdair MacIntyre, the best and most reasoned way to reconcile conflict in diverse traditions.[30] This is partly because he is open to the examination and dissection of contrary viewpoints as well as the fact that where he can find worthy themes in the antagonist's outlook, he will adopt and incorporate. The openness and capacity for inclusiveness of the varied traditions can only be described as the result of a mind in a state of permanent development and growth. Even the dialectical design of his masterpiece, *Summa Theologica*, reflects this tendency to consider all the potential avenues of explanation. MacIntyre relates:

> Aquinas was careful in each discussion to summon up all the relevant contributions to argument and interpretation which had been preserved and transmitted within the two major traditions. So biblical sources are brought into conversation with Socrates, Plato, Aristotle and Cicero, and all of them with Arab and Jewish thinkers, as well as the Patristic writers and later Christian theologians.

> The length and detail of the Summa are not accidental features of it, but integral to its purpose and more particularly to providing both Aquinas himself and his readers with the assurance that the arguments adduced for particular articles were the strongest produced so far from any known point of view.[31]

This is no ordinary way of tackling the thirteenth-century world any more than there was an easy method for Cicero to fall into compliance under the might and power of Roman rule during the time of republican upheaval. Each thinker was willing to engage the adversary for the purposes of argument but just as readily as a means to edify, learn, and encompass an idea or concept in the fullest of senses. In Cicero and Aquinas, the reader ascends by necessity not choice, for it is like "climbing a mountain"—hard to be sure but "going up a path made by a towering intellect" at the "summit is wisdom."[32]

Biographical sketch of Cicero

Marcus Tullius Cicero was born on January 3, 106 BCE, in the southeastern region of Italy—approximately seventy miles from Rome, in the town of Arpinum. By most measures, his family was economically well-to-do and politically connected to the more elite in Rome's social fabric. During this formative period, the Roman world was under major political stresses with competing visions about the role of the senate, its emperors, and national interests. Civil wars, factions of distinct military leaders, and challenges to its territorial integrity were issues about which both Rome and a young Cicero were quite knowledgeable. He lived "in stormy times."[33] In other words, Cicero received his education and training, as well as his socialization, in quarters that had to consider these dynamics. As a result, his political interests were shaped by the times in which he lived and the personalities he encountered.

At the age of ten his family moved to a fashionable part of Rome where he commenced his formal education, one that matched his pedigree and future ambitions. By his mid-teens, Cicero had been fully exposed to a variety of philosophical schools, such as Epicureanism and Stoicism, as well as other pursuits, all under the umbrella of an "Academy" education. In addition to studying under the great Philo, Cicero became more than comfortable with academic skepticism, which by its very nature rejects strict dogmatic conclusions about knowledge in general. Academic sceptics examine "all positions in order to find which was most probable, and this was always Cicero's method, so that just as he opposed all absolutism in philosophy, so also he opposed all absolutism, real or threatened, in government, whether the threat came from Sulla, Catiline, Caesar or Antonius."[34] During the period 88–81 BCE, Cicero furthered his education in two other significant directions that would impact his professional and personal life, namely in rhetoric and law. In the rhetorical arts, Cicero blended his legal advocacy to achieve the maximum results since the chief aim of rhetoric is to prove or satisfy the demands of a particular argument or line of reasoning. Hence, for most of Cicero's professional life, he was concerned with not only the factual truth of a given case, but also the manner in which a fact is posed or articulated and whether or not the arguments posed have the power to convince the listener. In the legal arts, as lawyer practitioner, Cicero excelled at building an extraordinary reputation in the early years of lawyerly life. Just as compellingly, Cicero's procedural tactics, his persuasive powers, and methods of articulating the advocate's substantive plan of legal argument became crucial to his skill as a member of the Bar. Not surprisingly, his first major publication, titled *Topics for Speeches (De Inventione)* was drafted around 81 BCE in the earlier part of his legal practice.[35] Early on, one discovers Cicero's passion for rhetoric and its obvious interplay with legal advocacy. By the year 77 BCE Cicero was in such demand as an advocate that he was overtaxed, "smelling somewhat of midnight oil"[36] and physically drained. In a self-imposed exile of a few years, Cicero took some time off to recharge and find happiness in marriage, have children, and revisit his numerous friends. In addition, he "visited various celebrated and fashionable teacher of rhetoric, [and] spent time on philosophical studies."[37] Eventually, Cicero returned to public life as an elected Quaestor in 75 BCE, a role primarily supportive to a Consul. His placement in Sicily caused some separation from his wife and new daughter Tullia, but Cicero carried out his task showing a "talent for competent and fair administration."[38] Cicero's political rise, coupled with his exceptional reputation as a lawyer-advocate, nurtured its upward trajectory until his appointment as Aedile, an administrative position one step below a Consul. The appointment confirmed what most already knew, he was a force to contend with.

Cicero's name grew far and wide with his continuing successes at the bar—none more corroborative than the prosecution of Verres. Verres resided within the upper crust of Roman society, a former governor of Sicily under scrutiny for the crime of extortion. Indeed the Verres case had captured the public's avid interest since his "corruption was notorious."[39] After a successful prosecution, Cicero moved on to other challenges in the world of litigation including Manilius, Cornelius and Catiline to name a few.[40] By 64 BCE, Cicero concluded that it was time to become a candidate for a Consulship, "the office most highly prized and jealously guarded by the nobility."[41] Because of his "tireless labors and brilliance in the courts"[42] Cicero assumed the role of Consul in the year 63 BCE. From this period forward, Cicero was touched by the tensions between absolute tyranny and dictatorship and the demise and diminution of power and authority of the senatorial function in the Roman world. During this time, his reputation for effective leadership was solidified by the end of the Catiline rebellion, an uprising that supported the disenfranchised and forgotten in Roman life as a result of "continuing class tensions and alienation of the lower orders because of economic hardship and the widening gulf between rich and poor."[43] Catiline was less effective in achieving his political goals and led an armed rebellion against the Roman Senate. Upon its detection, failure, and subsequent punishment, Cicero was lauded as the primary player in its unraveling. He also authorized the death, with minimal due process, of its members—a fact often cited as a rare lapse in procedural judgment.[44] His public reputation was at its high point being lauded as "Savior" of Rome and "Father of the Fatherland" although this elevated public opinion was short-lived given the coming tensions of Caesar, Pompey, and Crassus. This alliance was often referred to as the "First Triumvirate," the purpose of which was to balance the emerging tensions between a dictatorship and the historic republican form of government. Given all these political dynamics and Cicero's unfixed position trying to hold together traditional visions of Roman governance, Cicero imposed on himself a period of exile to Greece between 58 and 57 BCE.

As the dictatorial tendencies of Caesar became more evident, Cicero's concern and objections made his political elevation less likely in the decade to follow. As Caesar solidified his absolute rule, suspending republicanism in ways disturbing to the senatorial class, there is little question that dictatorship had won the day during this period. Trying to lay low and avoid the consequences of objection or resistance, Cicero's writing and philosophical pursuits took on added meaning at this time. His work on the nature of the state and government, *De Re Publica*, an affirmation of senatorial republicanism and resistance to tyranny, was authored from 54 to 51 BCE. During the same time, his insightful and original masterpiece on law, *De Legibus*, was published. His scholarly productivity was astonishing by ordinary measures throughout the previous decade, examples being:

45 BCE

- *Tusculan Disputations*
- *On Supreme Good and Evil (De Finibus Bonorum et Malorum)*
- *On the Nature of the Gods (De Natura Deorum)*

44 BCE

- *On Fate (De Fato)*
- *Duties (De Officiis)*
- *Foretelling the Future (De Divinatione)*

While Cicero mainly resisted quietly, through the bellowing of his books and texts, he could not remain an isolated figure during the reign of a tyrant. The toll on Cicero also seems to be evident in his personal life, his multiple marriages, the death of his daughter Tullia, and his own isolation, all of which impacted him deeply. Every effort to hold together a crushed republic seems to have failed at this time and while Cicero was not a direct participant in the death of Caesar, he approved of the action. By 43 BCE the complexities after Caesar's assassination, and the failed alliance of Cicero with Caesar's great-nephew Octavian, who turned on Caesar by aligning with Antony, culminated in the beginning of a very quick end. Antony labeled senators and their ilk "outlaws" and took their property.[45] Cicero was eventually found and executed upon Antony's orders; his hands cut off as symbolic punishment for this extraordinary man of ideas and logic. What is certain about Cicero is the perpetual influence his life, his works, and his ideas have had upon any democratic and republican form of government. The Framers of the United States Constitution, especially Jefferson, were deeply indebted to Ciceronian ideals. Later philosophers, in the mold of St. Thomas Aquinas, cited Cicero without hesitation. In the final analysis, Cicero's works gave "expression to many enduring ideals of Western culture, especially in relation to liberty, civil rights and humanistic education."[46] Cicero, aside from his political and philosophical ideals, while not being a sainted man, still valued the role of character and integrity in public dealings, a fact quite lost in our postmodern culture where self-interest is valued over all else. Thomas Mitchell sees this as his greatest legacy.

> He also adhered with rigid consistency to the standards of self-restraint and cleanhandedness that he prescribed for the good statesman, and his all-round moral integrity set him far apart from a great many of his contemporaries in the increasingly corrupt and amoral world of the late Republic.[47]

Biographical sketch of St. Thomas Aquinas

A life as rich and as productive as that of Aquinas (1225–1274) is difficult to summarize in a few pages. The life and times of Thomas Aquinas has been the subject of some exceptional biographies and other studies that highlight the enormity of his influence.[48] That he is a Doctor of the Church, Patron of Catholic Education, and designated the Angelic Doctor of Roman Catholicism[49] is both testimony to his spiritual depth and breadth and his immense intellect. On the flip side of these designations are a series of caricatures that follow Thomas wherever his thought is considered—Thomas the churchman, the papist, the theologian, and the dogmatic enforcer. Anyone who seriously encounters the body of work produced by St. Thomas can discern the folly of these descriptors for in Aquinas one encounters a philosophical genius.

The Italian family of Aquino was linked to Lombard kings and several royal houses of Europe. Landulph, his father, held the titles of count of Aquino and lord of Loreto, Acerro, and Belcastro. As nephew of Emperor Frederick Barbarossa he was also connected to the family of King Louis IX of France. His wife, Theodora, was the countess of Teano, a part of Sicily conquered by Norman barons. Hence, St. Thomas, born in Roccasecca around 1225, comes from a distinguished family with the usual high expectations for its offspring. From an early age, St. Thomas displayed an uncanny intellectual ability and as a result was sent to exceptional schools with high expectations for a significant career either in military, political, or clerical service. In his particular case, since his father's brother was abbot at the Benedictine Monastery at Monte Cassino, there was an expectation that Thomas might enter life with the Benedictines. After a classical education at Monte Cassino and subsequent enrollment at the university in Naples, St. Thomas surprised his family by his decision to join the Dominicans—a new order founded by St. Dominic. So distraught was his family about this choice, that his mother asked her other sons to confine Thomas at the castle at Monte San Giovanni Campano until his mind changed back to Monte Cassino. For more than a year, St. Thomas was kept within the castle walls and even subjected to temptations to lose his virtue with prostitutes.[50]

The decision to enter the Dominican order was never overturned by family or influence and his placement at the University of Paris in 1245 commenced an intellectual journey few have rivaled in the history of civilization. As a student, Thomas was exposed to his mentor, Albert the Great, whose influence and encouragement appeared unwavering from the outset.[51] While Albert witnessed an intellect in exceptional possibilities, most who had earlier encountered Thomas found him both quiet and unreservedly large and tall for his time. His student colleagues had labeled him the "Dumb Ox," to which Albert retorted: "You call him the dumb ox, but in his teaching he will one day produce such a bellowing that it will be heard throughout the world."[52]

During his tenure at Paris he worked closely with Albert and followed him on his subsequent appointment at Cologne. In his early professorial career, Thomas concentrated on sacred scripture and biblical studies. Author of nearly fifty original pieces of scholarly text, his first productions related to the Old and New Testaments including the following:

- *Expositio in Job ad litteram*—1260
- *In Psalmos Davidis exposition*—1272–1273
- *Expositio in Canticum Canticorum*—a lost work
- *Expositio in Isaiam prophetam*—1256–1259
- *Expositio in Jeremiam prophetam*—1267–1268
- *Expositio in Threnos Jeremiae prophetae*—1267–1268
- *Glossa continua in Matthaeum, Marcum, Lucam, Joannem* (The *Glossa* is commonly called the *Catena aurea*)—1263–1264
- *Expositio in evangelium s. Matthaei*—1269–1272
- *Expositio in evangelium s. Joannis*—1269–1272
- *Expositio in s. Pauli Epistolas*—1259–1272

At the same time, St. Thomas delved into all matter of theological and philosophical subject matter, working for decades to finish out massive compendium and theological and philosophical treatises. His first major synthesis on Peter Lombard's *Sentences* took three years to finish and delivered some early insights into Thomas's great penchant for ethical and jurisprudential ideas. Vernon Bourke relays:

> In his early thirties, Thomas Aquinas was already well known as a brilliant scholar and teacher. His preparatory studies had been more thorough than those of most of his colleagues. He had read widely and profoundly in the available literature of contemporary science, philosophy and religion. He had studies at four great and dissimilar centers of learning: Monte Cassino, the state University of Naples, the Dominican Institute at Cologne and the University of Paris.[53]

His two other tomes, *Summa Contra Gentiles* and *Summa Theologica*, compiled between 1261 and 1267, encompass the fullness and comprehensiveness of Catholic philosophical and theological thought. Other works, commonly labeled Academic Disputations, were produced at lightning speed during the remainder of his academic life at Paris, Colognes, and Naples. Those works include the following:

- *De veritate*—1256–1259
- *De potentia Dei*—1259–1268
- *De spiritualibus creaturis*—1269

- *De anima*—1269–1270
- *De unione Verbi incarnate*—1268–1272
- *De malo*—1263–1271
- *De virtutibus*—1269–1272
- *De immortalitatae animae?*
- *Utrum anima conjuncta cognoscat seipsam per essentiam?*
- *Contra impugnates Dei cultam et religionem*—1256
- *De perfectione vitae spiritualis*—1270
- *Contra pestiferam doctrinam retrahentium pueros a religionis ingress*—1270
- *De unitate intellecuts, contra Averroistas*—1270
- *De aeternitate mundi, contra murmurantes*—1271
- *De fallaciis ad quosdam nobiles artistas*—1244–1245
- *De propositionibus modalibus*—1244–1245
- *De ente et essential*—before 1256
- *De principiis naturae ad fratrem Sylvestrum*—before 1256
- *Compendium theologiae ad fratrem Reginaldum socium suum carissimum*—1260–1273
- *De substantiis separatis, seu de angelorum natura, ad fratrem Reginaldum, socium suum carissimum*—after 1270
- *De Regno (De regimine principium), ad regem Cypri*—1267

It is simply impossible to give proper treatment to the vastness of Thomas's bibliography, the scope of which "belong to many fields of activity and are a faithful mirror of his participation in the religious and intellectual life of his age."[54] Anthony Kenny correctly types Thomas as an intellect "of extraordinary power and industry."[55] From being and essence to kingship and tyranny, from good and evil, the full range of scholarly products cannot be readily catalogued for even world political figures and high-ranking Church personnel solicited the opinions offered by Thomas.[56]

By 1252, his tutelage under Albert the Great ended and he subsequently returned to the University of Paris for further study, culminating in the receipt of his license to teach theology at Paris in 1256. In 1259, Thomas was assigned to various teaching assignments in Italy at the Papal Curia as well as Orvieto, Rome, and Viterbo from 1261 to 1268. At this time, Thomas expended a great deal of intellectual effort commenting and critiquing the works of "The Philosopher" Aristotle with special and incisive analysis on his ethical and virtue theory.[57] Couple his conceptual affection for Aristotle with his respect shown for Arabian thinkers such as Avicenna and Averroes, as well as Jewish philosopher

Maimonides, and what emerges is a theologian/philosopher without match. This is a mind that can be best described as boundless, vivified, and in constant yearning, living in what Pegis calls the "historically social character of his own philosophical work. He lives and thinks in the company of others."[58]

It is this intellectual dynamism that gives fodder to his critics during his second term at the University of Paris beginning in 1268. Traditional Christian Platonists, operating under the blessings and agreement of the Augustinians, found much of the Thomist method a bit too radical for comfort. For example, Thomas's efforts to "assimilate Aristotelianism" seemed far more aggressive than necessary.[59] Others challenged the psychology of St. Thomas, whose vision of the human person and his or her potentiality was almost without boundary, for in Thomas the flourishing of the human agent is normative, not extraordinary. Critics of St. Thomas questioned whether man is free as a moral agent, whether or not man can really understand the complexities of the universe and its many operations, and whether it is proper to even consider the immortality of the soul.[60] To be sure, St. Thomas was not a shrinking violet but a diorama of flowers bursting with colors ready to tackle reality at every level in which it could be comprehended.

To his more traditional colleagues, St. Thomas was operating at the fringes by his very generosity of mind and thought. In his last term at the University of Paris, his productivity reached its apex culminating in the authorship of the second part of his *Summa Theologica*—over a million words in length—alongside the other texts he was simultaneously authoring. The sheer volume of his opus staggers even the modern observer. As Anthony Kenny remarks,

> When one reviews the sheer bulk of his output between 1269–1273 one can believe the testimony of his chief secretary that it was his habit, like a grand master at a chess tournament, to dictate to three or four secretaries simultaneously; one can almost believe the further testimony that he could dictate coherent prose while he slept.[61]

Despite his remarkable body of work and continuing reputation for exceptional theological and philosophical analysis, his second tour at Paris remained contentious until the end of his term. Thomas was asked by his Dominican superiors to create a Dominican house of study in Naples and during his travels he experienced a series of changes internally and externally that forever altered his once entrenched habits. Some have claimed that Thomas was mystically touched and capable of levitation. He exhibited signs of mysterious inner prayer and religious fervor.[62] In addition, during his travels, while riding in an open cart, his head was struck by a low hanging tree limb. In 1274, while recuperating at a monastery, his health continued its downward trend. After another mystical experience Thomas indicated to his colleagues that his enormous body of work, when compared in the context of true, divine knowledge "seems like straw."[63] On his deathbed, St. Thomas Aquinas's last words to the Cistercian monks signify his peaceful acceptance of his impending demise: "This is my rest forever and ever: Here will I dwell for I have chosen it (Psalm 131:14)."

Often called "The Universal Teacher," St. Thomas Aquinas died at the monastery of Fossanova on March 7, 1274.[64] While some of his philosophical opinions were challenged in a formal Syllabus of Errors in 1277, as advanced by Paris's Bishop Etienne Tempier, none of the challenges ever negated the brilliance of Aquinas. He was canonized by Pope John XXII in 1323 and declared an Angelic Doctor by Pope Pius V in 1567.[65] In 1879, Pope Leo XIII characterized Thomas's theology as the definitive exposition of Catholic doctrine and decreed that all Catholic seminaries and universities be grounded in Thomism. In 1880, St. Thomas was declared patron of all Catholic educational institutions.

The influence of Thomism has been subject to the ebb and flow of philosophical schools, none more compellingly antagonistic than those promoting ethical and moral relativity. In Thomas, the reader is exposed to a dependable system worthy of any intellectual; open yet resistant to chaos, fixed when it need be, and subject to fine-tuning if justified. In this text, Thomas provides a methodology of truth, one "profoundly religious, sensitive to the value of tradition," while "nonetheless an innovator in both philosophy and theology."[66] Anton Pegis labels Aquinas a "Giant."

> He stood on a giant past; and although he himself was a giant, he always looked upon his intellectual stature with the genuine humility of one who, even in his highest speculative reaches, accepted the fruits of philosophical victory as much as those who went before him as in his own.[67]

2

Nature and the Natural Order in Cicero and Aquinas

Introduction

Any examination of a natural law theory in the mold of St. Thomas, or for that matter any earlier visions advanced by Cicero, inevitably must start at the beginning with its definition and foundation. Critics and supporters alike always lay an intellectual foundation for why or how the natural law can be justified. For some, it will depend on the exclusive imprint of a Creator; for others the matter of natural law is fully discernable in scripture; for select groups the reliance might be human observation and behavior, cosmology, an orderly universe, and the nature of beings; or finally, some may preferably look to nature and natural order. In the last case, how things work, how a being functions or naturally operates, becomes a critical test for any subsequent conclusion about the natural law discovered. In essence, it is the nature of a being or thing that explains the parameters of moral and lawful conduct. When acting consistently with that nature, living compatibly and naturally with that nature, one is assured of proper moral choices in human activity. While a rock may have a way of acting as a rock, despite the complete lack of intentionality and choice, earlier natural law thinkers such as Cicero and surely up to and including Aquinas, it still has a nature, although easily distinguished from Homo sapiens. Jean Porter's masterpiece, *Nature as Reason*, concludes:

> In particular, the Scholastics gave special attention to those principles which appear to manifest themselves in other living creatures, as well as ourselves. They did not hold to the view sometimes attributed to them, according to which human beings simply imitate the behavior of nonhuman animals ... While norms for human behavior cannot be derived directly from animal behavior, there are nonetheless continuities between human morality and the behavioral norms which the other animals observe.[1]

As simple as this deduction might be, the complicated idea of exactly what nature constitutes will pester natural law thinkers during every age, starting with the most basic of notions—are nature and the natural law really one and the same thing? Is nature an individual observation or a collective observation in the cosmological sense? Is nature nothing more or less than how things work or how beings operate? Can we reach conclusions about ethical and moral standards by our observation of nature and the natural order? Does an orderly nature manifest or demonstrate a rational design or designer in the form of God?

Part of the task behind this project is to more specifically determine how Cicero and Aquinas construe nature and whether their overall approaches work compatibly or whether, once delved into, we discover vastly different worlds of interpretation. What is undeniable is that both thinkers grapple with the questions posed previously and our comparison points this out where instructive. What is less clear is if the point of terminus is identical, do Cicero and Aquinas not only travel a road that aligns, intersects, or even replicates the other, but also more crucially, do the roads chosen get to the same endpoint by arriving at a similar conclusion about human conduct and human affairs? Some, such as John Finnis, may glean some similarities in the approaches of Cicero and Aquinas, although in the final analysis, Thomas is unavoidably tethered to the question of God's "existence or nature or will."[2] Still other commentators are not sure that this conclusion is accurate. S. Adam Seagrave, for example, has sought to "reopen the question of a natural law in a strict sense, and renew the quest for its understanding, establishing a substantial basis for Thomistic natural law theory in a pre-Christian, classical philosophy."[3] Here the aim is joinder rather than division—unity based on commonality, not separation based on difference. Certainly the aim of this analysis is a grand inquiry that will likely raise far more questions than can be resolved. This complexity should not thwart the effort to link and bind, if at all possible, the pagan Cicero with the Angelic Doctor of Roman Catholicism, Aquinas, for such compatibility opens the door for a moral menu that most can order from and cause no harm.

In order to accomplish this, our attention turns to precise categories and definitions, or characteristics or traits, of what constitutes nature and its ultimate endgame—a moral code or measure for human action. In this way we shall consider both Cicero and St. Thomas in light of the following themes:

1. Nature as truth, science, and the natural order
2. Nature as correct function and biological use
3. Nature as being: dispositions and inclinations

4. Nature as efficient cause
5. Nature as a divine reflection, imprint, or creation

If our analysis demonstrates a commonly shared vision of Cicero and Aquinas in regard to nature, our attention turns toward other aspects of what is expected to construct a philosophy of natural law, namely reason and eventual conclusions concerning human action that can be universally agreed upon. Stated in a different way, we hope to discern whether Cicero and Aquinas are minimally "natural" thinkers about the propriety of human conduct. If this conclusion is reached, at least a starting gate can be opened when moral resolutions need to run the track, or as Martin Cook's "Ways of Thinking Naturally" posits, "Are there naturally preferred forms of human conduct and social organization that we tamper with at our peril? Can we look to naturally based considerations as a guide, if not a determiner, of morally correct action and judgment?"[4]

Nature as truth, science, and the natural order

Since the time of the earliest philosophical questions, the idea of what constitutes reality, the science of things so to speak, has challenged us. What is it that we see in our own space and time? Is the hard substance of matter and the form of this being or that being real or a manifestation of something else? Posed another way, can we truly capture the natural world, the nature of all forms of beings and corresponding essences? Can we decipher the way beings operate, how natural bodies move, and how the entire cosmos orders its own activity or are there other forces producing, designing, and creating the nature and natural order we encounter?

In this first form of inquiry, nature sits under our scientific microscope; nature, is scientifically and factually described as a series of laws and operations that we catalog and define. Whether the habits of a monkey, the movement of the constellations or the intricacies of human procreation, each of these processes is not only natural, but also part of a larger natural order in the universe; each works correctly in one way and not in alternate ways and as a result, the accuracy and reliability of any conclusions concerning these processes will only be true if known and understood. Aristotle's *Physics* offers an exceptional definition of nature:

> Of things that exist, some exist by nature, some from other causes. "By nature" the animals and their parts exist, and the plants and the simple bodies (earth, fire, air and water)—for we say that these and the like exist by nature … "Nature"

> then is what has been stated. Things "have a Nature" which have a principle of this kind. Each of them is a substance; for it is a subject and nature always implies a subject in which it inheres ... The term "according to nature" is applied to all these things and also to the attributes which belong to them in virtue of what they are.[5]

This knowledge about nature, science, and creation keeps the moral agent in the proper context in a scheme of being—especially as it relates to the place of Homo sapiens in a teleological and cosmological sense. Knowledge that is accurate, the "ultimate reality,"[6] Thomas concludes, keeps us in the proper station as dependent beings, caused by another and another, generating then corrupting, while only God needs no other cause. Hence, when the pagan worshiped the calf or lion, or the tribesman the moon or the winds, that reality or nature was destined to falter and fail on its own lack of logic and reason. When nature is properly scrutinized, when beings are examined in detail, there can be no rational conclusions that the First Being is a fire or planet but something not in need of anything—a being so simple yet so perfect that it lacks nothing. Aristotelian physics reached this conclusion about nature.[7] Knowledge of nature, science, and natural order can only contribute to our own reverence for the higher power thereby mitigating or minimizing the zeal for divinization and the assumption of characteristics that are inconsistent with our very being. Without knowledge of these truths, and "through ignorance of the nature of things" mankind cannot find his "own place in the order of the universe" or "to God as his last end."[8]

The plain assumption here holds that knowledge of nature must be an accurate reflection of exactly what nature really is. It would be folly to depend on a natural science, a defective biology, chemistry, or physics so to speak, as exclusive agencies for the discovery of truth. The assumption leads to other notions as well, such as if we know nature, shall we discover the possibility of higher beings, or at least gradations in beings? Shall we discern the truth about how life is to be lived? Is there a way of truth? Jan Aertsen's *Nature and Creature*[9] brilliantly lays out the intersection between knowing and living, or stated more keenly, understanding the nature of things in order to capture the dynamics of actual being. "It is a process of knowing by which the intellect conforms itself to that which is. The way of truth is likewise a dynamic of being whereby things are knowable for the intellect are 'unhidden.' "[10]

If we know "being" in all of its forms—contingent, dependent, or with or without necessity—"truth" cannot be far behind. Truth is knowledge that is scientifically correct and factually without doubt. That is why our understanding of nature and the natural order reap such rich and boundless rewards, for nature is the doorway to truth; it is the companion of truth and fully exchangeable with truth. "Truth is a relation between thought and reality."[11] From this vantage point nature takes on the possibility of providing a measure for correct action for nature, and assuming we are convinced, intersects with truth when properly understood. Nature and the natural order become the measuring stick of a defensible ethical system or moral code. D. J. B. Hawkins calls nature an ethical norm: "That the moral life is a life in accordance with nature is a venerable commonplace which has perhaps been given an even greater variety of meanings than most venerable commonplaces."[12]

The significance of this conclusion cannot be overstated especially in a world dominated by relativity rather than fixed principles. Then again, nature, it has been said, does not always provide the results that natural law thinkers hope and wish for, since not all of nature conforms to dogmatic reasoning and, in fact, may directly conflict with it. On top of this, thinkers such as Cicero were attuned to the role of socialization and community culture as either a sanctioning or a condemnatory force in decisions about the propriety of human conduct. Mark Jordan's analysis concludes: "So far as the virtues are assigned by Nature as roles or parts, moral life is governed by the theater's economy of approval, its booing and applause. The beauty of right action moves those watching to praise."[13]

So in every sense of the term, nature "instructs" either by our own rational discovery of what we are as beings or what the scientific world and order of things appear to be. It seems a safe bet that moral inquiry is appropriate within this innate and inherent domain of what constitutes or makes up the human player. Here, it is utterly natural to make those sorts of judgments and determinations.[14] "As for composition, Nature does the work for us … literally writes down for us to copy … This is nature as *ratio*, the source of invention."[15]

Instruction comes from other natural quarters too—how the animal kingdom carries on and how its diversity of creatures coexist under a survivalist mentality. In these operations, the science is fully open to the observer—the biology, chemistry, and physics—not a secret incapable of discernment. Couple this possibility with rational and reasonable inquiry, and the chances of cataloging rules for living may have just exploded with possibilities. Cynthia Crysdale joins the inner knowledge of Homo sapiens with the natural world that surrounds us day to day,

> Reason, that is, human meaning, while it certainly incorporates the changes involved in learning, is understood to have an ahistorical character to it. Likewise, the physical, chemical, biological and zoological cycles of nature,

while subject to certain changes such as growth and reproduction, are assumed to be explainable in terms of unchanging regularities.[16]

Herein lays a hope for nature to be the measure of good and bad human conduct. Is it capable of delivering a standard by which human acts can be measured? Are the "cycles of biology and animal sensitivity that humans have in common with other sentient species"[17] instructive and worth our moral notice? Finally, before examining the approaches taken by Cicero and Aquinas on this topic, is it reasonable to conclude that even the most rudimentary form of moral reasoning shall require the most elementary knowledge of science and the natural order? Indeed, Crysdale argues that any possibility of a natural law theory will come to depend on said knowledge, no matter how basic it might be. Hence, "knowledge of the natural world—reproductive processes, ecological systems, medical diagnoses, is an imperative for a responsible ethics."[18]

Cicero on nature and the natural order

There can be no question that the concept of nature and its corresponding order plays a major role in the Ciceronian worldview. Nature finds its way into literally every text Cicero ever authored—though not for identical reasons, although there are identifiable threads of commentary. To be sure, nature is not a foreign idea in Cicero's time, but a critical concept with an already long genealogy—from the Greek storehouse of ideas to his Roman contemporaries. That Cicero was influenced by such figures as Aristotle and Plato is undeniable for his texts are not remiss in their mention.[19] Just as evident is his persistent commentary on the various schools of philosophical thought debating nature and all sorts of other manner of philosophical content—groups he expressly mentions such as the Stoics and Epicureans as well as the followers of the original and revised Academics.[20] Other thinkers such as Xeno, an influential Stoic, and Antiochus, an Academic who rejected parts of the Stoic tradition, were just as influential in shaping Cicero's perspective on what nature really is.[21] In the Stoic mindset, one could come to understand and know nature cognitively, by what Xeno calls the "cataleptic impression." Xeno held that a correct impression of nature is "one that [a] comes from what is, and [b] is stamped and impressed in accordance with what is, [c] in such a way it could not come from what is not."[22] The aim here, at least in a definitional or epistemological sense, is to perceive nature as it is, as best we can. Stoics lumped a good many things together, namely nature, the cosmos, God and gods and in turn, since there is a pantheistic view that predominates the thought of the

Stoics, there must also be a universal law or common prescription for human life. "The Stoic tradition understood the universe as a vast state governed by reason or law inherent in nature . . . and identified this universal reason with God."[23] But to simply label Cicero a Stoic is at odds with his overall approach in diverse works for his hierarchy of being and order is immensely more complicated than the unified Stoic template, where everything rotates in unity and as one. The Stoics saw God and nature as one and the same, by way of example, while Cicero proposes a God that is metaphysically transcendent—overseeing a universe He created, not just existing. The consequences here also are significant for it leaves open another plausible way of seeing nature—as derivative, reflective, imaged in God's creative power and force rather than just moving in time and space. In the end, Cicero is much more than a Stoic and as his position on nature demonstrates "there was a good deal of mixing and borrowing between the schools."[24]

Questions involving impressions, the accuracy of apprehensions or conclusions, are not settled by these claims since to be bound by nature requires more than our impressions. In its place, what is necessary, according to Cicero, is that nature be defined and identified truly; that this truth of nature and natural order be corroborated by one's own experience and tradition and finally, that our impressions correctly represent "the state of affairs that is its object."[25] In addition, Cicero was not, according to Richard Horsley, comfortable with the natural determinism residing in Stoicism—a whole universe governed under a unified series of players whether those participants are human beings, the other animals, or God for in the last instance, the universe and God are synonymous.[26] This baseline of knowledge and its reliability will be crucial to any eventual conclusions about the propriety of human action. Cicero characterizes this sort of fact-finding as essential.

> Do you not think it important for our homes that we should know what is happening and being done in that home which is not shut in by the walls we build, but is the whole universe, a home and a fatherland which the gods have given us the privilege of sharing with them? Surely it is important, especially since, if we are ignorant of these matters, we must remain ignorant of many other important things. Besides, the mere learning about the facts of nature and their investigation gives me at least the greatest pleasure.[27]

Cicero persistently looks to the natural world trying hard to pin it down accurately, for such a methodology gives comfort to the decisions he will make at a later time about goodness or evil in human action. Nature, if we understand it correctly, provides a blueprint for the "conduct of life."[28] In *De Legibus*, he observes how nature provides a measure:

> When a farmer judges the quality of a tree by nature, shall we not use the same standard in regard to the characters of young men? Then shall we judge character by Nature, and judge Virtue and Vice, which result from character, by some other standard? But if we adopt the same standard for them, must we not refer the honorable and the base to Nature also? Whatever good thing is praiseworthy must have within itself something which deserves praise, for goodness itself is good by reason not of opinion but of Nature.[29]

If nature is studied long and hard enough it will deliver a body of systematic knowledge that can be dependable for nature does what is needed and necessary for its own preservation. In describing the design of the human person, by way of edification, Cicero holds:

> Nature has likewise not only equipped man himself with a nimbleness of thought, but also given him the senses, to be, as it were, his attendants and messengers; she had laid bare the obscure and none too [obvious] meanings of a great many things, to serve as the foundations of knowledge, as we may call them; and she has granted us a bodily form which is convenient and well suited to the human mind. For while she has bent the other creatures down toward their food, she has made man alone erect, and has challenged him to look up toward heaven, as being, so to speak, akin to him, and his first home.[30]

At this juncture another thread of Ciceronian nature emerges—that of natural function, natural design, and natural use.

Natural function, natural design, and natural use

Cicero expends considerable energy describing why something is designed and functions the way it does in his collection of works. To edify—how does a person's eye work, where are those eyes placed, and what protections against injury does the eye possess? What of the human hand, the design of the human torso, or other bodily construction? For Cicero, observation and analysis of the human person, its constitution and construction, are part of a larger circle of influence, for example, the developmental capacity of that person, the benefits from such a form, and finally, the wisdom of said design. Germain Grisez understands how function, design, and the corresponding human activity manifest what is good for the human person: "Human nature is prior in reality to the basic human good that fulfill it. However, because nothing is known except insofar as it is in act, we can come to know human nature only by knowing the whole set of human capacities, and those capacities are manifested only by their functions and the proper objects of those functions."[31]

Throughout his body of work, Cicero dwells on this issue with regularity, always searching for logic in how things are put together, operating under the assumption that there must be a creative design that arranges matter and form with an undeniable aim, end, or ultimate purpose. The full range of animals, beyond its rational version, does not escape Cicero's attention whether it be pigs or frogs, cats or dogs, horses or fish—all of these have messages about how beings live in conformity with nature.[32]

Everything in nature should make sense if we study it enough, and indeed anecdotally this is quite true. When we bemoan fires in the forest, we eventually discover, after wearing our observational hats on the natural order, that fire is essential to renewing forests and in the propagation of future seedlings. Weigh the ravages of a hurricane in a coastal region, which modern scientists readily explain as necessitous for the maintenance of estuarine ecosystems and surrounding environments. Tragedy and disaster become, under Nature's function, design, and overall order, acts that obviously have no intentionality, good or bad, but are critically needed to assure the longevity of these natural systems. What happens naturally usually makes sense when put in the vernacular. Of course, it might be argued that what happens unnaturally reaps the opposite result, moral or ecological. In any event, the idea that nature has specific functions, from the biological to the astronomical, from the ecological to the chemical and physical, should give us reason to pause—even if to be set powerless against the majesty of these events. Cicero eloquently remarks in the *Nature of the Gods*:

> Thirdly, there is the awe inspired by thunderbolts, storms, cloudbursts, blizzards, hailstorms, floods, plagues, earthquakes or sudden tremors of the earth, showers of stones, and raindrops as red as blood: from the subsidences and sudden fissures on the earth: from monstrosities in man and beast: from fiery portents and comets in the skies ... Terrified by such events as these, men came to see in them the working of some divine and heavenly power.[33]

Natural functions and events can lead to specific conclusions about how human beings should live and operate. To illustrate, Cicero painstakingly describes the wonders of the procreative process, from the initial conjugal act, to the care and feeding of the newborn.

> Their division in to males and females has been devised by nature for the propagation of their kind. They have parts of the body perfectly adapted for begetting and conceiving, and both male and female have a strong desire for physical union. Then, when the seed is planted in its place, it draws almost all the nourishment to itself and so builds up the embryo within the womb. When the child is born, almost all the food of the mother is turned into milk and the new-born creature seeks the mother's breast by instinct, without need of guidance, and fills itself from her abundance.[34]

Cicero will evaluate even smaller parts of Homo sapiens to confirm what he believes—that everything in human function and design has an express purpose and when they act in consort with nature, happiness will always trump personal distress for "nature is a guide in living."[35] Even specific organs of the body are devised with this holistic approach in mind. Cicero deduces when discussing eyes and ears:

> Our ears, unlike our eyes, are always open, for we need hearing even in our sleep, from which can be roused by any sound. The windings of the inner ear prevent anything going into to it as it could if the entrance were straight and simple. Nature has even provided that even the tiniest creatures which tries to creep in should be caught in sticky wax. The ears project outwards from the head, to shield and protect the organs of hearing and to prevent the sounds slipping past and being lost before they can affect the sense.[36]

Every imaginable function of the human body was evaluated for its purposes and design. Cicero evaluates the logic of the nose, the heart, the veins, the lungs, even how the body digests and expels food in order to prove the wisdom of the natural function and the natural design and "wonder of the natural body."[37]

The natural order

Another way of edifying the sense and sensibility of nature and its corresponding instructions for human living can be derived from the natural order. By "order" we measure how and why things work, if or whether nature tends to some particular end, or if one's chosen action is consistent or contrary to the order in the agent, its respective part or the universe itself. Order connotes logic in both individuals and worlds and for Cicero, as for many of his contemporaries, the proof of a transcendent power could be deduced from the wondrous logic of a cosmos or the progression of a life itself. At every level of human operation there is an order that cannot be changed or altered. To think otherwise, Cicero observes is a "fight against nature," which is "no different from battling the gods and the

Giants did."[38] There is no reason to fight the inevitable progression of growth, maturation, and human development for "man is not merely a creature native to the earth but is also an observer of all that happens to him in the skies."[39] Of course, one can always choose opposite than the natural dictate, which is part of the explanation why acts contrary to nature are termed grave and inhumane, even bestial by choice and intent. Such acts, are particularly shameful, Cicero concludes, since human "beings hide and conceal violations of nature, not before gods or beast, but before other humans."[40]

A human life has both a chronological and internal moral clock that ticks without any decision making. Cicero categorizes the various stages of human life as nothing more than a predictable order that we must not only accept as inevitable, but also embrace as part of nature's plan.

> Or do you think, perhaps, that young men ought to mourn their lost boyhood, and those a bit older their younger days? The course of life is clear to see: nature has only one path, and it has no turnings. Each season of life has an advantage peculiarly its own; the innocence of children, the hot blood of youth, the gravity of the prime of life and the mellowness of age all possess advantages that are theirs by nature and that should be garnered each at its proper time.[41]

Cicero's musings on old age are remarkably fresh and insightful—urging his readers to see time's passage as a "blessing" since it is the law of nature.[42] Fear not the body as it unravels and corrupts for that is exactly what it cannot avoid or fully prevent. Do not weary of the challenges of age because a life well-lived is a life full of accomplishments and mistakes, of joys and sorrows whereby we have had our "fill of life itself."[43] Old age, says Cicero, connotes an inevitable order that nature does not abhor, but embraces: "But life comes to its best end, when, with mind unimpaired and senses intact, nature herself breaks up the fabric to which she first gave form and order. Now in every case, things freshly put together are hard to pull apart; things that have gotten old come to pieces with ease."[44] Each human life has a natural order to its existence, and death, Cicero concludes, is the terminus for a temporal station. As such, it makes little sense for the old to "grasp greedily after those last few years of life."[45]

These same principles of order apply to the physical world, the physical universe that surrounds the human being. In describing the soil in which we grow our crops, Cicero equates the soil's willingness to grow with its nature of being soil. Argued from another slant, soil has a natural purpose or end result which it must be attentive to in order that it "be" soil. Cicero, when explaining crop growth, poetically describes the qualities of a soil as a "natural force"[46] and farmers who use the earth “make investments” in that earth—a deposit that “never balks at their orders.”[47]

To the higher planes of the universe Cicero extends his natural order—for everywhere there must be order if we assume a hierarchy of created perfection, an assumption that law and a transcendent God guides our universe and its inhabitants. “Cicero also uses the term *natura* to signify the governing principle or order of the world.”[48] Celestial revolutions, Seth Bernadette opines, “imply an intelligence beyond the heavens.”[49] Any reasonable being, after even the shortest period of human observation, will discover the continuity and flow of nature and those advising otherwise have chosen to disregard the evidence. Our planetary systems, stars, and every version of living being manifests order rather than chaos. As Cicero states: “Who cannot wonder at this harmony of things, at this symphony of nature which seems to will the well-being of the world? If there is such a man, then I am very sure that he has never thought of upon these things.”[50]

Moving outward in the universe, the same principles shall apply in the facts before us for there is order in the seasons, the oceans, the seas, the stars, and the planets—all moving toward their proper end and purpose—all doing so because there are no alternative motions to adopt or divergent roads to choose.[51] The stars preserve their “spherical form by the force of their own gravity” while the constellations, the sky, and the movement of material atoms take place without choosing options or differentiating multiple courses of action.[52] “The orderly motion of the stars, which is constant through all eternity, cannot be attributed to natural processes alone. Neither can it be attributed to accident which is the friend of chaos and the enemy of order.”[53] Nothing here can fulfill our destinies nor explain how the universe is a unified whole with transcendent oversight. Since all of these things are ordered, Cicero rightfully concludes that they are “subject to the laws of nature.”[54]

Cicero’s view of the natural order culminates in his divine interpretation of the gods or the supreme God’s role in how the universe operates. While some have argued that Cicero was questionable in sincerity regarding particular religious practices, there is little dispute, given the array of sources, that Cicero caps his orderly view of the universe with a divine power—a belief that a “Supreme Being was as at work in the world.”[55] Throughout his philosophical works, it would be impossible to escape the endless ways he describes this divine oversight. In some cases, it is merely a matter of governance, a “governor of the universe.”[56] At the endpoint, Cicero argues, an orderly system must depend upon a supreme power, a “divine intelligence”[57] for the sake of its systematic logic. Divine providence encompasses the critical and active role of God as "the ordering principle of the world."[58] In *De Re Publica*, Cicero clearly expounds this need for order which is evident in any idea of law when he states that "there will not be different laws at Rome and at Athens," and that law will remain the same "now and in the future."[59] Cicero concludes that the law is "eternal and unchangeable ... valid for all nations and all times" with "one master and ruler, that is, God, over all of us, for he is the author of this law, its promulgator, and its enforcing judge."[60]

At other settings, Cicero's placement of a divine force, a divine being, a providential God, streams throughout his many discourses. Trying to typecast the descriptions would be impossible, for in some cases the divine power is a force that not only guides, but also oversees; in other cases the divine power directly interjects himself into the affairs of humankind. Sometimes, the gods merely watch events unfold, while in other circumstances the gods are quite active in the affairs of mankind. In his *Defense of Milo*, Cicero relays energetically:

> There is, there is indeed, such a heavenly power. It is not the truth, that in these bodies, and in this feebleness of ours there is something which is vigorous and embued with feeling, and nothing which is so in this vast and beautiful movement of nature. Unless perhaps some people think there is no such thing in existence because it is not apparent, nor visible; just as if we were able to see our own mind.[61]

For Cicero, the order of things must end at a highest being, the Creator, the designer of all in the universe. In this way, the natural order has little alternative but to depend, for its own design and living existence, on a being that depends on no other for existence, lacks all contingency, and which is the First Cause of all living beings, the Prime Mover in a world of subsequent movement of all sorts and upon a being completely self-subsistent. This can be none other than God. In all of nature, Cicero's God is more than a blending or merger of functions, as if nature and God were one—a clearly Stoical view that Cicero never seems comfortable with—but in its place a God that fashions nature, gives it a creative sketch to operate so to speak and by his creative design and authority assures its quality control. Nature and God are not a Pantheistic One or Cosmological Unity as some have concluded in Cicero. Otherwise, Cicero's view of the natural order would not so regularly place God outside its operative powers. Nor would Cicero be as attentive as he is to the hierarchical structuring of beings, from rocks and stones, to fish and mammals, from human persons to divine entities or beings. Cicero never avoids the "specific place of human beings with a hierarchy of nature."[62] In *Nature of the Gods*, Cicero keeps God distinct from the creation he is totally responsible for. "If we could see all this panorama in a single glance with our eyes, as we can in thought, I believe that nobody, seeing thus the whole wide world, could doubt the handiwork of God."[63]

Aside from his governing attributes, Cicero terms God in the most generous terms relating to creativity and creative design. For Cicero, God is the master architect of the universe and every being residing within it owes both its living force and its design of operation to God. When speaking of the construction of the human being, Cicero employs words of wonder and astonishment:

> That animal which we call man, endowed with foresight and quick intelligence, complex, keen, possessing memory, full of reason and prudence, has been given a certain distinguished status by the supreme God who created him; for he is the only one among so many different kinds and varieties of living beings who has a share in reason and thought, while all the rest are deprived of it. But what is more divine, I will not say in man only, but in all of heaven and earth, than reason? And reason, when it is full grown and perfected, is rightly called wisdom. Therefore, since there is nothing better than reason, and since it exists in both man and God, the first common possession of man and God is reason.[64]

Here, Cicero lays out a God that creates with endless logic and justice, never wasting energy on designs that are contrary to the laws of the universe or the laws of God. Cicero sees man as a reflection of the supreme God who has "begotten and equipped man, desiring him to be the chief of all created things."[65] This preeminent position among all created beings, is neither accident nor chance but a structure of being intentionally envisioned by the God who creates all things. In order to be happy, Cicero argues, we shall have to become self-aware of our grand design and our even grander placement among the hierarchy of beings that nature offers. As Cicero relays:

> For he who knows himself will realize, in the first place, that he has a divine element within him, and will think of his own inner nature as a kind of consecrated image of God; and so he will always act and think in a way worthy of so great a gift of the gods, and when he has examined and thoroughly tested himself, he will understand how nobly equipped by Nature he entered life, and what manifold means he possesses for the attainment and acquisition of wisdom.[66]

To be certain, man has an elevated relationship with the God who created and designed his shape and form—these attributes Cicero described as "great and gracious benefits"[67] and a "spectacle"[68] unique to Homo sapiens.

Aquinas on nature and the natural order

Given their very distinctive methods, a perfect alignment of Cicero and Aquinas on any topic would be impossible. Cicero's dialectic and poetic style is a far cry from the Angelic Doctor's systematic dissection of question, objection, and response. To be sure, we are dealing with thirteen centuries in which philosophical method moves from Platonic dialogues to the Article formatting. St. Thomas, if asked to explain and educate the masses on the behavior of small animals, would already have the topic indexed and systematized. That is part charm and part demand on behalf of St. Thomas for nothing is easily resolved in the argumentative arena that Aquinas creates. In the bulk of St. Thomas's philosophy we witness an acute form of conceptual dissection that lays bare any idea. With that approach, comes more science than poetry or prose. For example, we rarely find Aquinas wandering the grounds gazing at the stars, in awe of how quick the horse's gait might be or inspired by the majesty of a waterfall. This seems not Thomas's style for his general penchant is to pose a question for speculation and then reduce every imaginable dimension to that question into a myriad of parts and components. Each piece of the inquiry will be painstakingly asked and answered. Each theme in the grand scheme shall be methodically parsed to discern the propriety of any response. Hence, as Cicero stands in awe of harmonious planets and stars, Thomas cannot envision a planetary model operating with anything but scientific logic and divine order. It is glaringly apparent that Thomas favors the Aristotelian way while Cicero the Platonic vision of reality. Hence any discussion of nature, in the former case, relies on Aristotle's *Physics*, on *De Caelo*, or *Parva Animalia*, while Cicero would be more comfortable with *Timaeus*, the *Republic*, or Plato's *Laws*.

Thomas starts at the beginning by asking the most fundamental of questions: What is being? Why is this so? Being makes up the natural order. If being is composed of matter and form what is its composite of parts? Being and the essence of things are intertwined and the sum total of nature and the natural order. Being connotes what really is or what potential might be. Being is both "ens," what actually exists and is, or "ens possible," that is "anything capable of entering the world of concrete existence."[69] In the former category Thomas admits that the being is really a composite of matter and form. Erecting a reality based view of nature, Thomas assembles being into its proper categories and concludes that "whatever has been, or is, or will be, or could really be, under whatever mode or manner, is comprised under the object of metaphysics … even that which is affined to the concrete order of things by way of privation or negation."[70] Being is thusly reduced to its essence (ens) and its existence (esse) whereby the human actor knows of some beings and encounters its very existence in reality. In this way, St. Thomas proposes, in the broadest possible sense—where the mind or the intellect knows something to be and recognizes it when we encounter it—a type of realism that can be confirmed or corroborated.[71] As such, of all beings, only God is not a sum of ens and esse but rather "is." Therefore, although we know God exists we must look to the causes, effects, or the contingencies of being a dependent creature, rather than God's complete self-sufficiency as an independent being. For all other forms of being, simplicity gives way to parts. St. Thomas holds:

> A proposition is self-evident because the predicate is included in the essence of the subject as "Man is an animal" for an animal is contained in the essence of man. If, therefore the essence of the predicate and subject be known to all, the proposition will be self-evident to all.[72]

In the highest form of being, God is "His Very Godhead,"[73] or alternatively described, God "is the same as His essence or nature."[74] While we surely cannot claim that man is man as descriptive of the nature of man, we can be readily comfortable with assuming that God is God because He is God. St. Thomas qualifies the difference:

> To understand this, it must be noted that in things composed of matter and form, the nature or essence must differ from the *suppositum*, because the essence or nature connotes only what is included in the definition of the species; as, humanity connotes all that is included in the definition of man, for it is by this that man is man, and it is this that humanity signifies, that, namely, man is man. Now individual matter, with all the individualizing accidents, is not included in the definition of the species. For this particular flesh, these bones, this blackness or whiteness, etc., are not included in the definition of a man. Therefore this flesh, these bones, and the accidental qualities distinguishing this particular matter, are not included in humanity; and yet they are included in the thing which is a man.[75]

Using this line of reasoning, Aquinas delineates a theory of being and nature that further looks to whether being is self-subsistent or dependent on others for its existence. Here too, only God's being is completely and without equivocation thoroughly self-sufficient, for his existence and his essence are identical, unified, one and the same for God is "his own essence … his own existence … a non-participatory being, a first being … having nothing added to it."[76] To conclude in any other manner, St. Thomas declares would be "absurd."[77]

From his analysis of God, St. Thomas develops a hierarchy of being in a very general sense. As noted, only one form of being is self-subsisting and self-sufficient, in need of nothing and absolutely perfect. God is the First Cause in need of no cause; the Prime Mover not requiring any movement from another source and the fully perfect being without need of anything in way of addition or subtraction.[78] Everything else needs or depends on some other force of nature like movement, or cause, or a path to perfection.[79] As a result of this conclusion, St. Thomas describes every other type of being as:

> Of things that exist, some exist by nature, some from other causes. 'By nature' the animals and their parts exist, and the plants and the simple bodies (earth, fire, air, water)—for we say that these and the like exist 'by nature'. All the things mentioned present a feature in which they differ from things which are not constituted by nature. Each of them has within itself a principle of motion and of stationariness (in respect of place, or of growth and decrease, or by way of alteration). On the other hand, a bed and a coat and anything else of that sort, qua receiving these designations i.e. in so far as they are products of art—have no innate impulse to change. But in so far as they happen to be composed of stone or of earth or of a mixture of the two, they do have such an impulse.[80]

Every type of being is contingent or dependent except for God, St. Thomas declares. While only rational man images the Creator and displays, in common with the Creator, his or her intellectual powers and reason as part of the person's superstructure, as in Cicero there are descending levels and types of being, all of which make up the natural world.[81] St. Thomas further finds that all beings except for God are subject to motion, generation, and corruption for nothing in a temporal being can escape change since the passage of time is not a matter of choice. And since being is generated, it cannot be God since it depends on other human actors to generate its very form and essence. Everything generated, St. Thomas deduces, is "imperfect."[82] Within this Thomistic framework, being and nature always are evaluated in a hierarchical construct, descending downward from the highest life form to the lowest object. All lower forms are moved by the higher and this movement is perfectly "natural to the lower bodies to be moved by the heavenly bodies, which are higher in the order of nature, as is it natural to any creature whatsoever to be changed by God, according to his will."[83]

Natural function, natural design, and natural use

When compared with Cicero, Aquinas is much less descriptive in matters of natural biological function, the actual design of natural parts, and how that function and design relates to actual usage. As a result, Cicero expends extended time describing the makeup of the human body and its various components while Aquinas seems to assume the naturalness and orderliness of the eyes, ears, and the arms. This biological inquiry does not consume the writings of St. Thomas in the same way as Cicero, although here and there, throughout his extraordinary body of work, we find examples.

First, Aquinas cannot imagine a Creator who creates man devaluing the body to the advantage of a soul over all else—for some have argued that the body and soul are not unified to make up the composition of man. Others have claimed that the body cannot operate without the soul, though most would concur that the body of man needs the soul for its vivification, so to speak. What Aquinas makes plain is that man needs the connection of his physical body to his incorporeal soul in order to be man. "Some have thought that man's body was formed first in priority in time, and that afterward the soul was infused in to the formed body. But it is inconsistent with the perfection of the production of things that God should have made either the body without the soul, or the soul without the body since each is a part of human nature."[84] Thus, while the soul remains after the body's very corruption, in theological circles, the body retains its crucial place in the makeup and operation of the human person. In this worldly orb, humanity cannot function without a bodily artifice and yet that body lacks a living, breathing humanity without the soul. We are not, St. Thomas concludes, just "angels."[85]

In a more particular sense, St. Thomas queries whether the body of man "was given an apt disposition?"[86] As Cicero does, Thomas evaluates the overall construction of the human person and finds the arrangement proof of an intelligent designer. Labeling man as "natural" St. Thomas concludes that our design arises from "Divine art" and God, like every artist "intends to give his work the best disposition,"[87] it only makes sense to conclude our design most fitting and apt. Aquinas also evaluates our design by evaluating our natural end or purposes for human existence—so much so, that our engineering leads to divine understanding better than alternative constructions, and that our sensory and appetitive powers make our interaction with the intelligible world an easier encounter, and our stature affords greater opportunity to gaze rationally at the wonders of the universe and inevitably discover the orchestration by the divine.[88] God, St. Thomas holds, "fashioned the human body in that disposition that was best, as most suited to its form and to such operations … and suitably proportioned to the soul and its operations."[89]

Our brains, St. Thomas finds are just the right shape and size for "freedom of action in the interior powers required for the intellectual powers" and its temperature, its capacity to control and regulate other parts of the human physique and anatomy, does not happen by chance or accident.[90] Man's sense of smell, capacity of hearing, and other sensory abilities represent the "perfect equability of his temperament."[91]

This line of biological inquiry seems even more a hot topic in the twenty-first century than the thirteenth as observers attempt to find an ethical naturalism in the biology itself, or proof of God's very existence by the scientific complexity discovered or whether or not there is a DNA or genetic formula for right action. Jean Porter's *Nature as Reason* delivers a splendid debate about these possibilities, though never reaches a final conclusion about any of it when she remarks:

> It might be said that the fact that species and higher levels of kids really exist in nature, taken by itself, does not necessarily rule out the possibility that they are simply the products of chance developments. But if species and higher taxa actually do exist in nature, that is to say, if our concepts of kinds of creatures are not just projections, but reflect real features of the world—then species cannot be just random groupings of individuals.[92]

St. Thomas, on the other hand, appears comfortable judging biology by the wisdom of its ultimate artist or designer. If God is the creative power in all being, what end would be served to design a defective or deformed body? We have what we need to be harmonious with body and soul and the God who crafted our design for "nothing belonging to the completeness of human nature would have been lacking."[93]

Comparatively, St. Thomas looks to other mammals to discern whether their anatomical designs make sense for Homo sapiens. He notes that human beings do not need "horns and claws," nor a "toughness of hide," nor a substantial "quantity of hair and feather" since these additions "do not suit the nature of man."[94] However, man needs what he and Aristotle term as the "organ of organs"—the human hand—which is "capable of conceiving an infinite number of things, so as to make for itself an infinite number of instruments."[95]

Contrarily, animals do not need what man possesses, for their design would have little practicality, for its inherent makeup cannot employ such traits as an upright and erect stature. Here St. Thomas painstakingly lays out the brain's extraordinary placement—most appropriate in the upright human species but not so in the four legged mammal. To be upright rouses the necessary sensory powers that trigger and stimulate the brain, that provide greater range of motion being upright rather than facing downward and hence stimulating because all parts of the body are lifted up. In addition, to be upright encourages the use of hands, speech, and eyesight.[96] In the Thomistic view, as in Cicero's vision of how the universe and its creatures work, it would simply not be possible for the Creator to design functions without the being's overall end in mind. "Therefore God gave to each natural being the best disposition; not absolutely so, but in view of its proper end."[97] Jean Porter goes a little further, and correctly so, when she argues that both Aristotle and Thomas move toward a biology of beings that encompass the whole of nature—looking to the "natures of specific kinds of creatures, regarded as the intelligible principles of their existence and their causal powers."[98]

The natural order

On the second front of comparison, the natural order, Cicero and St. Thomas deliver a stunning array of similarities and differences. Differences are not typed as disputes but matters of coverage, for just as Cicero mulled the cosmos in more poetic terms when it comes to the placement and design of man, so too will Thomas display his undeniable scientific realism as any Aristotelian would. Again, Cicero is a grand social, political, and cosmological figure while St. Thomas clearly projects an emerging scientific empiricism blended with theological groundings. That a natural order exists in being would not be denied by St. Thomas. His overreaching term, used with regularity, is the idea of Divine Government.[99] Nothing happens by chance and "always for the best" and hence some sort of "providence direct[s] nature towards good as an end; which is to govern."[100]

For St. Thomas the best place to commence the concept of "natural order" is the highest and most perfect of beings—God. From this perspective, everything, once God is properly stationed in the universal scheme of beings, descends from God. In this sense, "the order of nature signifies the notion of origin in general."[101] Using the logic so often witnessed in St. Thomas, of first cause, the unmoved mover, and the supreme good, one can easily discern why an orderly governance of the universe cannot be denied. Thomas connects the Governor with the end of governance:

> For it belongs to the best to produce the best, as it is fitting that the supreme goodness of God should produce things without giving them perfection. Now a thing's ultimate perfection consists in the attainment of its end. Therefore, it belongs to the Divine goodness, as it brought things into existence, so to lead them to their end: and this is to govern.[102]

This is evident in his findings on worldly governance being the product of one rather than many players, and how all things are subject to governance and how impossible it is for anything to escape the oversight of God's governance. For in God, there is an "essential good" where "no addition is possible."[103] In God, no human being can resist or avoid the care and watchful eye of the Creator, "every inclination of anything, whether natural or voluntary, is a kind of impression from the first mover."[104] The universe, the natural order, by reason of God's governance, is properly and perfectly ordered.

Aquinas also wrestles with the concept of order in the natural law portion of his *Summa Theologica*—that section commonly known as the *Treatise on Law*.[105] The bulk of the natural law content follows in Chapter 5 of this text, but for the moment an analysis of his eternal law category is a central feature of the principle of order. In Thomas's legal theory, the entire legal infrastructure and superstructure is subject to oversight by the supreme exemplar in law—the eternal law—which governs the "whole community of the universe."[106] The same universe is guided and overseen by divine reason and its "conception of things is not subject to time but is eternal ... therefore it is that this kind of law must be called eternal."[107] As in other cases, the eternal law can be only one version for to conclude differently undermines any rational theory of a prime mover or first cause. The eternal law commands and oversees all things in the universe for God's power and omnipotence simply cannot be measured or plotted in boundaries. The eternal law extends its jurisdiction to all the natural order, when Thomas asserts:

> Now just as man, by such pronouncement, impresses a kind of inward principle of action on the man that is subject to him, so God imprints on the whole of nature the principles of its proper actions. And so, in this way, God is said to command the whole of nature ... And thus all actions and movements of the whole of nature are subject to the eternal law.[108]

Second, Thomas holds that the eternal law governs literally every human activity undertaken by man. Citing Augustine, he remarks "Nothing evades the laws of the most high Creator and Governor, for by him the peace of the universe is administered."[109] The eternal law of God is the exemplar, the template, the perfect jurisprudence for human operations for this law "is nothing else than a type of Divine Wisdom ... directing all actions and movements."[110]

In the same commentary, St. Thomas directly concurs with Cicero's *Nature of the Gods* when he observes: "Wherefore, the unfailing order we observe in things is a sign of their being governed; for instance, if we enter a well-ordered house we gather therefrom the intention of him that put it in order, as Tullius says quoting Aristotle."[111] At every line of reasoning, the human being is subject to the ordering that God creates without motion or cause—this mysterious yet logical Prime Mover of the natural order. Man is subject to this oversight without a choice in the matter Gilson claims, "first, as a natural being he is subject to the overruling of providence as is all creation; then, as being with mind and capable of sharing in an interior notion of this exterior divine law which rules him."[112]

Since nature and the natural order are not subsistent but relational to a higher Creator; it is not pantheistic or strictly a matter of cosmological soup giving rise to life accidently, but instead a growing, living, maturing, and especially a moving reality triggered at its origin by the First Cause and Unmoved Mover.[113] "As a general rule Thomas formulates: that which comes first is always preserved in what comes later."[114] Order exists in all things God has created—even in the nature and operation of virtue. Virtue is said to be consistent with nature, with law, with reason, and with God's plan for the achieving of every being's end. Virtues, like charity, need order as when "some things [are] loved out of charity, which order is in reference to the first principle of that love, which is God."[115] And our love of God must be ordered to God before others and in the greatest possible fervor since God is the cause of all being including self and neighbor. In this way, there is order to granting and giving love since "God ought to be loved chiefly and before all out of charity."[116]

Finally, the question of what is consistent with and compatible toward the natural order can be measured and evaluated in light of conduct to the contrary—the unnatural. For St. Thomas and his contemporaries, until really the midpoint of the twentieth century, the definition and measure was a variable regularly considered when deciphering the propriety of human affairs. To live in accordance with nature—that Stoic exhortation for a happy life—has surfaced in many forms over many schools of ethical inquiry. To live naturally is to live well. To abide by the laws of nature, one is bound to stay true to acceptable human conduct. When veering off that path, the ethical agent runs many risks from the traditional social-moral constructs to familial and to even biological and physical harms. Most unnatural things, most journeys outside the norm of nature, produce negative results. In most American criminal codes, by way of illustration, until the 1950s certain forms of conduct were seen as especially immoral due to their direct confrontation with the natural order. For example, bestiality or buggery, sexual intercourse with animals, was severely condemned for its intense refutation with what is natural—often termed "contra gravissima natura"—a concept that is best described as the most grave, most hideous, or most shameful when measured against the norm of nature. So too with sexual abuse of children, with homosexuality, with other acts that undermine the general moral definitions that Cicero and Aquinas had become comfortable with. While today's ethicist might scoff at such suggestions or paint them as the rantings of the homophobic religious zealot, many moral and sexual condemnations were rooted in a naturalist theory—that this sexual organ has this purpose, that sexual activities with our offspring contradicts the nature and health of a family, or that homosexual activity contradicts the natural procreative possibility. Put aside the politics of these debates and consider from whence these conclusions come—a very ordered, structurally naturalistic vision of behavior.[117]

It is not enough to merely scoff on the one side or continue the debate autonomically on the other but consider the value of the arguments in the context of a Ciceronian or Thomist naturalism. Within these contexts is there room for the natural order to shift a bit, or the laws of nature to be scrutinized with a little more inclusivity? Or, St. Thomas declares, shall vice, which is always contrary to the natural order, become acceptable or tolerated even in small doses? All vice, all sin is contrary to reason, as we discover in Chapter 4, and hence, "contrary to the nature of man, as man; while whatsoever is accord with reason, is in accord with the nature of man."[118]

Unnatural crimes and the natural order

To round out the analysis of Aquinas on the natural order, it makes perfect sense to consider his particular scrutiny of criminal felonies that have historically fallen under the category "unnatural." To expect the thirteenth-century Dominican philosopher to accept the current challenges to sodomy laws, as recently liberalized by courts and legislatures, or to have any inkling of a tolerant libertarian perspective on incest and bestiality would be utterly absurd. Of course, as contemporaries we have witnessed a cavalcade of challenges sweeping away traditional moorings and that tendency has accelerated in the last decade.[119] Any once settled notions of the "natural order" have long been lost in this debate but a revisit to once broadly accepted views may be instructive or remind us what the building blocks of traditional morality were.

Sodomy

American jurisdictions possess an expansive menu of conduct that falls under the sodomy category. Although St. Thomas deals with sodomy in the larger framework of "unnatural vice,"[120] he recognizes how all unnatural acts fit into the category. Bestiality, "uncleanness" as to oral sex, "monstrous and bestial manners of copulation," and acts of homosexuality are all lumped together. Until

Lawrence versus Texas,[121] where the US Supreme Court struck down the definition, sodomy was equated with homosexuality.

For the Thomist, sodomy fails on multiple fronts relating to the natural order and the end of sexual intercourse. Acts of sodomy have no end except pleasure and pleasure for its own sake is not a defensible moral argument. Human sexual practices cannot be separated from its natural purpose for this is what nature dictates and commands. Aquinas reserves a special characterization for these sorts of human behavior. "Just as the ordering of right reason proceeds from man, so the order of nature is from God Himself; wherefore in sins contrary to nature, whereby the very order of nature is violated, and injury is done to God, the Author of nature."[122] Anal intercourse between two men, oral sex between two women, or copulation between man and animal, annihilate the true meaning of human sexuality.[123] In addition, St. Thomas labels sodomy as "the greatest sin amongst the species of lust,"[124] ranking as the most egregious of offenses. Sodomy, aside from failing to meet the proper ends of the human species, directly assaults nature, being "against nature are also against God ... and are much more grievous."[125]

Incest

Sexual intercourse between those related by blood or special affinity and proximity has been universally condemned for much of recorded history. Incest has few supporters, but given the collapsing sexual mores witnessed in the last fifty years, advocates are sure to increase. St. Thomas mentions various situations in his commentary and argues that sexual relations between relatives suffer from "unbecomingness."[126] He commences his condemnation by portraying the natural aversion humans possess to such activities.[127] This extends to relationships of affinity, though less severe when compared with relationships built on consanguinity. These behaviors are ruinous to individuals, the family unit, and the community at large, and produce shame and disgrace for its victims.[128]

Thomas also argues that incest fosters insularity that is damaging to the social structure of a community. Incest would breed intermarriage, undermine true notions of friendship and cause less social and human interaction with those outside the circle of the nuclear family. Inbreeding can predictably lead to corruption on many fronts. St. Thomas indicates "Since through a man taking a stranger to wife, all his wife's relations are united to him by a special kind of friendship, as though they were of the same blood as himself."[129] In addition, St. Thomas offers the idea of control and sexual parameters. Unbridled sexual activity within the family is a recipe for disaster. St. Thomas sets out the strict boundary that this form of sexual activity is off limits.[130] St. Thomas offers no insights on the genetic rationale for criminalizing incest for it is likely that this sort of biogenic thinking was foreign to the medievalist.

Bestiality

Although Aquinas never directly addresses bestiality, his broader coverage of "unnatural sex" fully encompasses the practice. The *Summa* enunciates a clear definition of the offense: "Secondly by copulation with a thing of undue species, and this is called bestiality."[131] Any sexual action with animals in the lower order of nature offends the author of all creation—our eternal God. Bestiality consists of nothing more than a grievous vice "against nature," which in turn offends God. St. Thomas cogently writes: "Vices against nature are also against God … and are so much more grievous than the depravity of sacrilege, as the order impressed on human nature is prior to and more firm than any subsequently established order."[132] Hence, as nature has been erected, any alteration of that nature will be as condemnable as the damage caused by the unnatural act. Referencing the Book of Genesis, St. Thomas displays no diplomacy in his condemnation of bestiality. "He accused the brethren of a most wicked crime … that they copulated with cattle."[133] That bestiality was criminalized at the time of St. Thomas is not in dispute.

Comparative conclusion: Cicero and Aquinas; nature and the natural order

Granted the methods employed by Cicero and St. Thomas may be vastly different in style and process, but despite these procedural differences, the substantive results appear to be more similar than not. In addition, each may employ differing stresses to prove their arguments. The larger questions appear to reach compatible conclusions that:

1. Both view nature as a barometer of moral agency.
2. Human conduct and human affairs can be measured against the backdrop of nature.
3. There is some sort of divine governance, government of oversight.
4. Ethical decisions culminate in higher rather than lower beings issuing moral and ethical constructs.
5. There is a natural way to do things, to use something and to design compatibly.

6. Each part of the human person has a natural, functional purpose and should be used in accordance with that purpose.
7. Every human being has a specific end to achieve.
8. There is a natural order in the universe.
9. The natural order is not by chance of accident but by divine providence or oversight.
10. The order of the universe assumes higher beings descending to lower beings.
11. Some human conduct is natural while some is unnatural.

3

Cicero and Aquinas: Nature and Reason

From Chapter 2 it is difficult not to find a series of common themes and approaches regarding the idea of nature and its corresponding natural order. Certainly, the stress may differ in the various texts of these thinkers, though the bulk of their outlook seem utterly compatible. Cicero's method is clearly less scientific and more qualitative than Aquinas. Compared with Cicero, Aquinas sees the world a bit more empirically and scientifically, as would Aristotle. Aquinas clearly prefers Aristotle's *Physics* while Cicero delights in Plato's *Laws* and his *Republic*. Despite the differences, both define nature; both conclude that nature is a creation of God—a reflection, an image of the creative God; both naturally conclude that nature and natural order, its function and usage, display an inherent logic that sets all being toward its ultimate end or purpose. So far, we encounter two vastly diverse upbringings and backgrounds at play in reaching very close conclusions. From this stage forward we examine whether or not the nature and reason in the human person correlate in the worlds of Cicero and Aquinas, and if so, what implications can be drawn from this framework in the moral domain?

Nature and reason

Precisely how the term and concept of human reason fits into the world of nature has been a befuddling and highly complex question.[1] On the one hand, nature imputes a biological character; while on the other hand, reason seems nothing but an intangible, almost "soul-like" component in the human person. If the soul vivifies the body, Thomas held, the connection is at least dependent.[2] We have already been exposed to the diversity of ways in which nature can be explained, but not so as to the concept of reason. First, the very concept of order implies a type of rationality, accepting that everything in nature works toward some logical or reasoned purpose and that nothing in nature is for naught. Good or bad results arising from natural events and circumstances are just what the natural order demands for nature does not intend any particular outcome; nature does not mete out punishment or reward; nature cannot make specific judgments among competing choices or alternatives; instead, nature manifests a rational orderliness that we glean and observe in human and temporal reality.[3] If the conclusion were otherwise, nature and reason would be part of a larger, pantheistic, self-determined system that had already been programmed toward a natural result. Nature and reason would be, as the Stoics essentially declared, and both Cicero and Aquinas rejected, a cosmological Godhead inside the very nature He created. Instead of a transcendent God, the Stoics confined God, fenced Him into a natural system. While it is fair to agree that there might be a "rational orderliness"[4] to the universe, that rationality reflects the Creator's imprint in every creative act, rather than the intentionality of nature and reason itself as God.[5] Cicero and St. Thomas both agreed that God was the Creator of all and existence yet still independent of, distinct from, above and transcendentally beyond, the creative result. Undeniably, there is an "internal harmony" in the universe and a "harmonious co-existence as well as interaction of every part in its relation both to the whole and to all other parts, where each creature assumes and holds its proper, that is, divinely ordered, place."[6]

From a second perspective, nature and reason are joined by what already exists in reason—its content to consider, weigh, and evaluate. For reason—a composite of the intellect, the will and other factors—has certain inclinations in what it knows or wants to choose. Intellect, from its inception, as composed by the Creator, knows without much scrutiny or analysis what is good or consistent with its purpose and the larger end of the human agent. Everything, as Thomas and Cicero conclude, is from the time of its creative inception, driven toward the good, the ultimate end of its existence and predisposed to proper choices in human actions. How else could it be, if we assume that nature reflects the creative power and intelligence of a perfect, designing God since "man is said to be to the image of God by reason of his intellectual nature."[7] Hence, when Cicero says that the human person "is born for justice"[8] the argument presupposes a nature leaning in that direction—to just action rather unjust action. Right action, Cicero proclaims,

> is based, not upon man's opinions, but upon Nature. This fact will immediately be plain if you once get a clear conception of man's fellowship with man and union with his fellow-men. For no single thing is so like another, so exactly its

> counterpart, as all of us are to one another ... And this is sufficient proof that there is no difference in kind between man and man; for if there were, one definition could not be applicable to all men; and indeed reason, which alone raises us above the level of the beasts and enables us to draw inferences, to prove and disprove, to discuss and solve problems, and to come to conclusions, is certainly common to us all.[9]

If this is part of our makeup, and surely Aquinas will be on a similar road when speaking of the natural goodness in all beings, the inclination of human beings to virtue rather than vice, and that each possesses a deposit of knowledge, an imprint of content that the intellect and will know and consider, then each human being must have some level of pre-rational content. Aquinas's entire natural law presupposes that we are born with justice, and pieces or bits of all the virtues imbued partially in our very beings.[10] It also presupposes that there is tension when arguing for the superiority of will in regard to moral choices. Thomas deduces that the intellect knows the content of moral choices and presents them to the will for consideration, and while knowing what the correct action might be, cannot guarantee on man choosing correctly. The desire for something that a person knows to be immoral may overwhelm the intellect when it comes to choosing correct action. This is why Aquinas, as Aristotle did, bifurcates the intellect into two parts, namely, the speculative intellect, which weighs and evaluates conduct, and the practical intellect, which asks the moral agent to choose in light of the choices given.[11] In this way, St. Thomas accounts for knowledge embedded in the human player that can only derive a realistic context when thought of in applied settings and situations. In other words, one may know in a dispositional sense, what it means to be just although the true test will be whether or not one can correctly apply moral decision making to particular applications. In the latter case, pre-rational gives way to understanding for intellect weighs what it knows and chooses by will to apply or not. As we see, Cicero lacks this method. However, Cicero is equally plain that our judgments must be in accord with nature, or the reasoning is defective, wrong, and not the "recta ratio," which rounds out the equation.[12] To correctly apply the inherent knowledge that nature provides we must rightly think, correctly conclude that right reason has the force of "Law."[13] Vernon Bourke delivers his usual keenness when summarizing the demand that we think in accordance with how we were made:

> The speculative reason judges rightly when it is conformed to the existing nature of its real objects. Practical reasoning, on the other hand, is ruled, or rectified, by the judgments of speculative reason. The rightness, or wrongness, of a practical

> judgment—and of the resultant moral act—is determined, not by a direct comparison of the proposed act with the natures of things, but by the conformity, or nonconformity, of practical reasoning with speculative reasoning, through which the real order is primarily known.[14]

Finally, the blending of nature and reason leads to the inevitable discovery, by both Cicero and Thomas, that how we are constructed, even down to specific parts, manifests the imagery of a creative force, a God that fashions beings unaided, and has chosen to share that portion of his being that connotes his superiority to all other beings—reason. Only God and man have this capacity in the kingdom of beings and both Thomas and Cicero explicitly correlate our natural constitutions with the power of a Creator. If we were merely a mass of atomic particles or a simple mound of flesh, the comparison would falter miserably; therefore, the intellectual side of our composition, the rational attributes that are patently obvious when surveying the composite array of beings residing in nature, only man and his God possess the faculty of reason. Only Homo sapiens, as the name implies, can achieve true and meaningful intellectual development and understanding culminating in wisdom. Every other creature labors with such rational shortcomings that neither Cicero nor Aquinas could find the "image and likeness of God."[15] In this manner, Cicero concludes, only man participates at any level of divine imitation.

> That animal which we call man, endowed with foresight and quick intelligence, complex, keen, possessing memory, full or reason and prudence, has been given a certain distinguished status by the supreme God who created him; for he is the only one among so many different kinds and varieties of living beings who has a share in reason and thought, while all the rest are deprived of it. But what is more divine, I will not say in man only, but in all of heaven and earth, than reason?[16]

For St. Thomas the discussion here depends more strenuously on his hierarchy of laws—from the eternal to the human. In eternal law, which only God can completely comprehend because he is the law, the human actor receives an imprint of understanding by the status of reason. Only man is capable of grasping the complexity here and while there may be differing levels of illumination and understanding as the eternal law plays out in the affairs of men, there can be no denying that the rational creature partakes, participates, and encounters the eternal law of God. St. Thomas declares:

> A thing may be known in two ways: first in itself; secondly, in its effect. Wherein some likeness of that thing is found: thus someone not seeing the sun in its

> substance, may know it by its rays. So then, no one can know the eternal law, as it is in itself, except the blessed who see God in His Essence. But every rational creature knows it in its reflection, greater or less.[17]

For God and man, as Cicero concludes, there is shared reason—an attribute operating in both while leaving the remaining array of living beings out of this unique and exclusive club. God has "impressed" certain knowledge within reason, the intellect, and the mind, and since this is so, the human agent cannot advocate his own ignorance on proper human action. This imprint, universally stamped on each human agent, provides a rough sketch about what is to be done and what is to be avoided, or in natural law lingo—that "good is to be done and pursued, and evil is to be avoided."[18] Just as in Cicero, God has shaped and fashioned the human being with the tools and artifices that reflect the Creator—not by chance or accident but by a designing intelligence that seeks, as Cicero mentioned, a communion to develop between God and man.[19]

Discussions of imprints, impressions, inherent content, virtue, and vice—all will take on added importance as this treatise seeks to bridge a divide between a humanist in the mold of Cicero and a Philosopher-Theologian at the ranks of the Angelic Doctor in Roman Catholicism. Thus far, the similarities appear curiously striking. In the pages to follow, we discern whether those two worlds can meet regarding right reasoning about correct or agreed upon moral action.

Cicero on reason

Among the many choices for what nature and the natural order connects itself to, reason signifies the most dependable of choices. Other options would produce curious results in the search for moral order.[20] Consider if Cicero deduced that only emotion be the arbiter of moral choice—or what of sense alone—our touch, our smell, or our sight? What type of ethical construct would this be except utterly individualistic and relative—person to person? Choosing reason represents, at a minimum, the hope for thought and intellectual grounding, for rational rather than irrational reaction, and for a process whereby the human person can make choices and defend the logic of the choice. Emotions or senses falter in that mission, as would desire and will, passions, whim, or dependence on other forces to make deliberate judgments. Cicero's system elevates reason above all these alternatives and does so without any reservation or equivocality. He is certain that reason provides the grounding for all subsequent moral discussions, "Therefore, just as that divine mind is the Supreme Law, so, when reason is perfected in man, that also is Law, and this perfected reason exists in the mind of the wise man."[21]

In the mind, Cicero finds solace because actual knowledge is less influenced by the fleeting political realities, public opinion, or the clamor of the mob. In the mind, the moral arbiter encounters a deposit of knowledge that will contain the concepts, the ideas, the terms, and definitions of our moral discourse and debate about particular decisions. Reason knows while the will desires or wants, and in the former instance, the analysis takes place in a more predictable environment—and this is why Cicero is completely comfortable equating terms such as nature and law, being coupled with the idea of reason—both terms are a bit more fixed or stable than the emotive alternatives. When Cicero describes law, by way of illustration, the analysis is universal and unflinchingly dependable:

> True law is right reason in agreement with nature; it is of universal application, unchanging and everlasting; it summons to duty by its commands, and averts from wrongdoing by its prohibitions. And does not lay its commands or prohibitions upon good men in vain, though neither have any effect on the wicked. It is a sin to try to alter this law, nor is it allowable to attempt to repeal any part of it, and it is impossible to abolish it entirely.[22]

Reason, when compared with other measures, can weigh and evaluate human action empirically; it judges among a range of possibilities the best or better course of human action and it cannot, since it is a component part in the makeup of the human person, vary as wildly in said judgment as sensory, passionate, or emotional conclusions might. Moral choices are better scrutinized in a world less cluttered and more capably analyzed by a deductive rationality as to what is naturally known. Reason can also be described as a moderating influence in the being known as the human person—it is the defensive block against the baser instincts and inclinations that reside in every human person. Cicero finds that reason keeps the human person completely human and resistant to beastly tendencies. "But that power which is hidden in men's minds and forms part of them, and is called reason, controls and subdues not merely one animal, or one which is easily mastered—that is, if it ever does that which is rarely possible; for that fierce beast must be held in check."[23]

For Cicero, the beastly attributes are multiple and readily witnessed in human activity—in greed and lust, in cowardice, fear and cruelty, as well as "merciless cruelty."[24] Reason, when properly employed, should rule over the lower powers of man, exercise dominion as if "it rules over the body as a king governs his subjects, or a father his children ... whereas it rules over lust ... restraining it and breaking its power."[25]

Cicero finds that reason works the same no matter where a person may be, just as a law, in order to be a law at all, must exhibit these predictable and universal tendencies. Reason, in its proper position and place, provides the mind with the knowledge necessary to defend against the temptations that seem good but are imitators of the good. Reason, in the same way that God rules over man, "the mind over the body"[26] contains and mitigates the impact of evil vices and conduct that undermines the human condition. Cicero never hesitates when he argues:

> And there will not be different laws at Rome and at Athens, or different laws now and in the future, but for all nations and all times, and there will one master and ruler that is, God, over us all, for he is the author of this law, its promulgation, and its enforcing judge. Whoever is disobedient is fleeing from himself and denying his human nature.[27]

Encompassed with this sentence is the rich rationality and role of reason that will be the undergirding of the Ciceronian ethic. Reason will never be taken lightly by Cicero but properly placed at the center of his moral system, his legal analysis, and his ethical measure. Reason will never be subordinate to the sensory and appetitive counterpart that often deludes and tricks the intellect into thinking that bad behavior is actually defensible. Reason is, Cicero concludes "The restraint exercised by the best part of the mind, the reason, over its own evil and weak elements, such as the lustful desires, anger, and the other disquieting emotions."[28]

Reason, as part of our nature, and in a more cosmological context, as part of nature itself, provides the proper mechanism for making moral decisions, or the proper "idea of choosing."[29] Cicero could not have accorded reason a higher status when he notes:

> Law is the highest reason, implanted in Nature, which commands what ought to be done and forbids the opposite. This reason, when firmly fixed and fully developed in the human mind, is Law. And they believe that Law is intelligence, whose natural function it is to command right conduct and forbid wrongdoing ... Now if this is correct, as I think it to be in general, then the origin of Justice is to be found in Law, for Law is a natural force; it is the mind and reason of the intelligent man, the standard by which Justice and Injustice are measured.[30]

The rich tapestry of reason in Cicero's thought cannot be overemphasized. The conclusions about reason can be summarized as follows:

1. Reason exists in every human person
2. Reason reflects the Creator-God who fashioned the human person
3. Only God and man have reason
4. Reason exists in nature when the natural order is examined
5. Reason is naturally just because man is inherently just and born for justice
6. Right reason is the proper thought and analysis for moral decision making
7. Right reason is law in its correct form
8. Since reason is law, law is universal and unchanging
9. Reason is capable of providing a dependable ethical and moral framework when making moral choices

Reason, in Cicero's view, represents the most significant distinguishing characteristic in a series and typology of beings, for those possessing reason surely hold a higher or even the highest place in that delineation. The human person is undeniably a rational creature above all other descriptors and this intellectual vision of man is what identifies and marks man for his alignment with the higher order of the universe rather than its lower order. Cicero places reason atop the highest components in the makeup of man. "And since all things that possess reason stand above those things which are without reason, and since it would be sacrilege to say that anything stands above universal Nature, we must admit that reason is inherent in Nature."[31]

Cicero on reason and divine reflection

Cicero often grapples with a cosmology whereby God is nature and nature is God, and if this is so, reason as part of nature is both individuated and collective by design. In his brilliant discourse concerning the nature of the gods, Cicero kicks this concept around in so many passages yet eventually urges his readers to discovery outside the world that he created. Neither God nor the sum of his creations can be fenced in like other creative forces as if his inclusion were just another in a series of beings. And while God may providentially oversee and govern the creation of his doing, God is distinctively separated from the formal, natural world—a thesis of the Stoics that he rejects when he states, "But nothing is more excellent than the divine and to divinity must belong the government of the world. God is not subject to obey the laws of nature. It is nature that is subject to the laws of God."[32]

The significance of this argument lay not in the proof of God's external influence—outside the fullness of his creation, but in the sense that there is no collective mind—no universal reason, independently or inherently coursing its way through the cosmos. However, it is a safe conclusion that everything made by God makes sense and acts in cohesion with the natural order. Yet, this type of moral choice is neither intentional nor conscious but merely a reflection of God's creative rationality. Even so, there are individual beings, fashioned by God with a reason shared with the Creator, that are capable of moral differentiation. These beings, blessed and endowed with reason, share something in common with God, a rationality that no other creature in the universe possesses or has the potential to develop. Only the human person can share in this function of thinking and reasoning and because of this higher power, it is critical that we develop our understanding to its greatest clarity and certitude. In *De Re Publica*, Cicero refers to this relationship between God and man as a "privilege."

> Do you not think it important for our homes that we should know what is happening and being done in that home which is not shut in by the walls we build, but is the whole universe, a home, a fatherland which the gods have given us the privilege of sharing with them?[33]

For Cicero, the entire structure of his ethical, moral, and jurisprudential arguments harkens to a realm higher than secular or earthly considerations—"a path to heaven"[34]—and has a vastly different vision of God than his Stoic counterparts. Pantheism is not a position Cicero ever seems comfortable with for his descriptions of God are very, very Aristotelian. For example:

> For that which is always in motion is eternal, but that which communicates motions to something else, but is itself moved by another force, necessarily ceases to live when this motion ends. Therefore only that which moves itself never cease its motion, because it never abandons itself; nay, it is the source and first cause of motion in all other things that are moved.[35]

Adopting a sterile imagery of the Prime Mover/First Cause, Cicero rejects the purely cosmological notion of God when he comments, "Thus it follows that motion begins with that which is moved of itself; but this can neither be born nor die, or else all the heavens must fall and all nature perish, possessing no force from which they can receive the first impulse to motion."[36]

Within this creative realm, man labors under an obvious rule of the being creating the species but in ways shared that paint an intimate picture of the relationship between God and the human person. From his creative design, God fashions the human person to be "prudent, intelligent, complex, and keen, capable of remembering, of reasoning, and of planning."[37] God and the human person, as if foretelling a Christian conception of sacrament, and because of reason, are in "communion" with one another.[38] Because of reason, Cicero argues, man knows the content of the right and true and fully comprehends correct moral choices among competing choices. Since reason exists in both, "their sense of right is common to them."[39] Reason delivers a fixed series of moral concepts that can be universally understood and applied with predictable dependability rather than a relative series of edicts that vary from circumstance to circumstance, or from human agent to human agent for "goodness itself is good by reason not of opinion but of Nature."[40] Nature, as we have seen thus far, reflects the logic of its Creator too, and for this reason, it would make little or no sense to author a rational process inconsistent with truth, or as Cicero remarks:

> For all to whom Nature gave the power of reasoning have received from her the ability to reason correctly. Thus has arisen law, which is right reason as expressed in commands and prohibitions; and from law has come justice. Therefore, since Nature gave us all the ability to reason, she gave us also justice.[41]

In this way, Cicero portrays reason as a divine spark, a divine illumination, a divine part of the person's constitution and "since there is nothing better than reason"[42] it is a component part we should feel comfortable relying upon in moral decision making. Only the human person is even capable of reaching this level of ethical scrutiny and of differentiating courses of ethical choice all of which is due to the presence of reason in the mind of man. Cicero fully appreciates superiority and supremacy of the human beings in the earthly hierarchy of beings when he notes:

> Therefore among all the varieties of living beings, there is no creature except man which has any knowledge of God, and among men themselves, there is no race either so highly civilized or so savage as not to know that it must believe in a god, even if it does not know in what sort of god it ought to believe. Thus it is clear that man recognizes God because, in a way, he remembers and recognizes the source from which he sprang.[43]

That Cicero emphasizes reason as part of the divine reflection of an active, perfect, and creative God surely cannot be denied even with a cursory reading of his primary texts. Cicero expounds on this communion and commonality—of shared rationality at nearly every corner of his prolific body of work—for in the final analysis, there is no possibility of happiness or human fruition without attending to his metaphysics of God and his rational beings. Cicero exhorts the human player never to forget this crucial step in personal understanding, "For he who knows himself will realize, in the first place, that he has a divine element within him, and will think of his own inner nature as a kind of consecrated image of God; and so he will always act and think in a way worthy of so great a gift of the gods."[44]

In the end, self-knowledge depends upon the full comprehension of our divine reflection, our created imagery that mirrors the only piece of our design that bespeaks of something divine, namely reason. In reason, Cicero urges a discovery beyond self, of a whole universe without limitation. Our happiness is assured when we understand our placement and relationship with the divine being who created us, our destiny as free beings, authored and crafted by a divine God. To understand the fullness of our nature and the whole realm and kingdom known as nature, we have to leap past the physical world alone and tread into a higher, spiritual plane. With his usual poetic clarity, Cicero lays out the task at hand:

> And further, when it has examined the heavens, the earth, the seas, the nature of the universe, and understands whence all these things came and whither they must return, when and how they are destined to perish, what part of them is moral and transient and what is divine and eternal; and when it almost lays hold of the ruler and governor of the universe, and when it realizes that it is not shut in by [narrow] walls as a resident of some fixed spot, but is a citizen of the whole universe, as it were of a single city—then in the midst of this universal grandeur, and with such a view and comprehension of nature, ye immortal gods, how well it will know itself.[45]

Cicero on reason and virtue

Just as the Greeks so laboriously pondered before him, there is no question that Cicero's musings on reason tie to an examination of the good life, the happy life, and most importantly the virtuous disposition. Cicero never skirted the topic of how to live well, and this tendency, already discovered in the mantra of living well, or living naturally or in accordance with nature, was just the beginning of a more grandiose picture where reason and human virtue lay side by side. Cicero searches hard for the happiest possible life, and this he admits has a correlation to the moral qualities of every human agent, but this conclusion is not shared by his contemporaries. For one can display moral goodness yet still be tormented or punished for its very exercise.

Living in accordance with nature, with reason's own deposit of knowledge, may or may not, Cicero indicates, assure happiness in temporal circumstances, but it is a fair bet that even the most naturalistic person may be unhappy for other reasons. Virtue is the missing ingredient that assures moral goodness and in turn nearly guarantees the happy life. In his *Discussions at Tusculum*, he poses this exact dilemma in the early pages:

> So, you really mean that moral goodness is not capable, by itself, of creating a happy life? ... Are you saying, then, that when staunchness, dignity, courage, wisdom and all the other virtues are hurried along to the torturer, and do not flinch from even the most dreadful torments and pains, happiness stays behind on the threshold outside the prison walls?[46]

As Cicero debates his colleague at Tusculum, the question of happiness undergirds the entire discussion because happiness is "the most glorious maxim, the most magnificent and fruitful promise"[47] especially when we live in accordance with nature and virtue. Cicero eloquently correlates virtue and the happy life as if adhering to a series of laws as he similarly did when describing nature as a law or laws. For when the human actor lives in accordance with virtue, he has "obeyed its laws" and "shall never fail to be armed against all the hazards of fortune; that he shall possess and control, within his own self."[48] Virtue provides "every possible guarantee for a satisfactory and happy life."[49] In the broadest possible context, Cicero never abandons the idea that human happiness depends on a line of behavior that is consistent with nature, compatible with our very beings and natural to our dispositions. The world of vice, Cicero, properly deduces, leads to the opposite state of unhappiness, for greed and avarice—an excessive obsession with "wealth distinctions, great offices of state, power and glory"[50]—cannot lead to a state of true happiness. Those enslaved to lust, to "self-indulgence are slaves to their own bodies" who measure moral goodness on the "desirability and undesirability of pleasure,"[51] cannot discover the true essence of happiness. Pleasure for Cicero allures and deceives in so many circumstances that its measure can never be depended upon for moral assessment. Pleasure, Cicero extols, "lurks deep within us, entwined in our every sense—that counterfeit of good."[52] Nor will sensory perception lead to truth and certitude in moral affairs and the desired state of happiness, for the sensory realm is subject to external influences that "colour and bend them as they wish."[53] The Ciceronian view of happiness depends upon a virtuous disposition—one that values the proper ends of human life, the proper goods for human flourishing, and the adherence to a natural constitution in the human person that is inclined and predisposed toward virtue. Every other means of moral measure are subject to "corruption" or the "allurements"[54] that blind us from the correct path and roadway laid out by nature itself.

Reason, as we have thus far witnessed, accurately reflects the content of nature, and that our natural operations are fully discoverable within the rational sphere. For Cicero, the relationship between reason and nature could not be keener since reason, while "inherent in Nature," stands "above all those things which are without reason."[55] Reason is a natural component in the creature called the human person and therefore, ordered to the good, to the right, to the just and to the virtuous. Nature delivers a predictable, dependable, and universal formula for correct moral action since our natures are already inclined to the virtuous. We are, Cicero emphatically describes:

> [S]o constituted by Nature as to share the sense of Justice with one another and to pass it on to all men. And in this whole discussion I want it understood that I shall call Nature is [that which is implanted in us by Nature]; ... For those creatures who have received the gift of reason from Nature have also received right reason, and therefore they have also received the gift of Law, which is right reason applied to command and prohibition. And if they have received Law, they have received Justice also. Now all men have received reason; therefore all men have received Justice.[56]

Human beings are, Cicero observes, naturally inclined to virtue because of nature, in the global sense of the concept, and because we are naturally and rationally inclined to the virtues rather than the vices. Reason naturally knows virtue, and while it may subsequently chose vice over its content, Cicero never backtracks from this general thesis. The human person manifests far more in terms of universality than relativity at least in the question of makeup, for the virtues, like Justice, are "inherent in Nature."[57] Nature offers up a roadmap, a pathway for human operations, for moral goodness, that inevitably relies upon the full range of virtues for particular explanations for correct behavior. Virtues apply to particular circumstances such as when charity demands generosity versus a more measured response, or courage dictates sacrifice for fellows rather than the careless loss of life. Each virtue, from the moral, intellectual, and theological dimensions, applies to particular applications in human operations. In nature, Cicero finds answers and in reason, the correct deposit of principles for a virtuous life. In the end, both lead to moral goodness. In his *Discussions at Tusculum*, Cicero summarizes:

> That is the point where the second branch of study begins—the comprehension of moral goodness. The virtues blossom forth in their various forms and manifestations, and it is revealed to us what nature has ordained as the ultimate good and evil, the principles on which human obligations ought to be based, and the rules we must adopt for the conduct of our lives.[58]

Cicero's commentary displays an unrivaled eloquence and poignancy when he relays "Surely there comes nothing more valuable than the full realization that we are born for Justice, and that right is based, not upon men's opinions, but upon Nature."[59] This Justice is the binding force for the commonwealth of individuals that make up the collective, encouraging citizens to live in accordance with nature's laws and its overall virtue driven philosophy. Nature provides the certainty in moral matters where the relativity of men's opinions cannot. Without nature, Cicero envisions a chaotic moral state whereby just action would be evaluated in light of the "decrees of peoples, the edicts of princes, or decisions of judges."[60]

Cicero comparatively analyzes why nature and reason are the only reliable source for a virtue ethic. Those comparisons include the clamor of the mob or crowd, political power, military might, the principle of utility, cost-benefit analysis, as well as hedonism and personal pleasure. None of these measures, Cicero observes, offer an ethical system with dependable and universal principles and conclusions for "only a madman would conclude that these judgments are matters of opinion, and not fixed by Nature."[61] In reason and nature, Cicero finds a comfortable formula for discerning correct moral action, for nature has made these judgments "accurate."[62] Cicero comments:

> But if so great a power belongs to the decisions and decrees of fools that the laws of Nature can be changed by their votes, then why do they not ordain that what is bad or baneful shall be considered good and salutary? Or, if a law can make Justice out of Injustice, can it not also make good out of bad? … For virtue is reason completely developed; and this certainly is natural; therefore every honorable is likewise natural.[63]

From this perspective, Cicero propounds a view of reason that mirrors the nature of being—not just that reason is a part of a person's natural composition, as are the body and its parts, and that added to reason would be the mind, the soul, the intellect, the will, and the appetite. This is also because the logic of a nature and the natural order could not envision or hold fast to any form of reason inconsistent with what nature and the natural order commands. For nature and reason both are bound and inclined to those ends most conducive to flourishing and the development of being. For nature and reason are both reflections of a creative God that authors and designs reflections of the image of God the Creator. Reason would not or could not think incorrectly, or evaluate in error or mistake about what it knows, or erroneously distinguish and differentiate the just from the unjust, nor be in "agreement with that primal and most ancient of all things, Nature."[64]

Aquinas on reason

The role of reason in the philosophy of St. Thomas Aquinas is definitely central to his overall plan and system, for Thomas, just as Cicero concludes, construes the human person as the only earthly being that is properly termed rational as compared with irrational creatures such as mammals and creatures of the sea. Even in the continuum of moral deliberation, where the debate concerning the supremacy of reason and will has raged for millennia, St. Thomas determines that moral action cannot occur without a preeminent content, a knowledge base within the intellect itself being fully considered.[65] To choose a particular course of moral conduct will come after that knowledge; the choice being willed after the rational or intellectual consideration of the subject matter. In this intricate psychology, St. Thomas will paint a sophisticated picture of a moral being making specific choices, deliberating and choosing, electing and consenting, and finally realizing the fruits or detriments to that moral choice.[66] Here one encounters a moral being consisting of a body and soul. In the latter category, the soul vivifies matter, gives life to this being and is the "substantial form of the living man."[67]

Throughout his discourse on the nature of man, St. Thomas examines the rational being from an internal perspective, parsing up parts and dissecting the very elements and components that are sum and substance of this most intricate creature in God's creation. So while Thomas will concur with Cicero on the hierarchical complexity of the human person, a being at a higher station than any other, he will cover very little on man from a cosmological perspective. Cicero's penchant for describing man in the order of the universe clearly represents a main theme and thread in his analysis, while Aquinas treats man in an ontological sense. For instance, categories of what the human person is composed of—body, soul, intellect, reason, appetites, senses, and emotions—receive Thomas's rigorous scrutiny against the backdrop of an ultimate end for human life.[68] So in the case of the soul, we are treated to a deep, incisive examination on every aspect of the human soul from its incorporeality and incorruptibility to its complex union with the body. Each part of the greater design of the human person is fully and almost microanalytically examined, and this observation is especially telling when compared with Cicero's grander evaluation of what constitutes the human type. Cicero was no metaphysician and never really showed any tendencies in that direction. Instead, Cicero weighed and considered the human player from a more biological perspective against the larger framework of nature, hierarchy of beings, and divine reflection.

In the case of St. Thomas we encounter a great deal of sophistication yet simultaneously more imprecision than modern thinkers are comfortable with.[69] For example what, precisely, is reason? Is reason a rational function? Does reason depend upon "pre-rational" functions in order to carry out its business? Does reason depend upon the intellect alone for its functionality? Does reason utilize or employ will as part of its overall design and mission? Is thinking proof of reason's existence? Does reason depend upon "intelligibility" of beings or things for its overall function or can reason function without an observable, intelligible world about which to make judgments? Is reason descriptive of a process—a form of discursive thinking—whereby the human agent merely moves from the intelligible world to conclusions about what has been encountered? In the last case, St. Thomas may be clearest, for he states reason is undeniably a process dependent on the intellect, both speculatively and practically, and the will, which picks and chooses among alternative conducts. It could be easily gleaned from Thomas, that the term "reason" combines the intellect, the mind, the human brain and its various neurological functions. Thomas states plainly, in quoting Augustine, "[T]hat in which man excels irrational animals is reason, or mind, or intelligence, or whatever appropriate name we like to give it. Therefore, reason, intellect and mind are one power."[70]

Hence, the rational-irrational comparison, which is part of Cicero's method as well, leads to the inevitable conclusion that the thinking, understanding being, and the reasoning being is surely superior to all other forms of being, except for God. St. Thomas, therefore, marks reason to be the highest evidence of our superiority to other creatures in the natural world because these other creatures are not able to "attain to the knowledge of truth, which reason seeks."[71] These other beings are equally incapable of any path that reason might take—the discursive one—which St. Thomas describes thus:

> For to understand is simply to apprehend intelligible truth; and to reason is to advance from one thing understood to another, so as to know an intelligible

> truth ... But man arrives at the knowledge of intelligible truth by advancing from one thing to another; and, therefore, he is called rational. Reasoning, therefore, is compared to understanding, as movement to rest, or acquisition to possession; of which one belongs to the perfect, the other to the imperfect.[72]

In this way, reason encompasses a host of possible tasks and descriptive functions, however imprecise the actual definition may be. What we do know is that reason is both a process and a function, a power that applies its content to particular settings and situations. Jean Porter suggests, "Reason stems from these intelligibilities even as it determines the appropriate forms for their expression. By the same token, reason never operates in isolation from the intelligibilities informing pre-rational nature, nor can the normative force of reason be understood apart from its grounding in wider forms of intelligibility."[73]

For St. Thomas, reason operates at two distinct levels—a higher and a lower level; and it operates in two differing ways—speculatively and practically. In the former case, St. Thomas systematizes what most know that the mind deals with already—higher, contemplative abstractions—and yet is equally capable of applying knowledge to specific circumstances, or discerning what works in the intelligible world. In the same way, St. Thomas indicates that there are two types of intellectual activity that reason employs: speculation and practical knowledge.

The higher-lower schema, as to the power of reason, provides some timeless observations on how the human mind operates. At the higher level, the subject matter concerns things that are contemplative by nature, or eternal as much as we can comprehend, while at the lower reason, our examination concerns the "disposal of temporal things."[74] St. Thomas also uses the higher-lower forms of reason, not as disconnected, unrelated, distinct powers, but in unison with one another and as part of the same power. Higher subject matter can be interpreted in light of temporal effects, such as the proof of God's creation. In the case of lower reason, this too can be elevated to the highest science or understanding once we exhaust the contemplation of the temporal thing, since that temporal thing cannot explain the ultimate wisdom, or cause, or movement but by our knowledge of it, we are inevitably led to it. When considered in this manner, what emerges is a unity of knowledge whereby higher and lower depend upon one another. Reason, in this analysis, continues its unceasing movement, from one topic to another, St. Thomas explains. "But the power of reason is such that both medium and term belong to it. For the act of reason is, as it were, a movement from thing to another. But the same movable thing passes through the medium and reaches the end."[75]

When dealing with speculative and practical intellect, St. Thomas lays out another way of appreciating the eclectic nature of reason itself and, at the same time, how reason proceeds from understanding to pure human application. Knowledge for its own sake, in St. Thomas's eyes, is always a worthy endeavor but the test of its application assures a more accurate and dependable contemplation. Practical wisdom or knowledge is not some downtrodden category for Thomas but a coequal in his analysis of reason, mind, and understanding. This is the basis for a two-fold intellect in Thomism—namely, a passive intellect that receives and processes all information; and second, an active intellect that takes the knowledge and applies it to real world settings. "The intellect proper, the intellect *possibilis*, is the intellect which actually understands."[76] This bifurcation of intellect, Jean Porter claims, is a highly creative departure from traditional Scholasticism, for she concludes that contemplative reason alone is insufficient for a completely developed human life. Porter finds, "Even more strikingly, Aquinas denies that reason operating by itself leads to action. On the contrary, he holds that practical reflection and action always take their starting points from some desire."[77]

Stated another way, Aquinas resolves, in a radical way, that thought alone will not suffice; or to know is simply not enough because the human person finds his or her real purpose or meaning in actual agency, real movement, and concrete moral action. Rather than being a passive lump of flesh without meaningful activity, the human person does more than just think. In fact, the entire natural law edifice of St. Thomas depends more upon the practical intellect than the speculative because the content of the natural law is about doing this or that—preserving and procreating, caring and loving, and living and flourishing. His natural law principles, whether labeled "first," "primary or secondary" or other designations, are all grounded in "basic reasons for action, the sorts of ends and goods that are not means to or derived from other ends or goods."[78] It is practical reason that knows the goods that are naturally complimentary to a full, fruitful, and developed human life—those courses of human activity that assure the most productive and complete human existence. John Finnis, when discussing the role of practical reason, indicates that this type of reason is quick to identify the inclinations, the predilections, and dispositions that are natural to the human person.

> So we have an inclination to preserve ourselves in existence as the sort of beings we are; and we understand human life to be a good to be served and preserved. Elsewhere Aquinas refers to this good as conservation of oneself and refers to

> the good[s] most intrinsic to life (and to its conservation) as health and bodily integrity. The basic good in question can, then, be described as human life, in (if possible), maturity, integrity and health.[79]

In Chapter 4, the analysis of the natural law and its content, and the crucial role of practical intellect will be readily apparent. Despite this prominence, Thomas does not dispense with speculation, for within the speculative realm resides the truth as best a mortal man can discover it. Speculative intellect, speculative reasoning, is the jumping-off point for the ethicist in search of a moral code because the "speculative intellect becomes practical."[80] St. Thomas additionally concludes that speculation and practical application eventually must depend upon one another for the former is about "apprehension" and the latter about "operation."[81] Looked at from another angle, it would seem that neither form of intellect can ever find true meaning in a human life for the human agent must not only identify the truth about human existence, but also live out an existence in conformity with that truth. Thomas holds, "For it is the speculative intellect which directs what it apprehends, not to operation, but to the consideration of truth; while the practical intellect is that which directs what it apprehends to operation."[82]

The coverage posed here cannot do justice to the intricate and erudite Thomistic view of human reason and its various parts. Surely, just as crucial about reason, is its dominant position when compared with the will. St. Thomas holds that while the will is moved by a host of things, the intellect always stores the content of knowledge while the will evaluates that content and makes decisions. In this sense, the intellect is rightfully construed a "higher" power over the will, for the "object of the intellect is more simple and more absolute than the object of the will."[83]

Aquinas on reason and divine reflection

That Aquinas's ultimate end for the human person is his or her connection to God, by and through the Beatific Vision, as intimately as a human being can be to God, can be discovered consistently in his body of work. Part of this pining for an end which results in a reunion with the Creator God has tugged at us all during our time in the temporal sphere.[84] For St. Thomas, the natural law assumes that we believe in a God, we believe naturally and inherently in a being higher than our very corruptible selves and we yearn for a final participatory mode with Him, sharing in His "likeness … in a uniquely close and fulfilling way, through understanding God."[85] Aquinas relates this final aim in the *Summa Contra Gentiles*:

> Since all creatures, even those without understanding, are ordered to God as to an ultimate end, all attain this end in so far as they share something of the likeness of God; intelligent creatures attain him in a more special way, by their own operation, in understanding him. So the intelligent creature's end must be: to understand God.[86]

Thomas also deals with the dilemma of whether the all-powerful, all perfect, and all omniscient God can have any relational qualities with that which he creates. From another perspective, how can God, as perfect being at all, have any relationship or reflection on any of creation since these beings are by nature less perfect? Thomas finds that the relational quality of the being's nature may preclude it from establishing a relationship with the perfect God, but God does not exclude any being from his love and care. God, as First Cause, can relate to all beings as his effects. In this sense, God has a special relationship with his creative domain, although none reaches the immediacy of a relationship as God's role in the life of every human person. Here it is fair to say that God has created a being in his likeness—a being that has reason, that thinks rationally, and is the only being in the entire universe that possesses this trait or capacity. St. Thomas declares:

> Now since power is proper to God in relation to His effect, and since power, as was said, has his character of a principle, and since principle expresses relationship to that which proceeds from it, it is evident that something can be said of God relatively, with regard to His effects.
>
> Further, Likeness is a certain kind of relation. But God, even as other agents, produces something like to Himself. Therefore, something is said of Him relatively.[87]

Hence, God relates to his beings not as equal measure or identically, but by one, sole characteristic in the human person: reason. Both God and man reason, think, and speculate, and nothing else in the creative world can make that assertion. Even though the comparison falters due to the natural inequality that exists between a First Cause and a subsequent effect, there is still a likeness, though admittedly an "imperfect" one.[88] For Aquinas, the relationship between God and man is undeniable for man has been shaped and crafted in the image of God, while simultaneously accepting the extreme differences in a perfect being and a mere mortal. St. Thomas types the term image as being at "distance."[89] Even so, that chasm is scalable because of God's extraordinary love for all creation and the condition both beings share—a working intellect and processes essential for a reasoning being. St. Thomas accepts the formula of comparison easily, "Now it is manifest that in man there is some likeness to God, copies from God as from an exemplar; yet this likeness is not one of equality, for such an exemplar infinitely excels its copy. Therefore there is in man a likeness to God; not, indeed, a perfect likeness, but imperfect."[90]

This image and likeness is further tested under a series of challenges posed by St. Thomas. Are irrational creatures subject to the same rules? If we accept that God creates all beings, should there not be an image of God in lower creatures without reason, without intellect and working minds? Is not all creation an image of a creative God? To these questions, St. Thomas will qualify and keenly define the ideas of image or likeness while at the same time accept that all created beings can be traced back to the Creator. The matter of image and likeness assumes a similar condition or characteristic and since human beings are rational creatures, and the only other identifiable rational creature in the universe is God, that likeness can be confirmed. In irrational creatures, the likeness or image cannot be supported because the structure of rationality, namely intellect, mind, and reason itself, is completely missing. Only in "intellectual creatures" can any image be discerned.[91]

Support for this line of reasoning continues when he examines the comparative imagery of angels and men. In angels, incorporeal creatures with much higher intellectual clarity and knowledge, the image of God "is more perfect … than in man, because their intellectual nature is more perfect."[92] Citing Gregory, St. Thomas designates angels with a more eclectic definition of image, calling it a "seal of resemblance" where the "Divine image is wrought with greater expression."[93]

Thus far, St. Thomas affirms, without any equivocation, that the human characteristic or part that mirrors and images the Creator is reason and this conclusion he universally reaches about each and every man. God and man are intellectual creatures. All men are intellectual actors, and this being so, all share in the image and likeness of God. St. Thomas poses the dilemma, "Since man is said to be the image of God by reason of his intellectual nature, he is the most perfectly like God according to that in which he can best imitate God in his intellectual nature."[94] Throughout his discourse on the image of God in man, St. Thomas never leaves the parameters of these basic arguments, that the image is a shared capacity in both God and man whenever matters of intellect and mind are shown side by side. So too with the incorporeal soul that God and man both possess granting vast differences in scope and application. Not even the worst critics of St. Thomas's theory of image and likeness will be capable of a critique due to inconsistency. Thomas never buckles, for God's "image means a likeness which in some degree, however small, attains to a representation of the species."[95]

Reaching this conclusion on the image shared between God and man will inevitably lead to a few other features of this shared capacity, especially when it comes to knowledge of the precepts of the natural law and the infused virtue that need not be taught to the human agent. In addition, the likeness of God might be quantified by a view of the soul's incorruptibility, the presence of free will and self-movement, or the love of virtue or natural intelligence.[96] All of these comparisons say something of image and likeness though none more compellingly than our knowledge of the eternal and natural law.

For St. Thomas, the natural law is known by all, imprinted on all, and discoverable by all because with just a bit of introspection, an ad seriatim listing of moral do's and don'ts emerges. For law, as a general proposition, is the "rule and measure of reason"[97] and a "dictate of practical reason."[98] This content of the natural law, its principles, precepts, ordinances of operation, can be discovered in reason—that same shared characteristic between God and man. St. Thomas poetically describes it as, "the light of natural reason, whereby we discern what is good and what is evil, which is the function of the natural law, is nothing else than an imprint on us of the Divine light. It is therefore evident that the natural law is nothing else than the rational creature's participation of the eternal law."[99]

In this relationship between God and man, reason weaves its way into every facet of the discussion. Reason provides the bridge between the Creator and his created rational beings—those that think and deliberate, those that ponder and evaluate, and those that apply speculative knowledge to a more refined practical application. In the human person, reason provides the glue that attaches man to God and allows what Thomas calls as our best chance to "participate" or to be in communion with God. Thomas points out:

> Now among all others, the rational creature is subject to Divine Providence in the most excellent way, in so far as it partakes of a share of providence … Wherefore it has a share of the Eternal Reason, whereby it has a natural inclination to its proper act and end: and this participation of the eternal law in the rational creature is called the natural law.[100]

While our coverage of the natural law is brief here until a later chapter affords its proper due, the aim and purpose here is to demonstrate that reason again binds us to not only God, but also makes possible a natural law system. Reason, the intellect, and the mind, are all the locus for the divine imprint—that impression left by God in every rational being which includes the basic content of the natural law. Aquinas understands that this content, imbued into the mind of the human agent, represents the truths of moral agency and the correct formula for living right. Aquinas comprehends that this imprint, placed in the portion of man where image and likeness have real meaning, mirrors the truest and most meaningful participatory role that one can have with a perfect God. Aquinas captures this relationship at its most intimate and loving point, where "every rational creature knows in its reflection, greater or less" the eternal law of God[101] and also realizes that the "knowledge of truth is a kind of reflection of the eternal law, which is the unchangeable truth."[102]

Aquinas on reason and virtue

Any reader of Aquinas will quickly encounter a deeply developed and intricately woven virtue theory in much of his philosophy and theology.[103] Whether it is his analysis of the "good," the end or purposes for human life, or the purpose of law and legislation, St. Thomas regularly and consistently offers up a virtue theory as part of its construction. Virtue, for St. Thomas, represents a proper and comparative ordering of reason, a disciplined disposition to do what is good for the human person, the power and strength to achieve the suitable ends of the created being. In his analysis of love and friendship, St. Thomas puts virtue on a pedestal when compared with other earthly goods. "Virtue is much more honorable than money, whence those who feign virtue are more malicious than those who counterfeit money."[104] Gilson succinctly analyzes this aspect of St. Thomas:

> Each thing's good is what is suited to it in view of its form. Each thing's evil is whatever contradicts this form and tends, consequently, to destroy its order. Since man's form is his rational soul itself, every act conforming to reason must be called good, and every act contrary to it called evil. If we consider each individual act which conforms to reason, we shall find that it does so insofar as it is ordered to an end and to a series of means which the reason, after some investigation, declares good. So, the many particular good acts which man does are an ensemble of acts ordered to their end and justifiable by reason.[105]

Virtue is a power that stimulates the human agent to perfect. Since the "good for anything whatever consists in the fact that its action is in agreement with its form."[106] Virtue is the means by which reason will act in accordance with the essence of the being and avoid those things "repugnant to the nature of reason."[107]

That reason is the conduit for virtuous activity is consistent with Thomas's overall philosophy. Reason, if correctly applied, only deliberates and guides activities compatible with preservation. Virtue is critical to the unfolding of human capacity, and influences contrary to it, must be cast off. Even longtime friendship "should be dissolved toward those who do not remain in virtue."[108] Since the rule of reason is the measure of human activity, "the virtuous habit, for St. Thomas, is its agreement with reason. Man is marked by rationality as his specific difference: to become a morally perfected human being is to develop all four moral powers in accord with right reason."[109]

No thinker, except Aristotle, has so aggressively and decisively advanced this theory of virtue relating to reason as has St. Thomas. In the soul of man, we find either virtue or vice. In reason, if acting in accordance with our form, we find an inclination, a disposition to do good, to achieve proper ends. Virtue is the "perfection of a power,"[110] to perfect oneself according to our nature. Virtue's prime act is what is true "in making man's deed good."[111] Remembering that law, according to Thomistic jurisprudence, is nothing more than reason's rule and measure of human activity, it makes perfect sense to integrate the doctrine of virtues. Man's very essence is in the form of a rational soul and as a result there is in "every man a natural inclination to act according to reason: and this is to act according to virtue."[112]

In Thomas, virtue powerfully connects to the human person's quest for living the correct and moral life, as a recipe and formula for identifying and achieving the goods and ends that are consistent with our nature and as a pathway to the best perfection possible for the moral creature.[113] Human behavior is adjudged as virtuous because it is what is good, not merely what we claim is good for human operations. This is a fact lost on the moderns, those of the alleged Age of Enlightenment and the contemporary deconstructionist who find no value in anything universally. If anything, Aquinas sees virtue as the blueprint consistent with the design of the human agent, not something forced because of theological dictate or dogma. Alisdair MacIntrye's magnificent *After Virtue* captures the dilemma:

> But once the notion of essential human purposes or functions disappears from morality, it begins to appear implausible to treat moral judgments as factual statements.

> Moreover the secularization of morality by the Enlightenment has put in question the status of moral judgments as ostensible reports of divine law.[114]

Detached from this traditional mooring, contemporary virtue theory represents a lesson in pure contradiction—for on the one hand we are to live in accordance with a virtuous life, while on the other hand, one asks by what measure are we to decide what is virtuous? For Aquinas, virtue theory is about living compatibly with our nature, the natural law, the inherent design of the human person, the content of intellect, body, and soul all in proper order. Compared with today, often referred to an "emotivist" culture of relativity, there is simply no way to know anything with certitude.[115]

Virtue connotes power, strength, capacity, and capability, an almost enduring perseverance to choose and do right action. John Osterle generally finds that Thomas will label virtue "wholly positive"[116] and an "activity of human powers at their best."[117] In order that these powers be perfected, the human person will have to regulate the competing interests often posed by sensory and appetitive influences that may or may not cloud our understanding of correct human action, as do passions or a will that makes choices in opposition to reason's dictates. For in Thomas, all virtue can be discovered in reason itself since reason "is the first principle of human acts."[118] St. Thomas is clear about this unity of reason, will, and the appetites when it comes to finding the virtuous path or mean, "Accordingly for a man to do a good deed, it is requisite not only that his reason be well disposed by means of a habit of intellectual virtue; but also that his appetite be well disposed by means of a habit of moral virtue."[119] Virtue, then, connotes a perfective direction—whatever is done in the name of virtue always advances rather than detracts from the perfection of the human person. St. Thomas, relying on Aristotle, defines virtue as "that which makes its possessor good, and his work good otherwise."[120]

Precisely what direction virtue will take depends on the subject matter of the virtue in question. For example, to exhibit courage requires constancy despite challenging situations; to love in charity calls upon the actor to love even one's enemies; or to be temperate means to do things with sense, with moderation, and never to excess or deficit. Of course this is why the virtues are delineated in major categories, namely the intellectual, moral, and theological virtues. In this way, as Jean Porter holds, every "particular virtue is linked to a specific kind of action."[121] The examples are as numerous as the virtue's designation and definition, although all of these perfections, lead to better character in that person. Finnis remarks,

> This is not some prim conformity to convention or rule, but excellence and strength [virtus] of character involving a disposition and readiness to act with intelligent love in pursuit of real goods—the basic human goods towards which the primary practical principles direct—and successful resistance to the ultimately unreasonable lure of bad options.[122]

The sophistication of Thomistic psychology is obvious to those familiar with the virtue theory of St. Thomas. Each human person has extraordinary, almost exceptional control of one's behavior, for despite knowing the better paths of basic human goods, human beings are free to choose despite the natural inclination to do good and avoid evil. Our DNA, imaged by a perfect, creative God, cannot be the sum and substance of error and vice but rather is by nature a good being, leaning and moving in naturally moral directions, yet simultaneously perfectly capable of choosing a life of vice as opposed to virtue. And while reason knows basic content, contained and encapsulated in what connotes the natural law, the human person is still capable of a level of corruption that leads to moral blindness.

Thomas indicates that most of the virtues we see in human operations are not inherent but acquired, developed behaviors and habituations that become second nature to us. Virtues, St. Thomas states are, in a word, "habits"[123] that can increase in power and strength through repetition, while at the same time decrease by neglect or repetition in a vice laden lifestyle. Not only do we have the power to choose conduct, but we also have the distinct capacity to ratchet up or dial down the behavior, which in turn leads to variable habituations. Even the mind, the content area of the intellectual virtues such as prudence, wisdom, understanding, and the like, is subject to this corruption. Thomas holds "Therefore a habit either of virtue or vice, may be corrupted by a judgment of reason, whenever its motion is contrary to such vice or virtue, whether through ignorance, passion or deliberate choice."[124]

Thus far we have established that virtues for St. Thomas are fundamentally habits, subject to addition and/or corruption, the majority of which are acquired by repetition leading to habituation or nondevelopment, causing a sort of neglect that undermines the development of the virtue. Learned too, is that there is a small portion of our virtues that appear to be inherent or infused, innately part of our "good nature."[125] The opposite result of virtue is the condition of vice, whereby the order of things in the species, and in reason itself, becomes disordered because the choices made about human operations are contrary to our proper development and flourishing. More specifically, vice represents a rejection of reason's knowing path to the preference of an errant will or appetitive attraction that undermines right reason. St. Thomas is completely clear when he articulates "The evil of drunkenness and excessive drink, consists in falling away from the order of reason. Now it happens that, together with this falling away from reason, some lower power is perfect in reference to that which belongs to its own kind, even in direct opposition to reason, or with some falling away therefrom."[126]

In reason Aquinas rests the heavy understanding of virtue in every imaginable form—not in its alternatives of passions, emotions, appetites, or the will. These latter categories are so utterly relative that virtue could never find a footing or framework to plant itself. Instead, Thomas chooses reason as the fixed position for virtue analysis for two reasons: first, there is no other possible alternative in the discovery of human behavior that instructs on what human goods and corresponding human operations should be; second, that these nonrational characteristics cannot stand on their own—cannot decide or know on their own or provide any knowing mechanism for choices in human operations. Only the intellectual qualities of the human person are capable of this. St. Thomas considers the possibility when he comments:

> For virtue is a perfect habit, by which it never happens that anything but good is done: and so virtue must needs be in that power which consummates the good act. But the knowledge of truth is not consummated in the sensitive powers of apprehension: for such powers prepare the way to the intellective knowledge. And therefore in these powers there are none of the virtues, by which we know truth: these are rather in the intellect or reason.[127]

For in reason, a measuring takes place, an evaluation of act and knowledge so to speak such as what conduct is the best choice among others posed. To illustrate, as in Cicero's "recta ratio" (right reason), St. Thomas will conclude that reason has a range of knowledge, degrees of wisdom, variations in prudential insight, and overall capacity to think correctly. In other words, it is not enough that we think but more emphatically that we think correctly, consistently with our ultimate end, our goods, and purposes. While everyone thinks, the variations in the quality and correctness of that thinking may vary widely. Hence, virtue, as applied to human operations, whether it is about our mind, body, or soul, has an appropriate rectitude, a mean achieved by balancing and applying reason to particular facts or settings. Virtues are the "mean," the balance appropriate in any human context.[128] This is not strictly a mathematical computation that finds moderation in this or that, but a final determination that a particular human action, carried out in moderation, represents the perfect balance of being, the good and the end of the human player. The mean is between, Thomas comments:

> In actions and passions the mean and the extremes depend on various circumstances: hence nothing hinders something from being extreme in a particular virtue as to one circumstance, while the same thing is a mean in respect of other circumstances, through being in conformity with reason. This is the case with magnanimity and magnificence. For if we look at the absolute quantity of the respective objects of these virtues, we shall call it an extreme and a maximum: but if we consider the quantity in relation to other circumstances, then it has the character of a mean: since these virtues tend to this maximum in accordance with the rule of reason, i.e., *where* it is right, *when* it is right, and for an *end* that is right.[129]

It is more appropriately termed the "mean of reason"—not a mathematical, computational, or political mean. This is true for intellectual virtues, prudential judgments, and theological insights as well. Every virtue is good only if it "consists in its observing the mean, by conformity with a rule or measure in respect of which it may happen to be excessive or deficient, as stated above. Now intellectual virtue, like moral virtue, is directed to the good."[130] Each virtue focuses on the just mean of human activity. To be in conformity with right reason the just mean is:

> removed from excess and defect in each given case. Sometimes it happens that the mean fixed by reason is the mean of the thing itself, as in the case of justice which regulates operations relating to external acts, and must assign to each his due, neither more nor less. Sometimes, on the contrary, it happens that the mean fixed by reason is not the mean of the thing itself, but one that is a mean in relation to us.[131]

In the end, virtue signifies a balance of action with moral knowledge discoverable in the rational being. St. Thomas lays out the formula:

> Now this happens in two ways. First, by reason of their suitableness or unsuitableness to nature. In this way, a good habit is specifically distinct from a bad habit; since a good habit is one which disposes to an act suitable to the agent's nature, while an evil act is one which disposes to an act unsuitable to nature. Thus, acts of virtue are suitable to human nature, since they are according to reason, whereas acts of vice are discordant from human nature, since they are against reason.[132]

At no place is this form of critique more evident than the Thomist view of law and its interrelationship with reason. In law, St. Thomas finds "rationality and orderliness."[133] In law, reason sits as centerpiece in his theory of jurisprudence when he asserts:

> Law is a rule and measure of acts, whereby man is induced to act or is restrained from acting; for lex (law) is derived from ligare (to bind), because it binds one to act. Now the rule and measure of human acts is the reason, which is the first principle of human acts … since it belongs to the reason to direct to an end, which is the first principle in all matter of action.[134]

From the earliest pages of the *Treatise on Law*, St. Thomas places reason in its primary place and context when judgments are rendered about acceptable human behavior. Laws, if effective and meaningful, must be the product of a rational being, using and employing reason to adhere to what nature demands of us. To live in accordance with nature, is to live a fully reasoned and virtuous existence for only "reason issues its commands as regards things ordained" to our proper end.[135] Aquinas never ceases to blend reason and virtue with his jurisprudence for he sees law as a "dictate of reason,"[136] its primary effect being to "lead its subjects to their proper virtue."[137] When Thomas delineates his theory of natural law, he commences that discussion by referencing how the human agent can naturally know its content and how by "the light of natural reason … we discern what is good and what is evil."[138] When connecting human law, primarily the promulgation of the legislator, St. Thomas characterizes these practical applications, these "particular determinations, devised by human reason,"[139] as dependent upon the identical theory of reason as does the natural law. Human law is still a "dictate of the practical reason" that depends on "human reason to proceed."[140] At the same time that reason is trumpeted as the rule and measure of law, its effects and impacts are directed to the good, to the virtuous, and ultimately our natural and final end—God. St. Thomas declares that the natural law prescribes "all acts of virtue" when he relays,

> [T]o the natural law belongs everything to which a man is inclined according to his nature. Now each thing is inclined naturally to an operation that is suitable to it according to its form; thus fire is inclined to give heat. Wherefore, since the rational soul is the proper form of man, there is in every man a natural inclination to act according to reason; and this is to act according to virtue.[141]

This same line of reasoning continues in the analysis of human law, whereby Thomas similarly deduces that human law, to be law at all, must uphold "good order, whereby the citizens are directed in the upholding of the common good of justice and peace."[142] Interestingly, Thomas cautions the lawgiver on zealous attempts to utilize the law as absolute control or repression of all vice, a use that he would consider implausible. Given the reality of human behavior and "according to the customs of a country"[143] the legislator cannot be expected to eradicate all human sin and vice by and through the mechanism of laws. The lines between absolute prohibition, tyranny, and repression may be closer than realized, St. Thomas finds. To control and dominate less than desirable behavior, even vice itself, may be unrealistic since these laws and precepts will be "despised, and those men, from contempt, break out into evils worse still."[144]

Hence, in union with Cicero, St. Thomas proposes an ethical system that depends foremost upon the supremacy of reason in human operations. When compared with the will, the passions, and sense appetites, reason delivers the most objective measure for a moral code. Next, this same reason is inexorably tied to the powerful virtue theory of Aquinas, which manifests itself across the great body of Thomistic works. Virtue is primarily a habit, and habituation will vary depending upon its subject matter, whether moral, intellectual, or spiritual in scope. Finally, just as Cicero expounds in *De Legibus*—the concept and idea of law inevitably weaves back to reason and virtue, just as the two thinkers agreed on in regard to nature. While Thomas may offer more theological rationales for these positions, and more microscopically examine specific issues—the major themes—of reason and nature are uncannily compatible.

The compatibility of Cicero and Aquinas: Nature, reason, and virtue

On close examination, it is difficult to discern extraordinary differences between Thomas and Cicero on these conceptual frameworks. While the emphasis may vary a bit, both Thomas and Cicero adhere to one another in generally identical ways. First, nature consumes their attention though it is a fair bet, as was said in Chapter 2, Cicero may expend more energy on a biologic nature, and his teleological tendencies belie that. Not the perfect Stoic, Cicero rejects a pantheistic God, though some may find otherwise, and relegates nature to an effect of a perfect and creative God. By contrast, Thomas will evaluate nature as a hierarchical construct of varying beings—all of which are good due to the God that created them. At top of the temporal order shall be the human person—the only creature properly described as rational. This rational creature is capable of using reason, which contains the necessary content for correct moral choices. Reason is as natural a part of our human constitution as a membrane, an eye, or other appendage, but can only be used properly when driven toward virtuous conduct and our proper and ultimate end. Reason is bound up in both virtue theories since each thinker discounts the alternatives—namely, sense, will, and emotions. Reason alone, is capable of delivering objective, reliable information on the content of virtuous human conduct. Reason contains a deposit of knowledge that constitutes virtue but also the law, and while some of this knowledge is infused in our nature; much of it is learned by habituation, repetitive conduct, and instruction. Cicero and Aquinas link reason and nature; both blend reason with knowledge of correct moral action, and both find that virtue is discoverable in the orderliness of nature, its beings, and its effects. In sum, Cicero and Aquinas are comfortable with first discovering the nature of being before it and then, "in tune with its fundamental nature, moving towards the proper end and objects of its very existence. God's 'architectonic plan' is part of God's reason, from the origin of the universe to the fluidity of the present."[145]

Second, the idea that reason in the human person mirrors the God who fashioned them appears adopted by both Cicero and Thomas. Surely there are fundamental differences in how each argument plays out, although the conclusions for the most part are eerily similar. In either camp, the parties accept that there is a Creator-God—a force designated a Prime Mover, First Cause, and the like. This being must be God and all other beings, following in sequential order, are secondary beings, moved rather than unmoved, and hence not a supreme God. So, even from a theological perspective, the result seems compatible. From this, it is fairly concluded, that the effects—that reflection of the Prime Mover—must be self-evident in every created being descending from this omniscient God. For Cicero and Thomas the unquestionable feature that connects God and man is reason, for only reason is the sole characteristic shared by God and man. Reason manifests that God and the human being are rational creatures, and no other creature has such capacity in the universe. As a consequence, given what we have seen thus far, this reason opens the door to other dimensions of communion between the Creator and the created rational person; both beings think, know certain and select content about virtue, and the natural law. Accepting all of this, it can be concluded that we are inclined and predisposed to certain behaviors. Since a perfect God created us, we must be designed with perfection in mind—with virtue on the front burner rather than the back. If we are crafted in the image of God, then we are "capable of rational knowledge and self-direction."[146] To have such intimate company with the Creator who creates all is, in a way, far more than a mere reflection, but as St. Thomas will expound in his natural law theory, a "participation"[147] by man in the very mind and life of God.

4

Cicero and Aquinas on the Natural Law

Introduction

Whether Cicero and Aquinas share a philosophy rooted in the natural law, frames an essential rationale for this text's analysis. In this question, one can posit the existence or lack of a shared vision despite their vastly different cultural, religious, and theological-philosophical outlooks. To be clear, can a pagan and secular thinker reach a similar series of conclusions about the idea and application of a natural law as those reached by the Angelic Doctor of the Roman Catholic Church? To answer this affirmatively depends on the considerations thus far covered on virtue, nature, reason, divine imagery, and illumination, but most critically as to a finding on the natural law itself. For none of these moral queries make much sense without a system to evaluate moral action. In St. Thomas there can be no dispute about his natural law design and systematic approach since the natural law serves as centerpiece for his moral and ethical framework. Natural law is indispensable to any conclusions or justifications regarding human conduct, and even the most minor of controls or bases for law and legislation will be assessed in light of its content and provisions. When St. Thomas indicates that all human law, even the seemingly insignificant provisions, must be evaluated in light of natural law, he is urging the evaluator to look to the pervasive and holistic influence of the natural law, not its limitations.[1] In every context the natural law has meaning and influence when it comes to moral scrutiny. So while an act like taxation may initially appear morally neutral, for St. Thomas even this governmental extraction will have natural law implications such as whether or not the tax is justly imposed, fairly enacted, an appropriate matter for assessment, and whether its imposition is properly proportionate to the citizen's capacity to pay. These are just a few of the natural law implications that can be gleaned from the act of taxing, illustrating how St. Thomas weaves a natural law perspective into literally every human action. He does so with an explicitness and clarity that most other advocates are incapable of. Aquinas recognizes, more than any other, how the natural law fully integrates with our psychology, our make up, and creative design and how uniquely we as creatures are attuned to its content. As Alisdair MacIntyre concludes, "What needs emphasizing is that in Aquinas' view the precepts of the natural law function in more than one way in the moral life. They are the expression of divine law as apprehended by human reason, and God in uttering those precepts in human beings is at once sovereign legislator and teacher."[2]

Hence, when analyzing St. Thomas, the discovery of a natural law theory will be an easy undertaking. The larger question, and the more relevant scrutiny, will be whether or not his theory of natural law and that of Cicero will be complimentary and compatible. In reviewing Cicero's literature, there are many scholars that claim the self-evidence of a natural law theory. To be fair, it seems almost impossible that this conclusion is not reasonable. However, the thrust and emphasis of Cicero's perspective may look identical in places, while at the same time the description employed by the great Roman orator carries a distinctively different message. Already referenced has been his Stoical tendency, his cosmological inclinations that tend to make law, and his belief that God or the gods are part of the created universe whereby God is merely nature itself—none of which is acceptable to any Thomist. On the other hand, Cicero discounts a good deal of this when he adopts the unmoved mover mentality and separates creation from the Creator, when he describes the image of God as a mere reflection in man rather than some essential identicality, or when he describes a hierarchical structure of law that ends in the human promulgation but begins before the world ever commenced. Other examples would fuel the debate, but suffice it to say there are both structural and methodological differences in how Cicero and Aquinas deal with the natural law. Discovering those differences, and possibly reconciling them, is the chief aim of this chapter.

Cicero on the natural law

To say that Cicero's influence on Western civilization, especially as relating to law, jurisprudence, constitutional republicanism, and the virtuous citizen, has not been "profound"[3] would be an egregious misunderstanding of his importance. Some have argued Cicero was the "father" of the natural law concept, which includes a "supreme law, prior to all human laws, the same everywhere in the world and recognized by all men, whose sanction is divine."[4] Frank O. Copely describes Cicero as a "towering, not to say overpowering figure whose brilliant statecraft, penetrating intellect, broad humanity, and rich literary gifts guaranteed him a commanding place in the intellectual life of all succeeding periods."[5] Though a few of his critics belabor his lack of originality in philosophical pursuits, that conclusion usually overlooks that Cicero blended what was known at his time, with what he had been bequeathed from earlier times. Hence, Cicero had an earnest reverence for Greek thinking and its perennial relevance.[6] When this is coupled with the later Christian thinkers, such as Augustine and Aquinas, it is readily apparent that his originality is not subject to question.[7] Aristotle provides little if any guidance on the natural law, nor can it be said that Plato delivers anything remotely as coherent on this sort of jurisprudence.[8] At no place in the Thomistic corpus does a pagan hold such sway as Cicero regarding a philosophy of jurisprudence. When speaking of a natural law or a law of nature, Cicero receives the reference, not his Greek forefathers. The "range and brilliance of Cicero's gifts"[9] becomes clear as Thomas unfolds his systematic jurisprudence rooted in the natural law. Cicero was quoted more frequently than any other Latin writer in the magnificent opus of St. Thomas and understandably so. For in Cicero, practical knowledge always courses through his dialogue and debate; the affairs of human beings remain centered in the discussion; the power and influence of law, legislation, and leadership sitting on the edge of his pen and his oratory at all times, for this was Rome's greatest lawyer pining for philosophical truth. Cicero was a man in search of the ultimate meaning for human life yet he could never detach his profession, his practical reality, and existence from those very questions. It is difficult to envision a more perfect match for his inquiry into law, and more specifically the natural law, than being the lawyer advocate coupled with the speculative philosopher. Instead the world is usually treated to one or the other—the thinker incapable of blending speculation with practicality—something Cicero brilliantly accomplished. Given today's blistering antagonism between those who disagree on particular moral issues, or even if we accept the misery of a plebiscite incapable of making moral judgments fearing offense to others because the judgment was made, or finally because the general citizenry is so morally numb it is incapable of this type of moral calculation, it may be time to visit the glory and brilliance of Cicero again—especially when evaluated against the backdrop of St. Thomas. These times, as L. P. Wilkinson puts it, are much like Cicero's:

> It so happened that the life of Cicero coincided with one of those tides in the affairs of men when the cross-currents come to the surface so that we seem to

> see more clearly than usual the pattern of cause and effect. We recognize similar conjunctions when they occur again, and are tempted to evolve hazardous theories of historical cycles. We must be aware indeed of seeing history through modern spectacles; and yet it is precisely the recognition of analogous situations that makes such periods particularly exciting.[10]

At the crossroads, the inquiry finds meaning and conceptual continuity. Was Cicero's natural law the same as that proposed by St. Thomas? Or are these propositions, posed nearly thirteen centuries apart, incapable of reconciliation?

Cicero: A law of nature or a natural law

Whenever we encounter Cicero's idea and concept of law, it becomes quickly apparent that promulgation of human law, alone and in itself, can never encompass the depth and breadth of his jurisprudence. Ciceronian law resides on various strata—at street level where promulgation occurs; at the moral level where law is scrutinized for its right action; and at a metaphysical level where law emerges as existent before any human affairs operate. In this last category, the metaphysical, Cicero's legal theory takes on a divine quality since his entire legal system depends on the higher to the lower. He states in *De Legibus*: "{L}et us begin with the Supreme Law which had its origin ages before any written law existed or any state had been established."[11] In the same text, Cicero repeatedly chides those who see law as moored in human affairs alone calling the conclusion "the most foolish notion of all"[12] for human customs, human laws, national and state laws mean promulgation for the moment alone. Today, with positivism reigning supreme in human affairs, it is almost incomprehensible that Cicero would discount human law as strenuously as he does. Law, in its most original and primal form is "not a product of human thought, nor is it any enactment of peoples, but something eternal which rules the whole universe by its wisdom in command and prohibition."[13]

While Cicero poses a hierarchical structure in his jurisprudence, a closer reading manifests an alternative stress—one with enormous emphasis on nature's laws and laws of nature. In other words, Cicero expends a significant amount of text discussing and describing the "law of nature" as compared with a "natural law." Even the Latin translation has some contrast whereby the former is "lex naturae" while the latter is "lex naturalis."[14] When discussing the "law of nature," Cicero tends to the biological order, and more particularly, how a being's design implies or expressly directs a particular usage or purpose. In other words, the law of nature always makes sense because nature never acts contrarily to its own preservation for in "this law of nature there is nothing which can be criticized"[15] since it "develops the fullest possibilities of the natural world."[16]

At first glance, one might argue this merely a matter of semantics or a distinction without major meaning or purpose. However, a review of Cicero's primary literature on law manifests an emphasis on the natural side of things, the natural meaning of how the world operates; how its creatures function and how the biological range of living and animate beings carry on their basic operations. Cicero's view of man is tightly wound up in an undeniably natural analysis when he finds:

> And you are wise, for you must understand that in no other kind of discussion can one bring out so clearly what Nature's gifts to man are, what a wealth of most excellent possessions the human mind enjoys, what the purpose is, to strive after and accomplish which we have been born and placed in this world, what it is that unites men, and what natural fellowship there is among them. For it is only after all these things have made clear that the origin of Law and Justice can be discovered.[17]

Put another way, Cicero integrates a natural biology into his legal theory and delivers a biological emphasis when laying out his jurisprudence. Cicero refers to a "Common Law of Nature"[18] with an expectation that each human being acts correctly when he or she "knows how to employ it and use it."[19] The laws of nature seem forever on the forefront of his analysis for "Law is a natural force"[20] and an orderliness that can be witnessed at every level of the living organism. Nature is not a sum set of accidental forces but a plan, a blueprint for the being's proper end and purpose. When Cicero references "Nature's road,"[21] he exhorts the moral agent to follow it since it leads to the "ideal condition"[22] for that person. This same observation is true even at the lowest steps of the biological order. In the *Nature of the Gods*, Cicero concludes:

> The providence of God has made wise provision for the preservation of the whole fabric of the world and for the perpetuation of all kinds of animals and trees and every plant that grows upon the earth. In all of these there is a seed which enables many to be born of one. This seed is concealed deep in the fruit of every tree. This fruit satisfied the hunger of man and the earth is filled with new generations of the tree. The same wisdom provides for the preservation of every kind of beast. Their division into males and females has been devised by nature for the propagation of their kind. They have parts of the body perfectly adapted for begetting and conceiving, and both male and female have a strong desire for physical union.[23]

Coursing its way through his legal analysis are a wide array of biological descriptions which, for Cicero, edify a logic, a rationality of order, a cosmic to ontological sense of how things are constructed. Hence, his intricate anatomical and physiological analysis of the human body is quite appropriately part of his law of nature. Our bodily form—a design of nature—is perfectly suited to our operative qualities Cicero argues:

> {A}nd she has granted us a bodily form which is convenient and well suited to the human mind. For while she has bent other creatures down toward their food, she has made man alone erect, and has challenged him to look up toward heaven, as being, so to speak, akin to him, and his first home. In addition, she has so formed his features as to portray therein the character that lies hidden deep within him; for not only do the eyes declare with exceeding clearness the innermost feelings of our hearts, but also the countenance, as we Romans call it, which can be found in no living things save man, reveals the character.[24]

The human body, according to Cicero, has been shaped and formed for sustenance, breathing, and movement. Our mouth, he claims, takes in food, drink, and air, and has been designed to eventually break things down by teeth and tongue, to push forward nourishment by the gullet and tongue.[25] Soon thereafter, food and drink are deposited in the stomach for further processing as Cicero microscopically dissects this and a host of other laws discoverable in natural operations. "Many marvelous processes take place in the stomach, which is a muscular complex, coiled and winding so as to hold and compress the dry or moist food which it receives so that it can be assimilated through the digestive process."[26]

In even more precise ways, Cicero meticulously describes the workings of the lungs, the liver, the kidneys, and the heart.[27] The law of nature is evident in a system of veins "interwoven through the whole body and bear{ing} witness to the marvelous power of the work of the divine artificer."[28] In the eyes and eyelids, Cicero describes a wondrous design commencing with the protection of "most delicate covering membranes, which are at once translucent to give clear sight yet strong enough safely to contain the fluid of the eye."[29] Cicero's biological descriptions are exquisitely detailed as he moves throughout the various functions of the human body. Eyelids are not random components, but intelligently designed pieces in the whole biogenic frame of the human being.

> Then there are the eyelids, very soft to the touch so as not to harm the sight, exquisitely designed by nature to open and shut quickly, so that nothing can get into the eye. The eyelids are fenced with a kind of palisade of hairs. These

serve to prevent anything entering the eyes when they are open, and when shut in sleep, and we have no wish to see, they rest intertwined one with the other.[30]

No part of the human anatomy, whether eyes, ears, or nostrils, escapes Cicero's keen scrutiny for each of these parts manifest laws of nature. This biological inclination, upon first reading, rests centrally in his overall philosophy of law and human action and it is fair to conclude that this style of discourse is distinctively different from that of St. Thomas. While nature shall play a crucial role in various argumentative fronts, its placement is secondary at best. Hence, when St. Thomas lays out his Five Proofs for God's existence, the order of nature from human observation gets less play than the other four arguments.[31] Comparatively, Cicero sets up a superstructure of nature and the natural order as the moral measure for human activity, so much so, that it is essential for man to place "himself under obedience to nature."[32] The human person must live by and in accordance with nature, in unity with its design and purpose, and never be antagonistic to its function and purpose. Cicero, while surely a figure who uses the term "natural law," argues more convincingly for a law of nature, at least in his earliest discussion of these concepts. What is plain is his emphasis on the natural, the biological, the biogenic functionalism, as to each and every piece that makes up the whole human person. From his upright stature to the measurement of his forehead, from the engineering evident in the hands, the feet, and the fingers, Cicero paints a picture of law that sweeps up all of nature.[33] Cicero remark:,

> Who cannot wonder at this harmony of things, at this symphony of nature which seems to will the well-being of the world? If there is such a man, then I am very sure that he has never thought upon these things. If we turn now from heavenly to earthly things, we find everywhere similar signs of a purposive intelligence in nature. The plants which grown in the soil have stocks which give them stability and strength and at the same time draw from the soil the juices by which the plant is fed through the roots. The trunks of trees are covered with bark ... Vines clutch at their props with tendrils like tiny hands.[34]

In the law of nature, Cicero proposes both wisdom and mindless inevitability. Either way, nature always makes sense for in death and old age, by way of illustration, the processes are good rather than to be disdained or purposively avoided. Anything coming about from "nature's law" is something to be embraced.[35] Even old age should be welcomed in accordance with nature's dictates. Cicero urges, "{F}or I count nature our surest guide; I follow her and obey her as I would a god, and it makes no sense to believe that she would be at great pains to map out the earlier parts of life and then, like a lazy playwright, give the last act a careless once-over."[36] The same conclusion can be reached concerning death itself. Cicero holds that the logical end station in the temporal world must be death. Death, for Cicero, is an act more in accord with the "Law of Nature"[37] than any other human action, except possibly birth.

Nothing escapes this natural ordering for Cicero for everything that operates naturally, operates wisely, and in accord with the fundamental nature that guides being. For Cicero, the law of nature is to do things right for in this "law of nature there is nothing that can be criticized"[38] as it is the "handiwork of God"[39] for nature is our "surest starting point . . . the common parent of us all."[40]

Natural law as imprint of the Eternal/Divine Law

Even if we accept that Cicero's law of nature displays greater biological qualities than theological ones, the journey through Cicero's jurisprudence provides many other insights than the Christian tradition of natural law most would anticipate. It is fair to conclude that Cicero's excursion does not end with nature itself but vigorously proceeds to a first phase of construction for natural law jurisprudence, "flowing from God, from whom man derives his nature"[41] because "human life is subject to the decrees of the Supreme Law."[42] It is just as obvious that once he moves past the natural operations of beings, he opens up territory not often considered in comprehensive terms until the time of St. Augustine nearly 350 years later.[43] Cicero states in *Nature of the Gods*:

> But what is such a greater being but a god? For if no gods exist, then what is there in nature greater than man? He alone is endowed with the supreme gift of reason. Only an arrogant fool would imagine that there was nothing in the whole world greater than himself. Therefore there must be something greater than Man. And that something is God.[44]

In Cicero we discover all sorts of themes and terminology not evident in either Plato or Aristotle and, most importantly, a hierarchical structure where human, natural, and supreme law is weighed, evaluated, and fully integrated. This is no small feat and by his intellectual contributions makes the Thomistic concept of the natural law all the more understandable. If the concepts were charted, comparatively, it would look a bit like Figure 4.1.

Cicero's legal philosophy will prompt an endless and rightful examination of how natural law works in the human experience and that conclusion will be reached once the role of God, in the creative process of fashioning the human

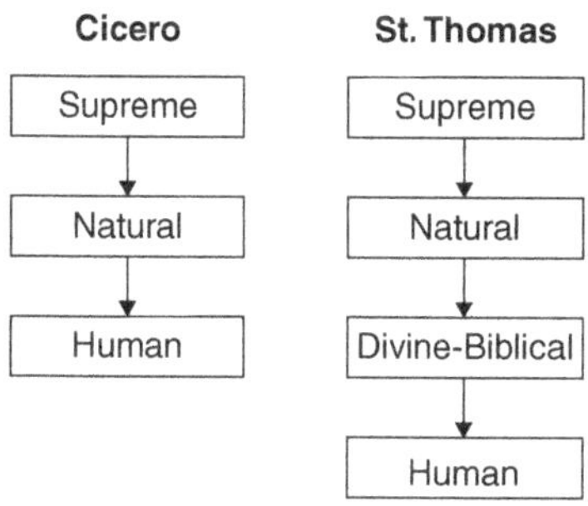

Figure 4.1 HIEARCHCHY OF LAW

person, is fully comprehended. For in both Cicero and Aquinas, God's creative power and capacity is what generates any meaningful theory of natural law: a Supreme, Eternal, and Divine Law descending to the lower forms of creation. Cicero observes that any notion of law commences with a higher order, a transcendent power, a God who oversees the creative results of his being. "Thus they have been accustomed to say that Law is the primal and ultimate mind of God, whose reason directs all things either by reason or constraint … it is coeval with that God who guards and rules heaven and earth."[45]

For Cicero a legal philosophy short changing the God of creation is a system bound to relativity and failure, for law is equated with what is right and true, what is universal and dependable, and derived from the "divine mind."[46] "To Cicero it seems self-evident that there must be a law above human law, otherwise society and morality would break up."[47] Within this context a jurisprudence of universality, dependable application, and predictable moral measures can be fashioned. The alternative would constitute an individualistic determination where both neighbor and the collective, because of the "variety of men's beliefs and by their disagreements,"[48] could never really determine the suitability of human conduct. Cicero urges his readers to jump past the promulgations of the nation-state to a higher metaphysics. The alternative to this, Cicero chides is "the most foolish notion of all,"[49] to believe exclusively in the "customs or laws of nations."[50] Cicero is forever suspicious of human promulgation that rests exclusively on its own justification and throughout his body of work critiques pure positivism in every imaginable form. History and time teach that people make wrong moral choices, or just as readily the correct or lawful choice, from the moral menu rooted and constructed in the temporal sphere. Citizens and their governments are too fickle and utterly too influenced by trend and societal pressures. A legal and ethical system demands more than the whimsy of the mob and the current fad or fashion of the moment. Otherwise, Cicero exhorts, "the decrees of peoples, the edicts of princes, or the decision of judges, then Justice would sanction robbery and adultery."[51] This tendency to look at the heavens is an inclination that Cicero advocates throughout his body of titles, knowing only too well how undependable the alternative method has to be. We witnessed this preference when nature was elevated to its superior status since it encompasses all created beings; we reached a similar conclusion of higher beings over lower ones since higher beings have rational capacity. Reason makes defensible decisions, "not of opinion but of Nature."[52]

Any plan for a natural law theory will not be rooted in the foundation of human affairs and needs instead a firm footing in the highest good to justify its universality, for true law "is of universal application, unchanging and everlasting."[53] Any effort to escape its guidance or undo its particular applications, Cicero labels a "sin." Neither can it be repealed or abolished in part or in whole, nor can we be "freed from its obligations by senate or people."[54] At no other place in his natural law discourse does Cicero blend with Thomism better than when he discusses these characteristics of what constitutes this higher law, applicable in all cases and to all human beings. Cicero portrays a natural law that applies to every context of human behavior.

> And there will be not be different laws at Rome and at Athens, or different laws now and in the future, but one eternal and unchangeable law will be valid for all nations and all times, and there will be one master and ruler, that is, God, over us all, for he is the author of this law, its promulgator, and its enforcing judge. Whoever is disobedient is fleeing from himself and denying his human nature.[55]

In this setting, the human person finds himself uniquely placed, among all other creatures, to discover and participate in a natural law—the content of which is known naturally to human reason. In Cicero's eyes, God has imprinted, impressed the natural law in his or her mind and "nothing {is} more precious and distinctive than his mind."[56] Human beings, Cicero holds, are granted "a certain distinguished status by the Supreme God who created him; for he is the only one among so many different kinds and varieties of living beings who has a share in reason and thought."[57] Here, and in other Ciceronian texts, he lays out the participatory characteristic of his natural law that connects God and his highest creature—man—in a very intimate and meaningful way. Since our very creation, each human person has "inscribed upon their minds that gods exist."[58]

The content of the natural law

Getting to the specific content of Cicero's natural law will not be as easy as the systematic delineation of St. Thomas. While the *Summa Theologica* explicitly asks whether there are precepts or principles in the natural law, and Thomas subsequently responds with particularity about what those first and even secondary principles are, such is not the case with Cicero. In Thomas's *Treatise on Law*,[59] the questions posed concerning the existence and content of the natural law, have long shaped philosophical discourse on exactly what the natural law entails. Yet current commentary tends to emphasize the theological attributes of the Thomist tract on natural law. Because of the natural law's inherent spiritual and theological traits in an increasingly secular world, continuing criticisms have taken a toll on its advocates and its placement in the wider circle of jurisprudential thought.[60] Cicero may be the suitable antidote to this conceptual malaise since he offers up a natural law theory that predates the Christian influence and mutes the critics who unceasingly type natural law into this theological corner. We have already seen how nature and the natural—the biological and the biogenic—encapsulate at least some portion of the natural law school. And if we believe that nature messages its beings, exhorting each entity to seek its proper end and best form of preservation, can these instructions alone be a compelling case for the a nontheological natural law? Labeling the content as "Nature's gifts to man," Cicero asserts that our minds already have fixed content concerning these natural and proper dispositions, "a wealth of most excellent possessions … to strive after and accomplish."[61] Would Cicero be more comfortable with contemporary natural law thinkers, such as John Finnis, who discover it without "the question of God's existence or nature or will?"[62] Or does Cicero's treatment of the natural law, according to S. Adam Seagrave, open up the possibility that St. Thomas would propose a theory of natural law rooted in a classical philosophical grounding alone?[63] Or does Cicero simply rephrase and restate a natural law as shaped by the Stoics?[64] Here too, the question posed belies both the depth of Cicero's thought as well as its extraordinary originality. Instead of the caricature of a Stoical cosmology, Cicero delivers a theory of natural law that depends on human reason for its discovery and divine participation for its legitimacy.[65] Its content will foretell a Thomistic vision of natural law that Cicero's contemporaries could never have anticipated.

Seeking the good—avoiding evil

In most natural law circles, the primary tenet of seeking the good and avoiding evil and harm undergirds a series of secondary precepts that make up the content of the natural law.[66] This version, while simplistic, is undeniably the premise upon which other principles are drawn and deduced. While Cicero lacks this sort of specificity, at least in a numerical sense, it is clear that his natural law theory usually follows this ordering—the good for the individual creature, the good for the collective, and the specific good or end that leads to the greatest development for both person and commonwealth. Thomas calls this the "first principle" of the natural law,[67] and this primary precept reflects the most basic of inclinations, dispositions, or predilections in Homo sapiens—to discover what is good and avoid what is harmful. Of course, Thomas fleshes out the primary precept of natural law by reminding us that the "ultimate good"—the *Summum Bonum*—every rational being seeks is God by and through the Beatific Vision.[68] In Cicero that conclusion is not only phrased differently, but it is also posed in a less rigorous way. However, Cicero's various commentaries tie together the good of the human person with the good of our natures and the good for our subsequent development. When describing even the earliest days of Rome's founding, Cicero remarks that nature itself "carried Romulus away to man's inevitable end … to heaven,"[69] "into the yonder realm of the gods."[70] In Cicero's eyes, the human being has an inherent sense of what is good and just coupled with an inherent understanding of what conduct in life to avoid, in addition to a built-in "sense of shame"[71] since "nature has given to man … a certain fear of justified censure."[72] Throughout his numerous works, Cicero sees the fixed relationship between happiness and the choices made in human activity. Choose the good and good things shall result, while the contrary is just as obvious. Living in accordance with our nature will inevitably be consistent with a life of virtue for the alternative paths chosen display a very different result in the sustenance and maintenance of the human person. Vice, by way of illustration, never leads to the goods Cicero urges but the extreme opposite result. The self-indulgent become "slaves to their own bodies, and test the desirability and undesirability of everything on the basis of pleasure and pain."[73] Epicureans are on the continuous end of biting condemnation for their order, built upon the edifice of pleasure and sensory delight directly contradicts his virtue and nature advocacy, for in pleasure alone, the human actor "may drown."[74] Nor would Cicero accept the school that claims that each choice made by each individual is equally good in its own right for, as already noted, some choices are inconsistent with our nature and the divine imprint known as the natural law. Nor will the utilitarian offer a satisfactory truth since today's utility becomes tomorrow's dread, for if an actor believes it will "be profitable to him will, if he is able, disregard and violate the laws."[75] In the end, a utilitarian good falters on its inevitable illogic and will be "overthrown by the very utility itself."[76]

Within the richness of Cicero, one discovers his overall abhorrence of relativity in ethics and moral postures dictated by mood, by mob, and by the public clamor. Over and over, Cicero reminds his readers that the goods sought by the human person are not the stuff of chance or changing mores but a fixed series of principles discoverable in our very natures. Any other formula for determining the appropriate goods would at best be arbitrary. Cicero declares:

> But if so great a power belongs to the decisions and decrees of fools that the laws of Nature can be changed by their votes, then why do they not ordain that what is bad and baneful shall be considered good and salutary? Or, if a law can make Justice out of injustice, can it not also make good out of bad?[77]

Cicero concludes that nature provides the parameters for what is good and beneficial to human development for only a "madman would conclude that these judgments are matters of opinion, and not fixed by Nature."[78] In this overall framework, Cicero identifies the goods that each human being must seek—those rooted in and consistent with virtue and those that culminate in the highest good, the ultimate good, the *Summum Bonum*—God himself. A life well lived will reach this conclusion in due course. Cicero explains, "And further, when it has examined the heavens, the earth, the seas, the nature of the universe, and understands whence all these things came and whither they must return, when and how they destined to perish, what part of them is moral and transient and what is divine and eternal."[79]

Self-preservation

If Cicero exhorts every rational being to live naturally, to choose virtue over vice and to seek out proper ends and purposes in day to day living, he has the self-preservation principle in mind. Cicero's exhortations are highly developmental—not just some sort of maintenance of life and living but instead a plan for life, a recipe for human enrichment with assurances that each human person evolves in his or her most perfected state. A virtuous disposition assures a life of continuity between human reason and human action. It "signifies the enjoyment of a life of due measure based upon virtue, or following nature and living according to her law."[80] Hence to drive toward perfection, either in mind, body, or spirit, is to assure a more productive and fruitful existence. This starts with the demand that one's life be maintained as long as feasible.[81] Throughout his analysis, Cicero argues the preserving, protecting, and advancing ethic that living naturally accomplishes. Stated differently, the exhortation, found in hundreds of locations in Cicero's works, to live in accordance in nature is not a hollow plea or empty argument for its own sake. Instead, Cicero urges the human actor to live the happiest, the longest, and the most beneficial of lives in accordance with the law of nature and natural law he expounds since "everything which is honorable is likewise natural."[82]

While the preservation of life may be utterly consistent with his natural law outlook in some ways, the application of these principles to his cultural context appears a bit more muddled. In the areas of abortion, infant exposure, and an honorable suicide, there is less clarity and consistency than one might expect in the Roman experience. Suicide, by way of example, a contrary act to self-preservation, seems an honorable choice depending on particular contexts. When Cicero's express language is evaluated, the plausibility of a suicide ethic seems impossible. In the *Dream of Scipio*, Cicero relays: "Wherefore, you Publius, and all good men, must leave that soul in the custody of the body, and must not abandon human life except at the behest of him by whom it was given you, lest you appear to have shirked the duty imposed upon man by God."[83] In suicide, as well as abortion,[84] we find a mostly silent Cicero, where the preservation of life is touted as nature's chief aim, yet in specific application, the texts simply do not provide a formula for resolution. Of course, in St. Thomas, these matters are explicitly and expressly dealt with.

Finally, while the record is not filled with self-preservation references, Cicero does tell us, on multiple occasions, that the consequences of acting and living outside the natural order are always negative. Even if the formal mechanisms existing for punishment for wrongdoing fail (the courts, the prisons, etc.) the unnatural actor will not advance in preservation but undermine its longevity. If one lives outside nature, or in contravention to its express purposes and aims, a toll will be exacted. Cicero poetically paints this inevitability.

> And so men pay the penalty, not so much through the decisions of the courts (for once there were no courts anywhere, and to-day there are none in many lands; and where they do exist, they often act unjustly after all); but guilty men are tormented and pursued by the Furies, not with blazing torches, as in the tragedies, but with the anguish of remorse and the torture of a guilty conscience.[85]

Procreation and sexual attraction

As St. Thomas typically will categorize his natural law tenets, line by line, and principle by principle, Cicero will not organize his thoughts in a manner easy to discern natural law precepts. Here again, much of his virtue-nature discourse will be helpful in a general sense but woefully inadequate in a specific way. Thomas directly states that sexual activity has an end in mind—that of procreation; Cicero does as well but in an obscure way. In *Nature of the Gods*, one of his clearer expositions on the topic, he notes:

> The providence of God has made provision for the preservation for the whole fabric of the world and for the perpetuation of all kinds of animals and trees and every plant that grows upon the earth. In all of these there is a seed which enable many to be born of one. The seed is concealed deep in the fruit of every tree. The fruit satisfies the hunger of man and the earth is filled with new generations of the tree. The same wisdom applies to the preservation of every kind of beast. Their division into males and females has been devised by nature for the propagation of their kind. They have parts of the body perfect for begetting and conceiving, and both male and female have a strong desire for physical union.[86]

Thomas tells us that sexual attraction is normal and natural for males and females, and Cicero shall as well, but his discourse is never business like. If anything, Cicero is more inclined to discuss how inordinate affections, a slavishness to earthly, fleshly desires in an extreme fashion, lust overruling the mind,[87] will surely produce the wrong person with the equally wrong ideals. Inordinate sexual desire can rouse "men's desires to fever-pitch" like "wild, unbridled beasts."[88] Pleasure, without restriction or moderation, causes "subservience to the body"[89] replacing the proper position of man's mind and soul. In this upside down world, when the spirit is "subservient to pleasure" insures a mind, a soul will endure "many ages of torture."[90] Cicero also adds another layer to sexual desire and affection by reminding us that the desire alone will never really satisfy, but that desire must be motivated not by what is nature's imperative, but by our natural tendency to be intimate with other human beings, our craving for love and friendship. Sexual activity in and of itself comes up empty unless coupled with virtue since it "is the source of the rational, the stable and the consistent element in life" for "to love but to cherish the person for whom one feels affection."[91]

In the area of sexual attraction, Cicero is worldly enough to appreciate how the senses are open to inordinate influence, suggestion, and even outright corruption. In sensory matters, especially human conduct at the sexual level, it is easy to see how vice can be rationalized as a good when only the opposite conclusion may be consistent with his natural law theory. Cicero recognizes this when he states:

> But, against our minds all sorts of plots are constantly being laid, either by those whom I have just mentioned, who, taking possession of them while still tender

> and unformed, color and bend them as they wish, or else by that enemy which lurks deep within us, entwined in our every sense—that counterfeit of good, which is, however, the mother of all evils—pleasure. Corrupted by her allurements, we fail to discern clearly what things are by Nature good, because the same seductiveness and itching does not attend them.[92]

At various points in his discourse, sexual attraction is often coupled with the virtue of chastity. While there is never any direct call for complete abstinence, nor a life of celibacy as superior to a life of moderation, he urges his readers to appreciate chastity for the proper rationales. Not because, if caught, it would be embarrassing or politically troublesome but more because of the measure of that conduct. In *De Legibus*, he interestingly lays out the correct motivations for adhering to the principle of chastity.

> Is it possible to call those chaste who are kept from a life of lewdness by the fear of disgrace, when the disgrace itself results from the inherent vileness of the deed? For what can be properly praised or blamed, if you have disregarded the nature of the things which deserves praise or blame? Are bodily defects, if very conspicuous, to offend us, but not a deformity of character? And yet the baseness of this latter can easily be perceived from the very vices which result from it.[93]

While Cicero can be accused of imprecision with his natural law tenets, his demand for a virtuous lifestyle courses its way through all his writings.[94] Side by side with this observation is Cicero's recurring admonition that a non-virtuous life will have its own series of punishments, even if these pains not be of a temporal or bodily nature. Cicero often represents the vice ridden character as one in turmoil or present agony—"the minds of the wicked always troubled by one thing or another."[95] What is lacking in Cicero, in specific delineations as to natural law precepts, is filled in by his general disdain for immodesty, a lack of chastity, immoderate behavior, licentiousness and blind sexuality. Cicero ties happiness to self-control. "For you will have courage your defense against distress and fear, and self-control to liberate you from sensuality and keep you free of immoderate cravings."[96]

Certainly, some of Cicero's mentality as to sexual conduct was shaped by his own cultural experience such as the existence of adultery, prostitution, brothels, and concubines, which when weighed against reason and the laws of nature, should produce a condemnation.[97] Even so, Cicero's silence or lack of condemnation likely impacts the purity and consistency of his natural law thinking when particular moral questions are impacted by historic conditions.[98]

Family and care of offspring

A well-ordered society is impossible without a strong family unit, with children that are properly cared for and raised to be good citizens of the empire.[99] Roman culture and tradition had been, during even the more decadent periods of the empire, cognizant of the interconnectedness of the strong, nuclear family and the strength of the empire.[100] Cicero offers up a connection between strong families and strong communities when he remarks, "But, as regards the practical conduct of life, the system provides for legal marriage, legitimate children … It is impossible to live well except in a good commonwealth, and nothing can produce greater happiness than a well constituted State."[101] In this way, Cicero sees the inevitable connection between a healthy collective and political reality and the healthy family. He urges statesmen to be forever concerned about this connection between these parallel realities, which in turn provides "his fellow citizens a happy life, fortified by wealth, rich in material resources, good in glory and honored for virtue."[102]

Family, procreation, and the care of offspring are skill sets known and developed according to Cicero. Much of the content we already naturally know—the remainder drawn from socialization and experience. Some of it happens automatically, such as the production of breast milk and an infant's instinct to suckle. There is, Cicero says, "nothing accidental here."[103] Family and the care of offspring are not mere social structures that can be orchestrated in directions unnatural or antagonistic to the natural order inherent to their makeup. At each phase of human development, Cicero declares, there is a time and a season. He comments in his *Treatise on Old Age*, "Each season of life has an advantage particularly its own; the innocence of children, the hot blood of youth, the gravity of the prime of life, and the mellowness of age all possess advantages that are theirs by nature, and that should be garnered each at its proper time."[104]

A social, communal life

That the human person is a social, political creature is just as compellingly accepted by Cicero as it was by Aristotle and Plato. Although many reasons exist for this preference, Cicero argues that man is not only born naturally social, but also bound to his fellow brothers and sisters by our inherent love of justice, truth, and the virtuous lifestyle. A social existence is a natural law for the human person since "Nature abhors solitude."[105] Nor will any human person be capable of full isolation since friendship and a social existence weaves its way "through the life of every man; no matter how he chooses to live."[106]

Indeed, virtue cannot be all that meaningful in pure isolation for it is difficult to demonstrate cases where courage, charity, fortitude, and the like, do not depend on others. The very idea of virtue itself assumes a "natural inclination to love our fellow-men."[107] The entire natural law superstructure, which integrates virtue theory, cannot stand erect without a corresponding social structure. Not even friendship can survive if a friend loves a friend for any other purpose than love of that friend, and loved "with the whole heart."[108]

If it is in our natural inclination to be social, human history has surely proven this tendency to live collectively rather than singularly. Living in virtue tends to maintain social living more than living in vice or sin. The corrupt and decadent undermine the social order and social and cultural stability. The corrupt care little about justice and in its stead serve self-interest at the expense of any collective. If the corruption is substantial enough, what nature has "kindled in us are extinguished by this corruption and the vices which are their opposites spring up and are established."[109] In *De Re Publica,* Cicero makes plain how natural and ordinary it is for the human person to live in a collective rather than in isolation. "The first cause of such an association is not so much the weakness of the individual as a certain social spirit which nature has implanted in man. For man is not a solitary or unsocial creature, but born with such a nature that not even under conditions of great prosperity of every sort [is he willing to be isolated from his fellow men.]"[110]

Belief in a deity

For Cicero's natural law theory to have a scintilla of certitude, it will have to admit to the role of a transcendent God, for a failure to do so relegates the theory to endless relativity. Ultimately, the jurisprudence must conclude that a higher power exists, and not just out of necessity but logic too. For example, an imprint does not come from a party coequal but from a being superior, a "Supreme God, above us rul{ing} the universe."[111] The fact that we know anything about the natural law and its content manifests a power beyond our present limitations, yet at the same time our "likeness" to God, our participatory capability to reason as God can. No other creature is capable of this sharing of knowledge that results from the imprint of the natural law by a higher, most perfect God in a lower, less perfect human person. In *De Legibus*, Cicero eloquently poses the need for a belief in God.

> Therefore among all the variety of living beings, there is no creature except man which has any knowledge of God, and among men themselves there is no race

> either so highly civilized or so savage as not to know that it must believe in a god, even if it does not know in what sort of god it ought to believe. Thus it is clear that man recognizes God because, in a way, he remembers and recognizes the source from which he sprang.[112]

So for natural law to be universal in scope, the same in Athens and in Rome so to speak, it need admit to an author of these precepts who impresses the content and base knowledge in every rational creature, in reason where the content is discoverable. This "unchanging and everlasting,"[113] "eternal and unchangeable"[114] law can only be fashioned by a supreme God and hence, part of the natural law's package of fundamental precepts must include a belief in a deity. In a hierarchy of beings, from lower to higher, from ascending to descending, at some locus God must rule over man. In *De Re Publica*, Cicero holds firm to this logic. "Do we not observe that dominion has been granted by Nature to everything that is best to the great advantage of what is weak? For why else does God rule over man, the mind over the body, and reason over lust and anger and the other evil elements of the mind?"[115] In *De Legibus*, the need for a transcendent God in his overall jurisprudence could not be more evident. "{L}et us begin with that Supreme law which had its origin ages before any written law existed or any state had been established."[116]

Contrary to popular perception, Cicero's God remains distinct and independent as the pantheism of his day was common to assert, nor is God a simple synonym with nature itself. Cicero's description of God places him above the "celestial system" for this is a "God of transcendent power."[117] His descriptions of God are amazingly Aristotelian in scope and design. At some junctures in his works God sounds eerily familiar to the Prime Mover argument posited by Aristotle and this God remains beyond the scope of a universal cosmology and more the unmoved mover that creates all that is seen and unseen. Therefore, Cicero types God as a being "which moves itself… nay, it is the source and first cause of motion in all other things that are moved."[118] Hence only that which moves of itself can be labeled as eternal, otherwise the "heavens will fall and all nature perish."[119]

Aquinas on the natural law

By the time of St. Thomas, the natural law conception had been developed in a systematic fashion and the clarity and measured manner in which it is discussed results in a very different discourse than the poetic, almost ethereal way in which Cicero reviewed the concept. To be sure, thirteen centuries is a great distance to travel in the history of ideas but the time continuum is something that should be remembered when making comparisons. Law, for St. Thomas, leaps far beyond the text or simple promulgation. For St. Thomas any conception of the natural law will be gauged in light of other influences commencing with the power and omniscience of God himself, by and through the eternal law. The Lex Aeterna—the eternal law—becomes the first and final arbiter of all human events and circumstances, a divine exemplar, manifesting the perfection of the supreme Creator. Eventually, God imprints some portion, part, or knowledge of what the eternal law contains and it is and the content of this imprint that encompasses what we commonly term the natural law. St. Thomas concludes that the content of the natural law is burned, impressed, and imprinted into our very reason—principles which we know naturally and with minimal introspection—also termed the "self-evident principles of the natural law." For example, the human person need not be instructed on the value of self-preservation, but knows this inclination or tendency naturally since each being seeks out what is naturally good for its maintenance and avoids that which is deleterious to its survival. With a bit more reflection, the human agent can easily discover the value and merit of the secondary precepts of the natural law—on procreation, sexual attraction, communal living, and so on. Other conclusions are discoverable in particularized settings. Hence, the natural law cannot be possible without the eternal law.

Nor will the natural law be fully understood, according to St. Thomas, without revelation and recognition of our salvific history as enunciated by the Old and New Testaments—which Thomas labels the divine law. God's message in the Old and New Testaments, sent as the divine law, provides revelatory guidance to the people of God. The content of these Testaments will course through all of the natural law commentary of St. Thomas.

The edification of exactly what natural law means and connotes will be discoverable in human applications and the laws which it seeks to regulate, advance, or inhibit. Rounding out his natural law theory will be the last of the four categories of law in his magnificent opus—namely, human law.

Given both our political and social inclinations, St. Thomas accepts both the value and the necessity of human law. Human laws are the glue that fastens the social and cultural commonwealth and assures that a reasoned orderliness in maintained among competing visions of values. Human laws, in order to be valid, need to be consistent with and aligned to the content of the natural law.

In this sense, Thomistic jurisprudence is an interlocking and interwoven system that depends on a perfect God that transmits truth about human operations to his rational creatures by and through the tenets of the natural law, and finds real world application in the promulgation of human laws. Human law, to be just, must be consistent with the entire hierarchy of laws posed above, or lack the status or nature of law. Despite the imperfection, human laws are essential to Thomas's theory of law since their content aims "at the ordering of human life … under the precepts of the life we have to lead."[120] Moreover, human law maintains its integrative place in Thomistic jurisprudence because of its relation to reality, to social and political living and governance, and to the advancement of temporal happiness. Undeniably, human or positive law can never be as comprehensive or as perfect as its relational superiors—the eternal, natural, and divine laws—and if its terminus and enforceability depend solely on its human, secular object, then such a law, if not today, will tomorrow exact an injustice. This inevitable tragedy that results when human law is the centerpiece of a legal system is easy enough to predict. Since human law is promulgated by human beings, it will always be subject to error and mistake. Nevertheless, human law is driving toward and is concerned with the same goods as its counterpart. Law, as previously defined, is an exercise of reason, a rule and measure of it. Human laws directly reflect the exercise of practical reason—assessing individual facts and circumstances and then deliberating, enacting, and infusing authority by actual laws.[121] It would be grotesquely inaccurate to type Thomas's human law as isolated or independent of its legal counterparts. St. Thomas, in response to whether there is such a thing as the human law, insists on its utility and its unbridled necessity.[122] Human law is not only language, but also the power to habituate, the strength to reign in the unreasonable and the untrue, as well as a prescription for the virtues. Indeed for Thomas, "it is difficult to see how man could suffice"[123] without it.

One of the most striking features of Thomas's discussion of human law is its necessity—a belief that human existence would fail without legal promulgations. Human beings need commands, proscriptions, and prohibitions to carry out their individual and collective enterprise. Laws serve as a series of parameters and controls for human conduct. Although human beings are fundamentally geared to the good, and by their rational nature can identify proper ends, experience delineates the value of control. Wills, passions, and appetites tug and at times, overwhelm the rational creature that chooses conduct contrary to their nature. Indeed, St. Thomas is bold enough to assert that a morally inclined individual has little need of human law because that person already adheres to the dictates of practical reason, the mandates of the natural law, the divine law precepts, and the blueprint of the eternal law. This type of character is rare, for the theory of necessity relates to the bulk of humanity.[124] Those already disposed to virtue have less need for legal regulation, while those "who are evilly disposed are not led to virtue unless they are compelled."[125]

The necessity of human law, as St. Thomas poses, "refers to the removal of evils"[126] from the world we inhabit. Law, in the human sense, is the purifier, the fortress against the onslaught of moral barbarism. From another perspective, the necessity of human law is manifest in human activity of every sort, especially in the communal setting. Positive law involves both the "law of nations and civil law."[127]

Neither in anarchy nor in isolation the human person carries out a social and political existence reliant upon law. Henle argues that human law is necessary not because of its own necessity, but because of the "state of fallen man."[128] The law is not inherently coercive, but is consistent with all its other purposes, "directive" of what ought to be done. To be sure, law has the power to coerce and mold, but since law is a pure exercise of reason, the human actor should be comfortable with its content. Those exercising behavior in accordance with reason are willing properly and thus not in need of the coercive power of the law. In this sense "the good are not subject to the law, but only the wicked."[129] Hence, human law is necessitous for both reasons of utility and man's current lack of perfection. It is, for lack of a better description, a libation that the virtuous can avoid and the wicked must drink.

Human law is derived from other sources, including the theological and philosophical underpinnings espoused by St. Thomas. Even speeding, jaywalking, taxes, and the like, have a derivative quality, especially in the justness behind their enactment. Kings, too, derive their authority from a higher power, although history is replete with examples of those who turn the crown into an anointing, who would "usurp that right, by framing unjust laws, and by degenerating into tyrants who preyed on their subjects."[130] Human law depends upon and looks to the eternal, natural, and divine laws. Using his integrative method, Thomas finds it impossible to separate human law from the natural law order so evident in rational creatures. At most, Aquinas places human law lower in his legal hierarchy because its enforceability depends upon human beings, while divine law "persuades men by means of rewards or punishments to be received from God. In this respect it employs higher means."[131] Since law is an exercise of human reason, and reason is the rule and measure of law, Thomas argues that human law is derived from the natural and eternal law. "Now in all human affairs a thing is said to be just from being right, according to the rule of reason. But the first rule of reason is the law of nature, as is clear from what has been stated above. Consequently, every human law has just so much of the nature of law, as it is derived from the law of nature."[132] Since positivism zealously excludes any rootedness beyond its promulgation, it has stripped away and gutted moral inquiry in human law analysis. Rights are based on codifications, the mutterings of "some tiny little minority of an elite,"[133] rather than inherencies or perennial truths.

The derivative relationship between the positive law and "higher" law is not one based on confrontation but one of unity and integration. Human laws that are contrary to the tenets of the natural law, are by implication, an affront to the eternal law, and not really laws in the truest sense. Radically, Thomas holds that every law is derived from the eternal law because of reason's role in the deliberation, and a law deviating from reason has not the nature of law in any sense.[134] A human law, inconsistent with the natural, does violence to the very notion of what law is and, ergo cannot bind in conscience.[135] Therefore, neither is it law nor can it be law as popularly understood. Human laws inconsistent with the divine law receive no recognition from Thomas since any enactment "contrary to the divine law … has not the nature of law."[136] Any human promulgation antagonistic to the eternal, divine, and natural laws will be an affront to any version of law and equity. To so hold is a radical error in jurisprudence. Thus, Thomas declares, "But in so far as it deviates from reason, it is called an unjust law, and has the nature, not of law but of violence."[137] On the other hand, the objective of human law is to look to the heavens, and to prod man toward a life of virtue. A Thomist discovers early on that law has a formidable relationship with virtue, and that every human law should contribute to the advancement of individual and collective virtue. Law should foster, not inhibit self-perfection.[138] Human law transforms the citizenry "who live under common legal institutions into perfect citizens."[139] The law, as an instrument of the state, wishes perfection and happiness for its community. The positive or human law cannot possibly extinguish human imperfection in every case, but it can gradually lead men to a life of virtue.[140]

Aside from this four-part typology, St. Thomas's vision for a natural law theory depends on correct definitions as to the idea and concept of law. A common conception of law is that of a rule, regulation, statute, or ordinance, a case issued by judicial authority, or some other concretization of a particular legal idea or principle. Laws are as numerous and meaningful as the scope of their coverage, and are, without much argument, juridical instruments. The law's juridical content commands, prohibits, enhances, advances, or restricts a good or end. As comprehended by St. Thomas, law is juridical,[141] but only partially, for law is synonymous with God, with rationality, and his plan for creation. Even the irrational creature, as directed by God through natural inclination, has a legalistic quality. Law pertains to not only the operation of the species, but also the beauty, sensibility, and magnificence of its design. In the *Summa Contra Gentiles*, St. Thomas lays out this sweeping vision of the natural law.

> Just as the acts of irrational creatures are directed by God through a rational plan which pertains to their species, so are the acts of men directed by God inasmuch as they pertain to the individual, as we have shown. But the acts of irrational creatures, as pertaining to the species, are directed by God through natural inclination, which goes along with the nature of the species. Therefore, over and above this, something must be given to men whereby they may be directed in their own personal acts. And this we call law.[142]

Therefore, Thomistic law defines itself in a more profound sense beyond promulgation, for the law's essence mirrors the fullness of God's creation, the nature of his creatures, and the unfolding of species and their corresponding operations. Law is supreme, divine legislation in addition to its positive codification or ordinance; it is the plan for a life consistent with this divine rationality—a life of virtue—and it is the order "whereby man clings to God."[143]

Only man possesses reason and rationality, and in Thomas's view, law is a "certain rational plan and rule of operation"[144] and found in "rational creatures only."[145] St. Thomas confidently asserts that "law is something pertaining to reason,"[146] and at the same time, a rule and measure of human activity. Law entwines and entangles with being itself. Stated concisely, the law represents rationality, and creates orderliness in individual and rational existence. Law, aside from its enactment, is the handmaiden of reason itself. When dealing with the law's essence, St. Thomas imparts primary stature to reason:

> Law is a rule and measure of acts, whereby man is induced to act or is restrained from acting: for *lex* [*law*] is derived from *ligare* [*to bind*], because it binds one to act. Now the rule and measure of human acts is the reason, which is the first principle of human acts, as is evident from what has been stated above; since it belongs to the reason to direct to the end, which is the first principle in all matters of action, according to the Philosopher.[147]

The natural law model St. Thomas poses holds that reason contains this knowledge of natural law precepts rather than desire, the will, or the appetites. It is reason alone that can be relied upon to deliver consistently accurate messages about proper ends in human conduct, not will as a matter of personal preference.[148] Thomas indicates that law is a *dictate*, an ordination of reason, standing in a superior position to human will. Reason mirrors the law of our being, our consistent and compatible dispositions toward particular good and ends.[149]

Aquinas: A law of nature or a natural law

The question whether Aquinas prefers the law of nature to his subsequent natural law analysis will not be as difficult to determine as was apparent in Cicero. Cicero frequently touches both boundaries and, at times, even confuses the parameters of natural law with a naturalistic biology, while Thomas never seems confused on the separation of pure science from a theory of natural law. Early in his work, St. Thomas grounded his natural law reasoning in nature itself: that which is compatible with nature will be lawful; that contrary to it, unlawful. In the *Commentary on the Sentences*, he distinguishes activity according to the ends nature mandates for "whatever renders an action improportionate to the end which nature intends to obtain by a certain work is said to be contrary to natural law."[150] Similarly, in the *Summa Contra Gentiles* he paints a picture of this legal barometer. "The operation appropriate to a given being is a consequent of that nature. Now it is obvious that there is a determinate kind of nature for man. Therefore there must be some operations that are in themselves appropriate for man."[151] In this way, one determines the lawfulness of conduct by its relationship to the actor's nature.

From this point on, St. Thomas expands the primary precept to an ad seriatim listing of what he terms "self evident principles." Nature as a biological phenomenon does not act, but the human person, using reason, exhibits certain inclinations and these inclinations are based on various goods. Thomas's theory of the natural law catalogues these inclinations as essentially self-evident, discoverable by all who engage in "slight reflection."[152] At Question 94, Article 2 in his *Summa Theologica* a list of these first principles is announced:

> Because in man there is first of all an inclination to good in accordance with the nature which he has in common with all substances: inasmuch as every substance seeks the preservation of its own being, according to its nature: and by reason of this inclination, whatever is a means of preserving human life, and of warding off its obstacles, belongs to the natural law. Secondly, there is in man an inclination to things that pertain to him more specially, according to that nature which he has in common with other animals: and in virtue of this inclination,

> those things are said to belong to the natural law, which nature has taught to all animals, such as sexual intercourse, education of the offspring and so forth.[153]

These inclinations of social existence, propagation of the species, self-preservation, the inherent desire to know truth and God, are universally true in all rational beings.[154] They are unavoidably consistent with human experience and are propositions, ideas known inherently and by and through us.[155] Unnatural activities are deductively inconsistent with nature. C. S. Lewis reminds us that when inconsistency lends to unnatural vice "it is a departure for the worse."[156]

Being self-evident propositions, the actor has no choice but to make decisions compatible with their subject matter. This is why a natural law theorist has little or no quandary reconciling the current debates over abortion, homosexuality, or assisted suicide. These first principles of the natural law set out a formula, a series of criteria that forbid each of these activities. While the doing of good and avoiding of evil is known in and of itself, these primary precepts of the natural law may be conditionally self-evident.

To be sure, there are places where St. Thomas argues scientifically, almost cosmically and astronomically, a reflection of how all movement occurs, whether that of the heavenly body, the animal or plant, or the laws of physics. Anton-Hermann Chroust discovers a universal cosmic orderliness in his natural law theory:

> First, the ontological order in which being as such tends towards the preservation of its own being in accordance with its ontological nature. In the case of man this inclination manifests itself in the preservation of life and in all of man's actions conducive to this preservation. Secondly, the vitalistic order in which being tends towards positive action. In the case of man this tendency becomes an inclination to act appropriately and in accordance with his own being and purpose. And, thirdly, the order of the rational and social animal which is also the domain of free moral self-determination.[157]

In this sense, Thomas is more psychological than anatomical for he is forever gauging the human person's inclinations, predispositions, ordinations—all of which drive toward some sort of proper end, a fulfillment of essence and a perfection of operation. Etienne Gilson eloquently corroborates this by starting at a vast universe and then descending toward man's particular features or characteristics—all of which signify the natural law at work in the human species:

> The first, and the most vast of all, is the universe. All beings created by God and maintained in existence by His will, can be regarded as one huge society in

> which all of us are members, along with animals, and even with things. There is not a single creature, animate or inanimate, which does not act in conformity with certain ends. Animals and things are subject to these rules and tend toward their ends without knowing them. Man, on the contrary, is conscious of them, and his moral justice consists in accepting them voluntarily. All the laws of nature, all the laws of morality or of society ought to be considered as so many particular cases of one single law, divine law. Now, God's rule for the government of the universe is, like God Himself, necessarily eternal. Thus the name *eternal law* is given to this first law, sole source of all others.[158]

Clearly, nature, in a scientific, physical sense has order, a series of operational rules and "in its purity . . . is rather like the word life, but this shall never be a suitable substitute for the natural law itself.[159] Even so, nature edifies a great many aspects of Thomas's natural law theory for the human person is undeniably a creature of nature and thereby subsists of rules and operational qualities. Lewis's critical mind captures the interplay of nature and the natural law when he points out nature's most foundational meaning. "By far the commonest native meaning of *natura* is something like sort, kind, quality, or character. When you ask, in our modern idiom, what something 'is like', you are asking for its *natura*. When you want to tell a man the *natura* of anything you describe the thing."[160]

Thomas gets to the core of nature in his work, *On Kingship*, noting that "whatever is in accord with nature is best, for in all things nature does what is best."[161] As author of nature, God could not and would not forge a creation of disorder and anarchy, but more predictably, infuses and imprints an orderly, lawful, natural sequence in each of his creatures. "The manifold and beautiful order of nature is the work of a designing mind of vast intelligence; and must be ultimately explained by the existence of a personal God."[162] Undoubtedly, human beings like other beings, display natural inclinations, preferences, propensities, and dispositions that mirror the wisdom of the author. Gilson artfully offers this analysis: "Granted this, it is clear that the precepts of natural law correspond exactly with our natural inclinations and that their order is the same. Man is, to begin with, a being like all others. More particularly, he is a living being, like all other animals. Finally, by the privilege of this nature, he is a rational being. Thus it is that three great natural laws bind him, each in its own way."[163]

Nature will never be able to explain the full dynamism of natural law theory, but it does explain part of the definition. The term, natural law, references two critical Thomistic ideas: (1) the nature of a being itself; and (2) law as an operation of that nature. To say someone or something has a nature is to typify its very existence. Then, apply law to that nature and that nature unfolds before us—doing what it must and should do to preserve its existence, signifies nature as well.[164] Nor is the natural law some changeable phenomena deposited in the creature for the moment. To prove the permanency of the imprint, St. Thomas resists efforts to call the natural law a "habituation" because habits increase or decrease while natures with corresponding imprints are fixed.[165] Imprints are poured into essence of being during initial construction. A loose and impressive comparison might be this: as the eternal law is God himself, the natural law is a mirror of really what we are as beings, because this is the eternal plan. The natural law is imprinted on man, infused into his or her nature, "written" in their hearts. How could it be otherwise when the creature reflects the maker? Regularly found within the body of St. Thomas's work, is the term "imprint," which represents the mark of the maker. The human person partakes and participates in the eternal law of God. Human beings "derive their respective inclinations to their proper acts and ends."[166] Rational creatures among all others participate most generally, Thomas remarks;

> [T]he rational creature is subject to divine providence in the most excellent way, in so far as it partakes of a share of providence, by being provident both for itself and for others. Wherefore it has a share of the Eternal Reason, whereby it has a natural inclination to its proper act and end: and this participation of the eternal law in the rational creature is called the natural law.[167]

St. Thomas's natural law travels farther than any strict biological theory or functional perspective because the rational being receives design. Nor is his natural law a compendium or codex of legal annotations, codifications, and enactments. More aptly, the natural law is a reflection of the whole, or as Ignatius Eschmann cogently defines the natural law as "not a statute enacted by the divine Legislator, but is the self-same act by which the Creator brought into being our rational nature."[168] Inclinations, tendencies, and propensities are not blank, intellectual exercises, especially since the natural law theory of St. Thomas centrally depends upon reason for its discernment. That water travels to its lowest point, or that bears propagate their species is not natural law activity as St. Thomas defines it. "It is nature itself that is, more precisely, rational nature; it is reason understood as the power of reasoning."[169] Only rational creatures possess the natural law. Natural law is about inclinations and dispositional tendencies—how the human creature lives in accordance with their overall constitution, yet most critically how one lives compatibly as the Creator intended. For St. Thomas, the natural law cannot be removed, "blotted out,"[170] moreover, it cannot be forgotten or denied on the basis of ignorance. Natural law is the human person's participation in the eternal law of God. "Thus man has a natural inclination to know the truth about God, and to live in society: and in this respect, whatever pertains to this inclination belongs to the natural law: for instance, to shun ignorance, to avoid offending those among whom one has to live, and other such things regarding the above inclination."[171]

From the Thomistic view, man is forged so tightly with the natural law that he cannot extricate himself from its influence. We can't even intend contrary to what we are, though we can will the difference—choosing evil, which "is a result apart from intention."[172] Wickedness, unlawfulness, does not reside in reason or our constitution, for "such a thing is not the necessary result of what is intended; rather, it is repugnant to what is intended."[173] St. Thomas does not compartmentalize the natural law's influence on human operations but recognizes its determinative power. Every inclination in the human actor, particularly those touched or controlled by reason, deals with our natural law imprint.[174]

Those who argue its relativity, inapplicability, and selectivity as to person or precept, would be at odds with Thomistic doctrine. Natural law, at times, accused of its absolutist tendencies,[175] is a nonnegotiable imprint. St. Thomas declares:

> It is therefore evident that, as regards the general principles whether of speculative or of practical reason, truth or rectitude is the same for all, and is equally known by all. As to the proper conclusions of the speculative reason, the truth is the same for all, but it is not equally known to all: thus it is true for all that the three angles of a triangle are together equal to two right angles, although it is not known to all. But as to the proper conclusions of the practical reason, neither is the truth or rectitude the same for all, nor, where it is the same, is it equally known by all.[176]

Natural law reasoning only insists that a man act in conformity with what reason instructs. That there is one type of human person—the rational one—is indisputable. Reason commands as natural inclinations enunciate. In this sense, it would be ludicrous to fashion another species of man endowed with another version of reason. Therefore, in human conduct reason rules and commands the other powers, and this universal condition labels permanently the natural law.[177] This unchangeable, immutable reflection of the eternal law, this participation, albeit imperfect, by man in the eternal law, this imprint, messaging inclinations and ends for the human person, is the essence of the natural law. Quoting Gratian, St. Thomas summarizes the permanency of the natural law as follows. "It is said in the Decretals: The natural law dates from the creation of the rational creature. It does not vary according to time, but remains unchangeable."[178]

Given all of this analysis, it is fair to conclude that St. Thomas propounds a natural law theory far more coherently and cogently than Cicero. Aquinas integrates a strong series of naturalistic observations on the propriety of human conduct in relation to its overall nature, but it is abundantly clear that a hierarchical natural law vision, heavily dependent upon reason and rationality is his supreme consideration.

Natural law as eternal/divine imprint

At the pinnacle in Thomistic jurisprudence is the eternal law of God, as author and architect of all being, the exemplar for man and his universe. The eternal law, as Gilson urges, is that which "makes us what we are."[179] The lex aeterna is the blueprint for an ordered existence, the benchmark for perfection in every facet of existence, and "the objective and absolute *a priori* of everything that may properly be called a rule and a measure."[180] As the Supreme Exemplar,[181] Aquinas foundationally posits God right where He should be—in a perennial, permanent, and immutable dimension. God, the artist and the craftsman, makes only good things, and as a result, molds creatures with lawful inclinations and components. Aquinas characterizes objects or beings by the "emanation"[182] from God's being, containing or being the law itself and the "extensiveness" of God's influence on reality itself. The perfection of God is not an unbridgeable valley, due to God's creative relationship with his authorship of the world. Creation possesses an artistic or demonstrative quality that inevitably and intimately bonds the Creator with the created. The divine God moves "all things to their due end,"[183] and "bears the character of law."[184] In the plan of God, the higher law descends to the lower law. Thomas sees lower forms of the law as derived from the higher form. This "derivative"[185] quality commences with the eternal law, the divine exemplar that is the blueprint for the universe and its law. Divine revelation, centrally exposed in biblical instruction, gives clarification to the people of God. Creation, especially the rational variety, participates in the eternal law by and through the natural law. Positive laws, the promulgations of man, are a necessary component for a civil society. Unified and interdependent in design, Thomistic law is complicated yet elementary. At its peak, God's eternal law watches over the other categories. "The type of divine Wisdom is the eternal law,"[186] Thomas relates, and as a result "all laws proceed from the eternal law."[187] At the human level, each derives its legitimacy from its superior counterpart. Within the *Treatise on Law*, St. Thomas offers a series of interlocking and interdependent categories of law—each form gauged in its relationship to the others before legal action will have legitimacy.[188]

The perfect God naturally has a perfect legal constitution, though his complete content and subject matter are unknowable, the effects of his acts can be gauged and comprehended.[189] Thomas recognizes the human inadequacy of knowing directly and primarily what the eternal actually is—since the law is God Himself. As imperfect beings, we can struggle only to know the effects of the eternal law. Thomas holds that we "cannot know the things that are of God, as they are in themselves; but they are made known to us in their effects, according to Rom. i. 20: *The invisible things of God . . . are clearly seen, being understood by the things that are made.*"[190]

Later on, man will get closer to knowing these effects by nature's instructions on the norms for human activity. St. Thomas is wise enough to equate the eternal law of God with that of God himself. All that is created by God, "whether it be contingent or necessary, is subject to the eternal law."[191] God's law is the supreme norm for all living beings and creation. Governance of the universe by God imputes a law of operations. Thomas uses the term "government" when God is described as "the ruler of the universe."[192] This rule has the quality of and the "nature of a law."[193]

When St. Thomas queries whether all human affairs are subject to the eternal law, only an answer in the affirmative is possible. Even the wicked and the perverse, are subject to the eternal law; even the "blessed and the damned are under the eternal law."[194] The ignorant cannot disavow some knowledge of the eternal law since their being still reflects the Creator by his effects. The lustful and the slaves of flesh cannot "dominate"[195] and destroy the good of one's nature, for "there remains in man the inclination to act in accordance with the eternal law."[196] No human person can evade the eternal law. Thomas labels God's law as truth itself; that "the divine intellect is true in itself; and its type is truth itself."[197]

St. Thomas's evaluation of law may begin with the eternal law although it cannot end at this station, for law has practical and pragmatic applications. As rational creatures, the human being will never encompass the domain of the eternal law but are given, in its place, a participatory role in its wisdom and perfection. This participation will be made possible by the eternal law's imprint—the natural law.

The content of the natural law

Any reasoned analysis of the natural law inspects the sum and substance of its content. Thus far, descriptive terms, like inclinations and imprints, have been employed to describe the natural law, but these alone do not sufficiently cover its content. Where our inclinations lie or tend to instruct as to the influence and direction of the natural law and in some ways, the content can be gleaned from what we do naturally, although choices of conduct may be more or less self-evident depending on the person. In addition, scholars of St. Thomas have long categorized natural law precepts into primary, secondary, and even tertiary levels. While the primary principle, "to seek good and avoid evil," provides the undergirding for more particularized determinations, the proximity of some of the secondary precepts of the natural law, such as self-preservation, are closely aligned to the language of this first principle. Stated another way, the secondary precepts of the natural law, on matters of procreation, care of offspring, and the like, are not splintered from the primary precept but inevitably descended from it. In this sense, the natural law for Thomas, favors application in specified settings and ethical quandaries. As a result, St. Thomas is doggedly determined that laws be instructional to man, laying out parameters of conduct, serving as an instrument in moral valuation.

Throughout his articulation, St. Thomas never falls prey to the general moral norm being the particular moral resolution, nor the particular being the general. Each case may have a general rule of operation, but particular circumstances may alter the applicability of the general rule. This is true in every legal scenario, including the principles that emanate from the natural law. St. Thomas is fond of the expression "light of reason" when discussing the effects of the natural law, and sapient enough to realize that light will vary in the human intellect. While no man "can have an erroneous judgment about"[198] the first principles of the natural law, those emanating further down the continuum are not as expeditiously discovered. These other principles are labeled secondary, or by some tertiary,[199] derivations of fundamental natural law principles. The clear-cut, undeniable tenets of first principles lose their punch, or at least their ease of discovery, as one moves to more particular cases. Despite this growing remoteness, many secondary conclusions are entangled with the primary precepts. St. Thomas even says that our legal reasoning "will be found to fail the more, according as we descend further into detail."[200]

Found within this arena of secondary principles will be more particularized moral and legal issues. For example, is it self-evident, or readily understood, that adultery is opposed to the natural law, or divorce, masturbation, polygamy, contraception, and so on? These questions can be reconciled using natural law reasoning, but their solution calls for more scrutiny than questions regarding suicide or abortion. Thomas labels these secondary questions "proximate"[201] to the first principles, derivable therefrom and even allows for a greater flexibility in the resolution of said cases. Hence, the natural law has the capacity to consider novel moral considerations as human behavior evolves, or de-evolves for that matter, and because of this flexibility, can adapt to new and emerging moral difficulties. Thus, Thomas could never have anticipated genetic, selective reduction in the matter of twin births, yet the natural law, when applied to its particular facts, will readily resolve the dilemma. In this way, St. Thomas calls upon the natural law advocate to discover a "closeness" of the secondary precepts to the overall natural law principles. To have a natural law resolution the secondary issue must be closely related to the self-evident principles of natural law.[202] There may even be times when following the natural law would create an ironic injustice, for example, the maintenance of the life of a fetus over the life of a mother, or the condemnation of a soldier who, by giving up his life for his comrade, fails to preserve himself. In these and other special cases "observance of such precepts"[203] will not be possible.

Secondary precepts are so designated because of their intimate relationship to the ends and goods suitable for man. Conduct, in the most particularized categories, can be evaluated for moral legitimacy and legality by the ends promoted. If the ends are contrary to human perfection, the conduct or law would be contrary to the natural law. Thomas writes splendidly about this interplay between lawfulness and natural law and ends in the *Summa Contra Gentiles*. "Now, it is good for each person to attain his end, whereas it is bad for him to swerve away from his proper end. Now, this should be considered applicable to the parts, just as it is to the whole being; for instance, each and every part of man, and every one of his acts, should attain the proper end."[204] Precisely what the tenets of the natural law were for St. Thomas is fully analyzed.

Seeking the good—avoiding evil

Since law is reason's rule and measure, and since all human beings seek the good, the natural law must be rooted in one, basic tenet. Invariably, St. Thomas calls this fundamental inclination, to do good and avoid evil, the primary precept or the first principle of the natural law. Any Thomistic understanding of law considers the concept of the good, whether temporal, temporary ones, or the ultimate good, the penultimate end of man—God. Holistic in style, universal in approach, Thomistic law pulls in all that is good, beautiful, and perfect and finds final solace only in the Beatific Vision. Thomistic jurisprudence embraces more than the functionality of utilitarianism, the artificiality of Marxism,[205] and transformative humanism. A theory of law, so says St. Thomas, is loftier, rising above "prejudice and passion,"[206] and fixing "upon eternal reasons to reaffirm a forgotten truth, formulate a new principle, or overturn an established error."[207]

To be consistent with reason, man seeks perfection in every category of life. He or she can will otherwise, but in the intricate and incomprehensible act of creation itself, God could not fashion a being who would command his or her own destruction. Since the Creator is all-good, so too the creatures molded in his image. These ideas are more easily understood in the context of Aquinas's various kinds of law, specifically the eternal, natural, divine, and human. Man's reason, the artifice of law itself, can readily discover these ends. Perfect, unreserved happiness resides only in the splendor of divine perfection. "Perfect orderliness,"[208] as Chroust terms it, is "declaratory of the *summum bonum*, that is, of God."[209] At every level of Thomistic thinking, legal or otherwise, God is the ultimate end of the reasoning, intellectual creature. St. Thomas urges us, "Now, from what has been seen earlier, it is established that God is the ultimate end of the whole of things; that an intellectual nature alone attains to Him in Himself, that is by knowing and loving Him, as is evident from what has been said."[210]

This initial principle that "good is to be done and pursued, and evil is to be avoided"[211] serves as the cog in Thomas's natural law philosophy. Practical reason naturally identifies the good to be pursued and the evils to be shunned. Of course, this position is consistent with St. Thomas's view of man's end or purpose in existence, and particularly logical as to previous definitions of what a law is. This primary and common precept is part of our very fabric of being, Gilson argues:

> To say that we must do good and avoid evil is not arbitrarily to decree a moral law; it is merely to read a natural law which is written in the very substance of beings and to bring to light the hidden spring of all their operations. We have to do it, because it is our nature to do it. Such a precept is but a verification of fact.[212]

This doing good and avoiding evil provides, at best, a generalized prescription for life, and at worst gives fodder to those who challenge or debate the content or ingredients of its recipe. In the first instance, this primary precept is only a call that the human actor "act in accordance with reason ... with the created pattern of our nature and species."[213] While only rational creatures intellectualize natural law precepts, every being moves toward its proper end or goal.[214] Few would contest that St. Thomas knows that human beings already know its content, because the natural law is the dictate of reason.[215] Admittedly, some persons may know its content better than others, but only in particular applications or specifications. This fundamental precept, doing good and avoiding evil, is known equally by all. St. Thomas exhibits an understanding of human differences in discerning, not truth, or the primary precept of the natural law, but the determinations of practical rectitude that are "not equally known to all."[216] This "golden rule of the natural law"[217] is effortlessly understood "without investigation ... known and approved by all humans."[218]

The matter of the natural law's instruction does not end with this common precept. Rather, Thomas turns his attention to human operations, those predictable, commonly observed, universally conducted types of behavior, apparent in all men and all civilizations. In the average case, and for the average person, moral guideposts and legal parameters are crucial. At this stage, all Thomas has argued is that every rational creature seeks its proper end—the good of temporal existence and the ultimate end of God. Reason is the rule and measure of human action and thus the conduit of law. Reason, as the eternal law and divine exemplar infused in it, drives toward the good. This is its natural law, which is man's participation in the eternal law.

Another way of characterizing the process is to do good and avoid evil. In order to do so, one must examine our natural tendencies, our propensities, and inclinations. After completing this speculative task, a series of self-evident, indemonstrable primary principles of the natural law emerge, for example, self-preservation, procreation, and the like. There are "certain things which the natural reason of every man, of its own accord and at once, judges to be done or not to be done."[219] Writing in theological terms, St. Thomas labels acts contrary to our nature as special sins,[220] for such conduct is contrary to what is proper for man, or against a "nature which is common to man and other animals; and in this sense, certain special sins are said to be against nature: thus contrary to sexual intercourse, which is natural to all animals, is unisexual lust, which has received the special name of the unnatural crime."[221] These self-evident principles of the natural law are so easily discerned and universally understood, that promulgation is not warranted.

Self-preservation

When weighed as a group, there is no precept of the natural law as instructive as the self-preservation principle. To live and preserve is an inherent tendency in every living being, from mammal to man. It is not that we merely desire to live on but that we preserve the quality of our natures and our existence, for self-preservation assumes a rational being's hope for continued life and for a productive and rewarding day to day existence. To wish for the contrary is to act and live unnaturally, or as St. Thomas so convincingly says: "Therefore this act, since one's intention is to save one's own life, is not unlawful, seeing that it is natural to everything to keep itself in being, as far as possible."[222] So too a person would not be guilty of murder if he or she killed in self-defense because it is "lawful to defend one's life" and to "kill another in defense of his own life."[223] In self-defense, the moral agent confronts a powerful precept of the natural law, namely self-preservation, and may permissibly violate its provision in order to save one's own life by taking another's. Aquinas relays the doctrine of "double effect" in this instance quite clearly: "Nothing hinders one act from having two effects, only one which is intended, while the other is beside the intention. Now moral acts take their species according to what is intended, and not according to what is beside the intention."[224] Thomas soberly rebukes those who would "turn the other cheek" in all cases, nor does he label self-preservation as some sort of charitable deficit. His analysis addresses those who would admonish the self-defender and prop up the alternative of salvation and martyrdom since avoidance of defense is "not necessary for salvation"[225] since the human agent is "bound to take more care of one's own life than of another's."[226]

Suicide provides ample ground for critiquing the role and importance of self-preservation in the natural law theory of St. Thomas. At no place, will suicide be accepted or tolerated under natural law reasoning, for to advance or aid or abet its commission is to act in contravention with self-preservation principles. St. Thomas lays out three rationales for why suicide, which would also include euthanasia and versions of mercy killing, would be contrary to the natural law.

> It is all together unlawful to kill oneself, for three reasons. First, because everything naturally loves itself, the result being that everything naturally keeps itself in being, and resists corruptions so far as it can. Wherefore suicide is contrary to the inclination of nature, and to charity whereby everyman should love himself. Hence suicide is always a mortal sin, as being contrary to the natural law and to charity.

> Secondly, ... he belongs to the community. Hence by killing himself he injures the community ... Thirdly, because life is God's gift to man, and is subject to His power, Who kills and makes to live.[227]

St. Thomas displays no leniency in the matter of self-inflicted death since each act is a sin due its injustice to self and others, and its complete lack of charity as to self and others. In suicide, the actor "departs from the order of reason."[228]

Abortion and infanticide are equally instructive regarding the self-preservation precept of the natural law. Since the chief aim of the procreative act, the conjugal joining of the married couple, is the propagation of the species, any interference with that furtherance works at odds with this principle. Over the last forty years since Roe versus Wade, though there has been a debate on the early period of conception as not having met the necessary stage of human development for the claim of murder to be alleged, there is little tolerance for abortion at any stage of development in the works of St. Thomas.[229] While it is true that Thomas declared that an animated fetus be essential to the charge of murder, there is no place where abortion is not construed an act contrary to the natural law and a mortal sin. The issue of ensoulement was a trickier question for the medievalist than the contemporary neonatal scientist. Hence, the earliest stages of human development, while more tolerantly construed by Thomas, cannot be read as a permissive stance on abortion. St. Thomas lays out the contrast:

> In the first case, the necessity of the action itself results from the form by which the agent is made actual, because in order for this kind of action to exist, nothing extrinsic, as a terminus for it, is required. Thus, when the sense power is actualized by the sensible species, it necessarily acts; and so, too, does the intellect when it is actualized by the intelligible species.[230]

If the soul provides the form for the human person, St. Thomas states that semen, as a physical composition, cannot transmit the qualities of a noncorporeal soul—that it cannot "extend its action to the production of an immaterial effect."[231] Thomas states that the soul "comes from without,"[232] and arrives at some undetermined time.[233] Admittedly, according to John Finnis, the crude biology of the time and the infancy of the science led Thomas to inevitable findings that are in opposition to current understanding of human formation.

Procreation and sexual attraction

Sexuality undeniably is a necessary component of the maintenance and advancement of the human species, but to be in line with natural law theory sexuality must take place in the marital state with procreation in mind, "for the welfare of the whole human race."[234] The sexual act has a specific purpose in the natural order, and should be undertaken in "due manner and order, in keeping with the end of human procreation."[235] St. Thomas states:

> Now just as the preservation of the bodily nature of one individual is a true good, so too, is the preservation of the human species a very great good. And just as the use of food is directed to the preservation of life of the individual, so is the use of venereal acts directed to the preservation of the whole human race.[236]

While obviously St. Thomas states that sexual activity in the proper context is good, motives that are rooted in "lust" are never a rational basis for sexual activity. St. Thomas states that lust creates a feverish frenzy where the actor loses all rational moorings and sows pleasure for its own sake and an obsession with carnal desire, seeking the wanton and the debaucherous. This urge wreaks the "greatest havoc in a man's mind, yet secondarily applies to any matters pertaining to excess,"[237] and promotes a warped and distorted view of the procreative act. This wantonness seeks only the sensory and cares not for the objects or the means of its pursuit, gravitating toward the lower rather than higher ends. Thomas states, "When the lower powers are strongly moved towards their objects, the result is that the higher powers are hindered and disordered in their acts. Now the effect of the vice of lust is that the lower appetite, namely the concuspicible, is most vehemently intent on its object."[238]

Many sexual acts run counter to the end human procreation. Acts of sodomy have no other end except pleasure, which is never a just act in the world of St. Thomas. Thomas articulates his position with passion, stating pleasure must be a lawful act with proper ends in mind: "Just as the ordering of right reason proceeds from man, so the order of nature is from God Himself; wherefore in sins contrary to nature, whereby the very order of nature is violated, and injury is done to God, the Author of nature."[239] As such, sodomy is determined to be an unnatural vice, a "special kind of deformity whereby a venereal act is rendered unbecoming."[240] In light of this, any activity between two men, two women, between man and animal, rest outside of the true meaning of human sexuality. St. Thomas argues that sodomy in any form is indefensible: "First, through being contrary to right reason and this is common to all lustful vices; secondly, because, in addition, it is contrary to the natural order of the venereal act as becoming to the human race."[241] Thomas categorizes sodomy as "the greatest sin amongst the species of lust,"[242] noting that "Vices against nature are also against God … and are much more grievous."[243] He further comments: "Therefore since by the unnatural vices man transgresses which has been determined by nature with regard to the use of venereal actions, it follows that in this matter the sin is gravest of all."[244]

Incest, sexual intercourse between those related by blood, affinity, or proximity, has historically been condemned. St. Thomas, as in modern times, shows no reservation in condemning acts of incest and outlines various situations in his commentary regarding these classes of sexual relations as immoral acts that suffer from "unbecomingness."[245] St. Thomas begins his denunciation of incestuous acts by portraying the natural aversion humans possess to such activities. "There is something essentially unbecoming and contrary to natural reason in sexual intercourse between person related by blood, for instance between parents and children who are directly and immediately related to one another, since children naturally owe their parents honor."[246] Although lower in severity when compared with relationships built on consanguinity, this unbecomingness extends to relationships with an adoptive parent, stepfather, stepmother, or guardian. Sexual activity with a blood relative can only be described as "unseemly" and "most prejudicial to charity."[247] Incestuous sexual relations cause "certain shamefulness inconsistent with respect"[248] for those we are related to.

As in the other categories of the natural law content, St. Thomas precisely deals with the moral implications associated with propagation and procreation. In the *Summa Contra Gentiles*, he deals with the biological and moral simultaneously.

> Now, though the male semen is superfluous in regard to the preservation of the individual, it is nevertheless necessary in regard to the propagation of the species. Other superfluous things, such as excrement, urine, sweat, and such things, are not at all necessary; hence, their emission contributes to man's good. Now this is not what is sought in the case of semen, but, rather, to emit it for the purpose of generation, to which purpose the sexual act is directed.[249]

Furthermore, a series of predictable ethical dilemmas can be speedily reconciled by adhering to these basic propositions. Polygamy is contrary to the natural law because "one female is for one male is a consequence of natural instinct."[250] Incestuous marriage is inconsistent with natural law precepts since "it is unfitting for one to be conjugally united with persons to whom one should naturally be subject."[251] Promiscuity, inordinate affections, and gluttony are distortions of the ends man normally seeks and to engage in such vice is a departure from "the order of reason."[252]

In this context, once legitimate behavior, in conformity with the natural law, such as opposite sexual attraction, with subsequent sexual intercourse, with a procreative aim, can easily morph into the illegitimate being replaced with promiscuity, illicit behavior, adultery, and the like. Licitness can evolve into illicitness because the initial goodness of the conduct might evolve or degenerate into excessive or compulsive behaviors, or because the conduct is undertaken contrary to its inherent ends. Thomas's distinction is fully developed in the *Summa Contra Gentiles*:

> Now, since the use of food and sexual capacities is not illicit in itself, but can only be illicit when it departs from the order of reason, and since external possessions are necessary for the taking of food, for the upbringing of offspring and the support of a family, and for other needs of the body, it follows also that the possession of wealth is not in itself illicit, provided the order of reason be respected. That is to say, a man must justly possess what he has; he must not set the end of his will in these things, and he must use them in a fitting way for his own and others' benefit.[253]

Family and care of offspring

Witnessed thus far has been the natural law's precept regarding the care of offspring. Just about every creature in the natural order already knows how to instinctually care for its offspring and while human beings may know, they have shown and demonstrated an extraordinary capacity to willfully avoid that responsibility in various historical and cultural stages. Modern life has surely edified the collapse of family with 61percent divorce rates and illegitimacy rates as high as 80 percent in selected communities. This collapse of care and nurturing is all the more inexcusable when we are already blessed with the basic knowledge of how to properly care for our offspring. St. Thomas saw the institution of marriage as the stabilizing force in sexual relations, but also the fortifier in health and longevity of communities. The alternatives spoke too loudly with opposite results. Marriage between the opposite sexes assures a continuance of the species; marriage provided parameters for sexual intercourse and it differentiated roles and responsibilities for the various players. Marriage, in St. Thomas's view, provides determinacy, dependable relationships, and assurances for its participants, in contrast to the instability of one night stands and cavalier sexual behavior. St. Thomas cogently explains the connection:

> The union with a certain definite woman is called matrimony ... Since, however, the union of the sexes is directed to the common good of the whole human race,

> and common goods depend on the law for their determination . . . it follows that this union of man and woman, which we call matrimony, is determined by some law . . . Wherefore, since fornication is an indeterminate union of the sexes, as something incompatible with matrimony, it is opposed to the good of the child's upbringing, and consequently, it is a mortal sin.[254]

Thomas also determined that fornication undermines future marital fidelity because a person with a checkered sexual past will have difficulty staying within the commitment of matrimony. Sexual intercourse must remain in the context of a loving marriage. Pursuing sexual activity outside of marriage leads only to sin and emptiness. Quoting the *Book of Tobias*, Aquinas makes the point most eloquently. "Take heed to keep thyself . . . from all fornication, and beside thy wife never endure to know a crime."[255]

St. Thomas staunchly condemned any attack on the sanctity of marriage and disrespect for the sacrament of matrimony. Marriage is a bond of unity, and any action which undermines that relationship is judged as immoral by St. Thomas. He describes this bond, stating:

> A joining denotes a kind of uniting, and so wherever things are united there must be a joining. Now things directed to one purpose are said to be united in their directions thereto . . . Hence since by marriage certain persons are directed to one begetting and upbringing of children, and again to one family like, it is clear that in matrimony there is a joining in respect of which we speak of husband and wife; and this joining, through being directed to some one thing is matrimony: while the joining of bodies and minds is a result of matrimony.[256]

The bond of matrimony instills the social and spiritual structure for a "common life in family matters."[257] Bigamy destroys the unity between the marital partners and undermines the very definition of marriage. The multiple marital relationships inherent in bigamy eliminate the bond and contractual promise that any marriage entails—to love and cherish one another till death. Bigamy creates coexistent relationships that operate in secrecy and fraud. The bigamist lives in the underworld of multiple relationships, instead of a world of "fidelity," boldly breaking the promise of charity in the marital state. St. Thomas states that bigamy leads to the ruination of marital integrity, and "causes irregularity, because it destroys the perfect signification of the sacrament: which is seated both in the union of the minds, as expressed by the consent, and in the union of the bodies."[258]

Bigamy runs contrary to the marital ideal because marriage "requires the husband to have only one wife, and the wife to have only one husband."[259] St.

Thomas also sees marriage in spiritual terms, as a holy alliance blessed by God that will de-evolve into lust and passion in a bigamous state. Bigamy is "incompatible with spirituality, inasmuch as it makes a man to be wholly carnal,"[260] and causes the spouse to be "unwilling to be content with one wife"[261] and more inclined to promiscuity and lust.

Polygamy is put to an aligned natural law analysis by St. Thomas. He finds the practice illegitimate, and recognizes all the players suffer in this scenario. St. Thomas determines that polygamy is unjust since the disproportionate relationship dooms the subservient parties. Each wife will never receive their due because the husband's obligation has been spread too thin. As St. Thomas finds, polygamy cannot "render those actions proportionate to their end."[262] It is unnatural to expect our species to take on more than we are intended to tackle. Polygamy, "he says, is opposed to the secondary precepts of the natural law."[263] A multitude of wives is antagonistic to "nature's dictate to every animal according to the mode befitting its nature."[264] This also applies to the children born from these unions according to Thomas. "Wherefore also certain animals, the rearing of whose offspring demands the care of both, namely the male and female, by natural instinct clings to the union of one with one, for instance the turtle-dove, the dove and so forth."[265] Polygamy leads to a state of confusion for the offspring who experience the uncertainty of multiple mothers. This state is utterly unnatural for the human agent. St. Thomas realizes that the "begetting" is merely the initial result of the conjugal act and can in no way assure the proper upbringing of offspring. St. Thomas lucidly enunciates this failure in polygamy. "[T]he principle end of marriage is, in one respect, entirely destroyed, and in another respect hindered. For the good of the offspring means not only begetting, but also rearing."[266]

In the final analysis, marriage and family are only assured in the context of a matrimonial bond and sacrament. In the contemporary world of minimalist marriage, neglected children, adulterous and fornicating partners, as well as the increasing rates of incest, bigamy, and polygamy, St. Thomas's natural law vision for marriage and offspring has never been more poignant.

A social, communal life

Since man is a social animal, any legitimate theory of law extends to a culture, a community, a civilization. St. Thomas is well aware that the ordinating influence of law does not terminate with individual activity, because it just as pertinently applies to the common good of a nation as it applies to the common good of its individual citizenry. In response to whether a law should be crafted for the individual or common case, St. Thomas indicates that every human law derives legitimacy from its relationship to the common interest. Laws consist of far more than individual applications but are germane to the life of a nation. "Hence human laws should be proportionate to the common good. Now the common good comprises many things. Wherefore law should take account of many things, as to persons, as to matters, and as to times."[267]

With keen insight, Thomas discerns the futility of a law that applies in the individual scenario alone. Laws are implemented not for the single person or the one-time circumstance, but instead law is a common precept applicable to a community of men.[268] It is for the multitude that laws exist, because laws for the community are nothing more than the social sum of its members. Law, particularly the human variety, "is framed for a number of beings."[269] Law is equated with the happiness in both individual and culture. If lacking a communal component, the enactment would be "devoid of the nature of a law."[270]

Belief in a deity

Thomas's recognition of the eternal exemplar, the divine intellect giving rationality to the universe, and the view that God's very being is the eternal law itself, is often considered the thesis of divine law. Divine law, while having the qualities of God's rationality and plan, is not the same as the eternal law. Divine law, in the most elementary framework, is the Old and New Testaments of the Bible. It is easy to interchangeably term the eternal law the divine, and the divine the eternal, for common parlance often does so. Instead, one finds St. Thomas fully cognizant of the role and purpose of scripture in the life of the Christian, and that this same scripture has revelatory qualities. Scripture explains the mind and particular commands of a transcendent, perfect God. Additionally, the eternal, natural, and human laws, while interdependent and unified in a teleological sense, do not, according to St. Thomas, directly bring man to happiness:

> [T]he end of the Divine law is to bring man to that end which is everlasting happiness; which end is hindered by any sin, not only of external, but also of internal action. Consequently that which suffices for the perfection of human law, viz., the prohibition and punishment of sin, does not suffice for the perfection of the Divine law: but it is requisite that it should make man altogether fit to partake of everlasting happiness.[271]

It is obvious that St. Thomas is not just paying lip service as to the divine law's value in his natural law jurisprudence. It is nearly impossible to find a topic where St. Thomas does not reference a scriptural authority; he is strongly dependent on the instruction, the divinely inspired education and guidance that the Old and New Testament provide. Man and man alone is simply incapable of operating without divine instruction for "[h]uman reason is not infallible and with the best will in the world people fall into subjective error in working out the details of right and wrong."[272]

It is just this quality of the "directing of human conduct"[273] that makes divine law central to St. Thomas. Accepting the condition of human frailty and imperfection, realizing the historical evidence for both success and failure on the part of God's people, St. Thomas looks to scriptural instruction as a guide in a world of competing moral claims. When in doubt, God's word can and does resolve dilemmas, legal or otherwise. To assure salvation, God's divine instruction helps man "know without any doubt what he ought to do and what he ought to avoid."[274]

Man's inability to do what is right and God's unbridled generosity in his revealing through scripture the plan for human operations, the divine law anchors human kind in God's great scheme.[275] Comprehensively, Thomas inserts the divine promulgations of both the old law and the new, so the "benefits of nature"[276] are not forfeited and the "benefits of grace"[277] are not lost through sin.

Even more persuasive is St. Thomas's argument of need as it relates to man's final end of happiness and God. Some might claim that God has equipped the human agent and instilled and imprinted in his or her nature, the blueprint for the happy life. Since we cannot comprehend the eternal law of God, understanding its effects alone, and since nature, the natural law of our operations, is for the most part, nontheological in design, St. Thomas never downplays this theological dimension. Aquinas himself argues that the principles of the natural law were "contained in the Old Law."[278] It is clear what he means. "By the natural law the eternal law is participated proportionately to the capacity of human nature. But to his supernatural end man needs to be directed in a yet higher way. Hence the additional law given by God, whereby man shares more perfectly in the eternal law."[279]

This supernatural end is just as compatible with the perception of St. Thomas on the natural end. Theologically, the divine law is a revealed message on how to achieve the end God intends for his creatures, and the end is not exclusively about function, machination. or bodily perfection "because it is by law that man is directed how to perform his proper acts in view of his last end."[280] Eternal happiness is an end that "is inproportionate to man's natural faculty"[281] and the divine law fills the void.[282] St. Thomas agrees with this relational quality of the divine law since its prime aim is leading man to God, "either in this life or in the life to come,"[283] for the foremost purpose of the law "is for man to cling to God."[284]

In short, the divine law directly enunciates the faith since human reason alone cannot fully discern the things of God.[285] In both the Old and New Testaments, St. Thomas declares the plan of salvation as proclaimed by the Creator. Whether by the Old Testament's stern deterrent mentality, or the New Testament's all-encompassing charity, both scriptural domains lay out a map for salvation. The Decalogue, as an illustration, represents the divine law's capacity to guide, to instruct, to lead man to proper ends, on the way giving one another their due.[286] Divine law continually serves as a reminder to the Christian citizen and moral agent, transmitting its luminous beacon of moral truth to those "habituated to sin"[287] and "obscured in the point of things to be done in detail."[288]

Much more could be said about this component of St. Thomas's legal philosophy, but suffice it to say, the divine law is yet another reflection of God's love for his creation. Like a father to his family, St. Thomas declares the critical function of divine law in the life of the human person. "As the father of a family issues different commands to the children and to the adults, so also the one King, God, in His one kingdom, gave one law to men, while they were yet imperfect, and another more perfect law, when, by the preceding law, they had been led to a greater capacity for divine things."[289]

In Thomas's framework, law constitutes more than codification or enactment alone, but an esoteric integration of God's plan, the supreme exemplar for all being. Law encompasses man's intellectual operations and rationality; it suggests a cohesive and unified plan for social, governmental, and personal living; it lays out a schema of moral and human rights; it insists upon an unbridled attentiveness to nature and endorses conduct consistent with our nature. More particularly, there is recognition that the law of God is neither severable nor any different from any other legal approach, for Thomas unifies and subsequently derives all from the eternal law. The Thomistic theory of natural law encourages the human player to imperfectly interact with the eternal law of God. Thomas's natural law, the blueprint implanted by God in his rational creatures, is driven by a fundamental theorem—doing good and avoiding evil. Other first principles and even secondary principles are deduced therefrom. Thomas's natural law jurisprudence posits "that there are right answers to moral questions and those lawmakers can and should be guided by such moral truths."[290] That this form of jurisprudence is allegedly out of the mainstream, supplanted by the trendy variations of positivism, makes it no less persuasive.

Compatibility on the natural law: Cicero and Aquinas

Thus far, this examination has clearly found more overall similarities than differences between Cicero and Aquinas. It is fair to continue the argument that both Cicero and Aquinas have a jurisprudence rooted in transcendence rather than mere temporal affairs. Their respective works are so full of these references it would be folly to argue otherwise. Second, that a law of nature continues to course its way throughout these many works and pages is evident—both thinkers quite frequently urge their readers to live naturally; to discover the nature of being; and to preserve that being in the most efficacious way. Impossible to dispute would be that nature and the natural order of things do not play a crucial role in the jurisprudence of both Cicero and Aquinas. Third, as for the natural law itself, there is more agreement than meets the initial encounter. At first reading, Cicero's template for the natural law lacks the systematic precision of St. Thomas and in places, the emphasis differs markedly. What can be concluded is that both figures hold similarly:

1. A natural law emanates from a Creator
2. A natural law imprint or reflection is impressed on every human being
3. Natural law precepts, inclinations, and dispositions are identifiable
4. The natural law is universal and unchangeable
5. The natural law is rooted in reason and not in will, passions, or appetites
6. The natural law is the same for every person
7. The natural law is superior to every human law, though subservient and dependent upon a higher eternal or divine law

While some disagreement exists, it may be explained as more stylistic and cultural than substantive. In other words, the natural law theory of Cicero is really in its infancy stage when compared with the life and times of St. Thomas. To be fair, Cicero seems, at times, to be an original proponent of these ideas while his philosophical world has yet to encounter or fully develop these arguments. Argued from another slant, Cicero is advancing a natural law theory—its most developed version to date—in a theoretical sense, still anticipating its application in particular situations. For example, while St. Thomas looks at suicide as being contrary to natural law, Cicero never touches the subject matter—due to ignorance, cultural tolerance of the "noble" suicide, or other reasons. The same could be said of adultery, fornication, and other cultural practices now so certainly in opposition to the natural law of the thirteenth century, although Cicero was silent on these same dilemmas. Hence, there is a gap between the theory of the natural law and its practical application to specific moral settings. In other words, Cicero lacks actual experience testing the natural law consequences of one form of behavior or another. The morality of pagan Rome was strikingly different from that of Christian Europe in AD 1275. Of course other explanations may serve better but to completely discount the differences regarding how moral problems are assessed and analyzed during these radically different times, would be indefensible.

In addition, the styles and methods of each figure are just as radically different. While St. Thomas continues his scientific approach to posing queries with the subsequent didactic and debate—Cicero continues to walk along his endless river trying to cajole and dialogue with his many peers to discover the ultimate truth of things. Cicero will always have a harder time pinning the information down than Aquinas. But in the final analysis, they both arrive at a remarkably similar station with even more remarkably similar results. And while this text cannot resolve all the chasms between the various ethical schools, it can encourage those brighter than most, the chance to sit and talk on a riverbed both call home.

5

Cicero and Aquinas: Compatibility and Contrast

General observations on Cicero and Aquinas: Nature, the natural order, reason, and the natural law

The primary goal of this work, to find commonality and difference in the natural law theories of St. Thomas and Cicero, was and still remains an ambitious project. Whether St. Thomas and Cicero share a natural law jurisprudence, a naturalistic outlook, a law of nature theorem that delivers a recipe for human ethics and human morality in particular affairs, present both traditional and distinctively novel questions. Is it possible for a Roman pagan and a secularist with vastly different and distinct cultural experiences, as in Cicero's case, and St. Thomas, to achieve uniformity in moral application and ethical systems? Questions like these presuppose many things, especially the possibility that natural law philosophy can blaze new ground—hoping for some guideposts that have universal, perennial, and immutable applications due to a consensus of opinion. After careful analysis, questions of compatibility and contrast find partial resolution, but a few challenges still remain. Some general observations are necessary.

Across more than a millennia, these central figures in the history and development of natural law philosophy can, at times, seem strikingly similar in their approaches and in the case of explicit and express text and language, their compatibility seems almost assured. The text of one, the words employed, and the language chosen to describe concepts often mirrors the other. To illustrate, both Thomas and Cicero unequivocally believe that nature has order; that nature has laws; that nature reflects the cosmic orderliness of the Creator who authored and designed the universe. Throughout all major works cited in this text, that conclusion is irrefutable. In addition, this analysis can only conclude that reason is a critical component each thinker's natural law jurisprudence. In reason is the deposit of content that makes up the natural law; in reason the intellect identifies that content identically as every other rational being derives said knowledge; and in reason, which is in fact a natural part of the human person's constitution, there is a dependable locale for natural law judgments—the same in Athens as in Sparta, as Cicero would say. Because of reason's preeminence, Cicero holds that reason perfected images nature,[1] while Aquinas triumphs reason as not only being a natural part of the human constitution, but also the "rule and measure of law."[2] In essence, each thinker rejects relativity in moral judgments and prefers a fixed series of first principles that have universal appeal.

Throughout their respective works, each rejects a moral system based on power, individual preferences, utility, feelings, passions, and sensations; the supremacy of will over intellect and reason, epicureanism, and other pleasure-pain arbiters; politics and military might, and every other imaginable explanation except the law of nature and the natural law. Each proves the existence of a God or gods using arguments about the summum bonum,[3] goods and ends, Prime Movers and secondary ones, and the imperfect to the perfect dimension. Aquinas and Cicero never hesitate finding "imagery"[4] of a God who impresses, imprints, and is reflected in every creature in nature, though none as keenly as his only rational being—man.

While these similarities are readily demonstrable, their respective theories on the natural law appear, at least as to its content and precepts, less uniform and more aptly described as less than perfect matches. The grandiose idea that a natural law exists for both nature and its chief inhabitant—Homo sapiens—is fully agreed upon. That reason is the proper locus for the content of the natural law is beyond dispute as well, and that this natural law directly reflects the Creator's active participation in our very makeup as an illumination or reflection cannot be denied either. Where the divergence occurs relates to the content of the natural law and its particular applications. Here the sophistication and certitude of St. Thomas wins the day for his theory of natural law delineates a series of precepts and tenets unlike any other thinker on the subject matter. In addition, St. Thomas applies these speculative principles to practical situations and conditions in a type of ethical laboratory as he scrutinizes specific moral and ethical dilemmas. Cicero lacks this sort of keen articulation and tends to naturalistic platitudes without specific application to moral dilemmas. Hence, while St. Thomas systematically dissects issues such as abortion, homosexuality, suicide, and promiscuity, Cicero fails to integrate his natural law theory into these specific ethical challenges. By contrast, Aquinas never considers a problem in the ethical thicket without turning to his ad seriatim listing of natural law precepts, so much so, and to the consternation of some, his natural law descends into a wide array of issues that get less and less self-evident by their very remoteness to the original rules of the game. Hence, when Thomas discusses whether every human law is tethered to the natural law in some fashion, he really means that it is. As he notes in the *Summa Theologica*, "Consequently every human law has just so much of the nature of law, as it is derived from the law of nature. But, if in any point it deflects from the law of nature, it is no longer a law but a perversion of law."[5]

Cicero never tends toward this specificity though he does not hesitate to argue that laws cannot be justified by mere promulgation alone—that the legislative process self-righteously defends any type of enactment for only the "absurd" would believe such a thing.[6] On the other hand, Aquinas will dissect every major, and even minor, moral problem in light of his theory of the natural law—for nothing escapes its relevance. In discussing whether or not theft (taking goods from another to share with the collective) is actually more reflective of the natural law of community ownership, St. Thomas bristles in retort when he states:

> Community of goods is ascribed to the natural law, not that the natural law dictates that all things should be possessed in common and that nothing should be possessed on one's own; but because the division of possessions is not according to the natural law, but rather arose from human agreement which belongs to the positive law, as state above. Hence the ownership of possessions is not contrary to the natural law, but an addition thereto devised by human reason.[7]

Thomas, unlike Cicero, will fully integrate his natural law reasoning into a host of matters never considered by Cicero, including but not limited to fornication, adultery, and divorce. Despite this author's best efforts to scan the full body of Cicero's works, the evidence clearly displays Cicero's less integrative style in his use of natural law reasoning when dealing with particular moral issues, and at the same time, the silence on so many subjects that at the time of St. Thomas were more vocally critiqued. When compared with today's ethical briar patch of selective reduction, same sex marriage, and genetic manipulation, neither Cicero nor Aquinas could ever have extended the reach of their respective natural law theories to modern day questions. To be sure, Aquinas has a much more prominent role to play in resolving contemporary ethical quandaries because he was willing to do so. Aquinas does not shy away from troublesome questions of morality and by most standards was evaluating the problems of his age. However, if he could not have anticipated the ethical challenges of the twenty-first century, it is no wonder; neither could Cicero's theory of natural law be applied cleanly to these difficulties. In a sense, what we witness is a developmental problem, a genealogical gap of morals and ethics where things have yet reached fruition or any sort of consensus. In Cicero's time, there was indeed a theory of self-preservation, which was part and parcel a tenet of the natural law, yet right next to this concept was the notion of an honorable suicide for leaders. By the time of Aquinas, suicide was precisely resolved as nothing but antagonistic to the natural law. Suicide is one example of this lack of continuity in time and ethical formation between these two giants.

When the last portion of this chapter is considered, it will become obvious that Cicero's theory of the natural law, a young, almost infant-like series of generalized observations on how the world works, how nature plays out, and how the Creator of this cosmos imprints his reflective force, will suffer from its inherent insufficiency and a type of cultural relativity that all natural law thinkers hope to avoid. In the final analysis, Christianity may have been, as some have argued, the needed glue to fix these propositions exactly where they needed to be.[8] In the meantime, let us consider in a more detailed way, where the consensus exists and where the contrast is more marked.

Whether Cicero and Aquinas agree on the role of nature and the natural order

The question whether nature and the natural order play a prominent role in the natural law philosophy of Cicero and Aquinas can be settled very favorably. Both figures rely upon a naturalistic perspective when weighing the suitability and sense in human conduct. Both figures discern that the entire universe operates with an undeniable ordering that reflects the logic and oversight of a creative being. As Cicero describes, man has "a divine element within him, and will think of his own inner nature as a kind of consecrated image of God."[9] Divine governance and divine oversight is presumed to be part of the natural system, and in place of a chaotic series of accidents and circumstances, both would conclude that God orchestrates with the perfection of each being in mind. Nature and the natural order provide instruction on how to live correctly. Opinion is not what guides nature or other variables subject to change but the order is inherent in nature. When Cicero says that only "fools" could believe that the law of nature can be changed, he obviously respects its permanency.[10] Cicero urges the citizenry to gaze at a God who fashioned the natural order. "Therefore, if you will only look on high and contemplate this eternal home and resting place, you will no longer attend to the gossip of the vulgar herd or put your trust in human rewards for your exploits."[11]

St. Thomas finds similarly by concluding that "God is Ruler of the universe"[12] and nature is something "common to man and other animals"[13] and because of nature, man is "inclined naturally"[14] to act in certain ways. Given the universality of nature and the order inherent in its operations, Cicero and Aquinas are comfortable with the finding that acts in opposition to nature are to be severely condemned; to be declared "special sins" or "unnatural crime."[15] In this way, nature becomes a barometer of moral agency whereby human conduct and human affairs can be measured against the backdrop of nature.

Although the agreement here is irrefutable, there are differing degrees of emphasis. Cicero clearly engages his readers with more biology than Aquinas ever does, for in Cicero the subject of human anatomy and design are intricately woven into his analysis of natural order and function. Cicero speaks of eyes and ears, the mouth, teeth and the tongue, the forehead, the gait, and posture of the human person as pressing evidence of how our design proves the logic of a higher moral power.[16] Everything for Cicero makes sense—nothing exists here by chance or random selection. Hence, how something works or the particular purpose for a human organ takes on a moral dimension. To illustrate, Cicero speaks of sexual attraction as being designed anatomically for heterosexual relations. Aquinas expends a bit less energy on the functionalist biology so dominant in Cicero, leaning more to his psychological reputation for understanding the dispositions, the predilections, and inclinations of the human player. While it may be true that our designs favor this form of sexual activity over another form, St. Thomas is likely to argue that since sexual intercourse must align with the possibility of procreation these consequences are natural. Hence, other sexual activities, between the same sex or gender, such as homosexual sodomy falter. As Thomas articulates, "Just as the ordering of right reason proceeds from man, so the order of nature from God Himself; wherefore in sins contrary to nature, whereby the very order of nature is violated, and injury is done to God, the Author of nature."[17]

Thomas types unnatural acts with an unusual ferocity calling sodomy, incest, and bestiality a "special kind of deformity"[18] and a matter "most grave and shameful to act against things as determined by nature."[19] In Cicero and Aquinas there is a natural way to do things, to use something, and to live compatibly with our natural constitution—the makeup of mind, body, and spirit, as well as the particularized parts and pieces of that whole, whether it be an arm, a foot, or an eye. Each part of the human person has a natural, functional purpose and should be used in accordance with that purpose. This same admonition relates to the fullness of our existence as well, that every person has ends and goods that should be sought and other ends to be avoided. As such, Aquinas argues that vices like drunkenness work against our nature because it hinders reason and to "deprive oneself of reason is therefore a serious fault."[20] Activity in accordance with nature is always compatible with our ultimate ends and goods while vice operates to the very contrary. As Cicero determines, nature shapes our character into what is "honourable," not base.[21] In sum, Cicero and Aquinas concur on the role of nature and the natural order in shaping their respective natural law jurisprudence.

Whether Cicero and Aquinas see nature and reason as essential to their natural law philosophy

At the second phase of this project, the role of reason and nature is evaluated—determining whether or not nature instructs the human person and delivers its universal content by and through the use of a person's reason. Coursing through the pages of his many works, Cicero repeatedly references reason as central to understanding nature's dictates. While nonrational creatures may work and operate on instinct and innate habituation, rational creatures are perched at nature's highest steps—with God at the apex and man clinging right below. Only man and God have reason and that is exactly how nature intended it. On close examination, it is difficult to discern extraordinary differences between Thomas and Cicero on these conceptual frameworks. While the emphasis may vary a bit, both Thomas and Cicero adhere to one another in generally identical ways.

Nature consumes their attention but Cicero seems to expend more energy discussing issues of a biological nature. Cicero rejects a pantheistic God, and relegates nature to an effect of a perfect Creator-God. Taking the opposite direction, Thomas evaluates nature in a hierarchical construct. At the top of the ladder is the human person, the only creature described as rational. This rational human is capable of using reason to arrive at correct moral choices. Reason is a natural a part of our human constitution, as deposited by our Creator, but can only be used properly when driven toward virtuous conduct and our proper end. Reason is central in both of their virtue theories, believing that reason alone is capable of determining virtuous human conduct. Knowledge of virtue and the law is contained in reason, and while some of this knowledge is embedded, much of it is learned by habituation. Both Cicero and Aquinas see the link between reason and nature and blend it with knowledge of correct moral action. Both determine that virtue is evident in the order of nature, its beings, and its effects. Cicero and Aquinas both initially uncover the nature of the creation before them and then, "in tune with its fundamental nature, moving towards the proper end and objects of its very existence. God's 'architectonic plan' is part of God's reason, from the origin of the universe to the fluidity of the present."[22]

Both St. Thomas and Cicero adopt the idea that reason in the human person mirrors the Creator-God. There are basic differences in the arguments both offer but the conclusions they reach are inherently similar. Both accept that there is a Creator-God. All other beings are secondary beings, moved by the Supreme God. Further they conclude that reflection of the Prime Mover is self-evident in every being created by this omniscient God. The unquestionable trait that connects God and man is reason, which is the sole characteristic shared by God and man. God and the human being are rational creatures, imbued with reason; no other creature in the universe has such a capacity. Consequently, reason opens the door to other similarities between the Creator and the rational person: that is, both think, know certain content about virtue and the natural law. In light of this, it can be concluded that we are predisposed to certain behaviors. Humans must have been designed with perfection in mind because a perfect God created us in his image. Because we are crafted in the image of God, we are "capable of rational knowledge and self-direction."[23] To possess such an intimate connection with the Creator is a "participation"[24] by man in the mind of God. In reason, there is the spark of divine reflection and divine illumination, for both thinkers agree that reason is shared by God and man. For Cicero and Aquinas, the natural law is an "imprint" impressed upon reason with specific content that reason inherently knows or can readily discover with the most basic of reflections. Cicero labels reason the "first common possession of man and God."[25]

Across the entire conceptual structure of their arguments, Cicero and Aquinas agree with this conviction. Each knows that reason is unique to the human condition and the divine Creator that fashioned them. Cicero shows his natural affinity with Aquinas when he comments, "Therefore just as that divine mind is the supreme Law, when {reason} is perfected in man that also is Law; and this perfected reason exists in the mind of the wise man."[26] Aquinas confirms that only man shares this capacity because "the rational creature partakes thereof in an intellectual and rational manner"[27] and as a result the human person participates in the eternal law. No other creatures have this capability and therefore, there is no participation in them, "except by way of similitude."[28] While approaches and emphases may differ, Cicero and Aquinas find that reason exists in the nature of man, and since this is so, reason is part of the natural order, and a component in how the human person operates. Because of this, reason is part of nature. Cicero goes as far as to say that reason is a "gift" from nature. In *De Legibus*, he places reason at a very high elevation in the natural scheme of things. "For those who have received the gift of reason from Nature have also received right reason, and therefore they have also received the gift of Law, which is right reason applied to command and prohibition."[29] Cicero could not be more emphatic when he states that "true law is right reason in agreement with nature … it is of universal application, unchanging and everlasting … And if they have received Law, they have received Justice also."[30]

Aquinas affirms that "natural reason" is "nothing else than an imprint on us of the Divine Light."[31] While Aquinas may concur in parts here, his approach is a bit more clinical since reason is part of the human being's composition and dispositional tendencies and because reason is guided by law, which is the "rule and measure of acts, whereby man is induced to act or is restrained from acting."[32] This law is the natural law. Further, St. Thomas declares that reason, and reason alone, is the "rule and measure of human acts," with reason being the "first principle of human acts."[33] Reason is the place to discover the proper choices in human activity, not the will nor the passions, not the senses or the emotive powers evident in every human person. The knowledge and content of reason has the "power of moving from the will … for it is due to the fact that one wills the end, that the reason issues its commands as regards things ordained to the end."[34]

Both Cicero and Aquinas choose reason as the most dependable measure of human action. Everything else leads to unbridled relativity because opinions can be wrong, emotions can taint judgment, and passions blind the truth of any matter. Reason, "when it is full grown and perfected" Cicero says, "is rightly called wisdom."[35] In the Thomist view, all of this may be true, although Thomas's dissection of the human intellect and reason into two spheres is more complicated, and more persuasively illuminating than Cicero's observation. For St. Thomas, reason has a more universal attribute when considering the loftier, speculative questions, such as whether each being seeks its own preservation or every creature has a particular end or good in mind. On this score, the content of reason and reason's powers appear the same for every person. Descending to matters of practical application and rectitude, Thomas declares the variety can be astonishing. "But in matters of action, truth or practical rectitude is not the same for all, as to matters of detail, but only as to the general principles; and where there is the same rectitude in matters of detail, it is not equally known by all."[36]

Reason can also be corrupted by excessive pleasure and hedonism; tested, Cicero says, by the basis of "pleasure and pain"[37] and led to erroneous conclusions that are not fully grounded and fully compatible with our natural operations. St. Thomas completely concurs with the power of the human person to corrupt the basic orderliness of reason, indicating that reason can be "perverted by passion, or evil habit, or an evil disposition of nature."[38] St. Thomas confirms this destruction of reason's usual operation is a mighty, although not impossible, task when he queries whether the natural law can be abolished or blotted out from man.

> As to those general principles, the natural law, in the abstract, can nowise be blotted out from men's hearts ... But as to the other, i.e., the secondary precepts, the natural law can be blotted out from the human heart, either by evil persuasions ... by vicious customs and corrupts habits ... and even unnatural vices.[39]

Hence in both philosophical figures, right reason and correct reasoning will produce dependable and reliable moral decision making. Reliance on any other human component, from the will to the sensory capacities, will never produce a reliable body of knowledge upon which to build a system rooted in the natural. Right reason—recta ratio—is what Cicero and Aquinas exhort as the exclusive way of moral resolution.

Given these characteristics, it is no wonder that this same reason must be dependable because of other endearing attributes, such as universality and immutability. In Thomas and Cicero, a reason that mutates by the moment will not be a moral barometer worth capturing. Reason, law, and nature are unified, which "binds all human society, and is based on one Law, which is right reason applied to command and prohibition."[40] For Aquinas, a similar deduction is inevitable for what is right, what is just, what is true "in so far, as they partake of right reason, are derived from the eternal law."[41] Aquinas's coupling of the natural law with the eternal further buttresses the unchangeability argument, for in Thomas, these general principles have everlasting qualities reflected in the human agent since the "natural law dates from the creation of the rational creature. It does not vary according to time, but remains unchangeable."[42]

In sum, Cicero and St. Thomas largely concur as to how nature and reason edify a moral framework for human action. Both agree on reason's placement as the superior means to achieve and gain moral wisdom when compared with will, the senses, and appetites. Finally, each propounds a theory of right or correct reasoning whereby the results are the same for all men in all settings but, at the same time, are open to suggestions of corruption as to reason in secondary moral matters.

Whether the natural law of Cicero and Aquinas are compatible

When the natural law theories of Cicero and Aquinas are placed side by side, the similarities outweigh the differences—at least as to express and explicit text. Neither thinker ever avoids the argument that there is a law above the law as traditionally understood; that no human promulgation can ever be inherently satisfactory because of the human law's tendency to whimsy and whim, public opinion and clamor, as well as shifting utility and personal preferences in moral decision making. Cicero and Aquinas are adamant that something greater than the civil law exists for the law of the nation-state or the conclusions of jurists and judges alike will never deliver a dependable ethical framework. Instead, each insists that a greater power, eternally, perpetually, and universally powerful, has been part of created history. Cicero could not be more unequivocal when he states that there is "one, eternal and unchangeable law will valid for all nations, and all times," with "one master and ruler, and that is God, over us all, for he is author of this law, its promulgator and enforcing judge."[43] In Cicero's worldview, this sort of law is incapable of modification and its tenets are discoverable in human experience, in human reason, and in nature itself. The law of nature/natural law is "fixed" and is the "standard" by which human conduct must be eventually measured.[44]

For St. Thomas, this broad characterization is something he fully agrees with. The natural law is transcendently placed above human laws and serves as a barometer on the ethicality and morality for any human promulgation. Thomas declares, "Consequently every human law has just so much of the nature of law, as it is derived from the law of nature. But if in any point it deflects from the law of nature, it is no longer a law but a perversion of law."[45] Natural law retains all the Ciceronian attributes of immutability and permanence in Aquinas.[46] Aquinas describes the natural law as something that "does not vary according to time, but remains unchangeable.[47] So ingrained and permanent is the natural law in every rational creature, that it cannot be "blotted out"[48] and eradicated for this law is "written in the men's hearts."[49] Even though the natural law is not codified or published, its content is still universally known by every rational creature who "knows, is conscious of what is good and what is evil."[50] While Cicero concludes that the rational creature knows this law and is naturally constituted to be just, he, like Aquinas affirms the "imprint" that God impresses on us in both the form and knowledge about the natural law.[51]

Hence, the natural law philosophies of Cicero and Aquinas, at least in a broad, very general sense, are remarkably similar. Even though critics of this idea hold that Cicero is a mere Stoic imparting a cosmological view, whereby God is nature and law is merely in the subset, this critique seems shortsighted and even erroneous when the full body of Cicero's texts are reviewed. S. Adam Seagrave's "Cicero, Aquinas and Contemporary Issues in Natural Law Theory" captures the inaccuracy of naming Cicero a pure Stoic and Aquinas something that radically departs from this school of thought.[52] For Seagrave and others, Cicero advanced a far more sophisticated vision of natural law than his predecessors such as Plato and Aristotle—neither really shaping as coherent a vision of the natural law as that authored by Aquinas. Cicero, instead of lacking originality, delivers a natural law schema that will support the eventual infrastructure that St. Thomas will build upon; the "continuation and culmination of this Ciceronian-Aristotelian natural law than as the inchoate expression of a 'new' natural law."[53] On the grander principles of the natural law, which Aquinas will label the primary tenets, such as "seeking the good and avoiding the evil," this tendency to agree will continue. When more particular questions emerge about the ethical and moral challenges that are evident in every period of human history, such as suicide, abortion, homosexuality, and other secondary questions, a pattern of distinct difference in resolution will appear. These differences will not be supported by contrarian systems laid out about the natural law but can be proven by Cicero's own assertions. Even so, why or how Cicero will diverge regarding particular applications relevant to the natural law remains a curious mystery.

Seeking the good—avoiding evil

The natural law's entire edifice is built upon the primary tenet whereby every creature seeks its proper goods and avoids those ends and objects ruinous to its maintenance and preservation. Cicero blends his naturalistic thinking, "living in accordance with nature, living naturally mantra," throughout this line of discourse for no person can be "richer than the man who lacks nothing that his nature requires."[54] To discover what is good for human operations requires a close look at the being's natural makeup because "everything that is best, to the great advantage" has "been granted by Nature."[55]

Cicero defines the concept of law, which surely includes his theory of the natural law, as a command to live in accordance with our natural essence, to choose the good over bad, to be assured of preservation and continuance rather than destruction and annihilation. In *De Legibus*, this most basic tenet of the natural law is precisely defined and described.

> Law is the highest reason, implanted in Nature, which commands what ought to be done and forbids the opposite. This reason, when firmly fixed and fully developed in the human mind, is Law. And so they believe that Law is intelligence, whose natural function it is to command right conduct and forbid wrongdoing ... for Law is a natural force; it is the mind and reason of the intelligent man, the standard by which Justice and Injustice are measured.[56]

Critics of Cicero claim the language does not mirror the passionate intentions of Cicero whose lofty language of "good" pleads for a unified view of nature and human operations.[57] Thomas West calls this a "grandiloquent foray"[58] without sincerity, since the Roman way of life appeared, at least in some categories, at odds with the principles of doing good and avoiding evil. But this is shortsighted given the repetitive power of Cicero's explicit language. In *De Legibus*, Cicero expounds, in full and unbridled detail, to know the composition of man is to discover the very essence of the natural law—a form of self-knowledge that makes up the political, spiritual, and social essence of the human person.[59]

The Thomist perspective is largely similar and a fair conclusion is that natural law rests its foundation on this principle that every being naturally seeks the good and avoids evil. "All other precepts of the natural law are based upon this"[60] Thomas declares. The good is what every being seeks, a natural yearning rather than its opposite, which would be a desire for destruction. This tenet, that "good is to be done and pursued, and evil is to be avoided,"[61] provides a substantial foundation for all other decision making in specific moral and ethical applications. Hence, questions regarding the propriety of suicide find resolution in whether a being should or should not maintain its existence under the larger theory of natural law—which directs that we seek the good and avoid evil.[62] In this manner, the primary principle of the natural law resolved the secondary principle that involved self-preservation.

The dilemma of self-preservation: Abortion and suicide

When discussing the primary principle of the natural law, seeking good and avoidance of evil, no other precept of the natural law touches its central makeup as self-preservation. Some have argued that these concepts are so fundamental as to be interchangeable, though that argument is beyond the scope of this analysis. What is relevant has to do with maintenance of life itself, which in turn, can be fairly said to be more of a primordial concern than sexual relations might be, or the choice of living in community over isolation. In these last two examples, we can safely label the content secondary or even tertiary.

Therefore, the analysis turns to the troublesome question of abortion and suicide/euthanasia, both dilemmas firmly wrapped up in the natural law mantle. For St. Thomas, the matters are not cumbersome by any means and are quickly resolved by prudential application. In Cicero, due to a variety of factors, including, distinctively different times and cultures, and varied theological approaches, the natural law answers are not second nature in his body of work. In fact, the bulk of his texts rarely, if ever mention the concept of abortion as it relates to natural law, and his evaluation of suicide manifests an obvious cultural relativity.

In Aquinas, answers regarding whether abortion and suicide/euthanasia are in opposition to the natural law are readily found in his diverse scholarship. St. Thomas authors a very unique and often times provocative argument on the unlawfulness of abortion when assessing its culpability in a criminal context. In general, his position is clear and unequivocal. "He that strikes a woman with child does something unlawful: wherefore if there results the death of the woman or of the animated fetus, he will not be excused from homicide, especially seeing that death is the natural result of such a blow."[63] From this perspective, abortion is unlawful—even being categorized as intentional homicide. The gravity of the offense will largely depend on its timing in relation to the age of the fetus. An animated fetus is one fully born and developed and incurs the law's most severe punishment. The term "animated" denotes the complete formation of the human person. By contrast, an earlier abortion, when the fetus is not yet "animated," would lack the evidentiary basis for a murder since the human fetus had yet to quicken. Animation connotes, according to St. Thomas an "ensoulement"[64]—that stage when the fetus took on the true shape of the human person, when a soul was deposited. In rough terms, St. Thomas designates the first forty to eighty days or so of fetal development as pre-ensoulement and as a result is not murder but an unnatural act triggering sinful culpability. John Doyle's translation of Vitoria's *Commentary* provides insight into how St. Thomas dealt with early term abortion.

> It may be remarked that the abortion of an animated fetus … Is here regarded as homicide. This seems remarkably anticipatory of present day laws in various

> American states which prescribe a charge of homicide in such a case ... In all probability his only questions would concern the species of sin when a fetus would be aborted prior to animation and the ecclesiastical penalties to be attached to abortion at different stages of fetal development.[65]

This conclusion was obviously reached during a time with an incomplete biological understanding of human development; neonatal science was nonexistent. However, St. Thomas espoused that the soul, which vivifies and gives life to the body, is the essential ingredient for a human person. Until that soul takes shape in that body, what remains is only a physical form, without full humanity. Thomas believes that a person develops in "successive stages" that in time lead to the formation of the intellective soul. The soul is the only ingredient that can actualize the human form into personhood. Whether the soul is created at the date of conception or at some other time is the question to be answered. This belief is in direct contrast with the instantaneous deduction of present day, pro-life advocates. St. Thomas states:

> In the first case, the necessity of the action itself results from the form by which the agent is made actual, because in order for this kind of action to exist, nothing extrinsic, as a terminus for it, is required. Thus, when the sense power is actualized by the sensible species, it necessarily acts; and so, too, does the intellect when it is actualized by the intelligible species.[66]

Because of St. Thomas's belief that the soul provides the form for the human person, he deduced that because semen is a physical composition, it is unable to deposit the content of a non-corporeal soul. St. Thomas states it is impossible for a material power to "extend its action to the production of an immaterial effect."[67] The intellect, the soul, "comes from without,"[68] and exactly when ensoulement occurs is unknown.[69] Finnis concludes that the crude biology of St. Thomas's era led him to findings that are in opposition to the current understanding of human formation. Finnis intelligently remarks:

> It seems clear that, had he known of the extremely elaborate and specifically organized structure of the sperm and the ovum, their chromosomal complementarity, and the typical, wholly continuous self-directed growth and development of the even more elaborate and specifically organized embryo or embryos from the moment of insemination of the ovum, Aquinas would have concluded that the specifically human, rational, (sensitive and vegetative), animating form and act (soul)—and therefore personhood ... can be and is doubtless from that moment.[70]

Current pro-life advocates, with an advanced understanding of the biology of the human person, believe ensoulement occurs at conception. Therefore, the modern pro-lifer sees murder in all cases of abortion, while Thomas was wary of this deduction in the first trimester. This reticence to apply felony charges should not be understood as approval of abortion. St. Thomas holds that abortion, except to save the life of the mother, is a practice in complete opposition to the natural law as well as a "mortal sin" punishable by eternal damnation.[71] Killing innocents is never justified in the universe of St. Thomas for "we ought to love the nature which God has made, and which is destroyed by slaying him."[72]

As to suicide, Aquinas is not receptive to any intervention that ends the natural cycle of human existence. When responding to the query whether it is lawful to kill oneself, St. Thomas poses three rationales for why suicide is inconsistent with the natural law. First, it is rejected because suicide is "contrary to the inclination of nature, and to charity whereby every man should love himself."[73] Second, since man is a social being, part of a larger community, the collective, he or she has obligations to the said community—from family to his neighbors. By "killing himself he injures the community."[74] Third, life taking by suicide or euthanasia undermines God's plan and his providence. "Hence, whoever takes his own life sins against God...For it belongs to God alone to pronounce sentence of death and life."[75] For the sake of expediency and the avoidance of pain and suffering, Thomas does not alter his position but remains resolute when he notes, "Therefore to bring death upon oneself in order to escape the other afflictions of this life, is to adopt a greater evil in order to avoid a lesser."[76] As with abortion, St. Thomas finds no room for tolerance for suicide or euthanasia under his natural law principles.

Cicero's assessment of suicide and abortion is difficult to pin down with particularity. Abortion never undergoes an evaluation according to natural law principles. Couple this lack of analysis with an almost infantile perspective on neonatal science, the lack of any inherent arguments as to human dignity, and a theological framework of legal and human rights, whereby every being is endowed by God with special protections, and it is no surprise that Cicero trails Aquinas in the depth of his examination. While Cicero may utter the words "made in the image of God," its importance as a basis for sanctity of life arguments has yet to be advocated. Cicero's view on abortion lacks the comprehensiveness of Aquinas and tends to be a manifestation of his time and station. In the Roman world formal proscriptions against abortion simply did not exist with any regularity or clarity. In the earliest days of the Republic, fathers could leave out to exposure any female child and by the time of Cicero, there were no formal criminal codifications that outlawed the practice. "In 65 BC, Cicero favored punishment for abortion, but his intent seems to have been the condemnation of widespread moral laxity, injustice to the father, and interests of the human race and state."[77] Most of the laws dealing with abortion had more to do with estates and heirs, the rights of the father without regard to the mother's choice, and the practical desire that the Roman empire grow mightily with a hyperventilating birthrate. Thus, any negative punishment assigned for the procurement of abortion is largely due to cost-benefit analysis rather than a "clear statement that the embryo/fetus was being protected."[78] Cicero also mentions in *De Legibus*, under the provisions of the Twelve Tables, that deformed babies, due to expediency, can be aborted if terribly deformed.[79] As to the matter of abortion, Cicero's natural law theory lacks any cohesive role in its evaluation and application as is the case in Aquinas.

In the matter of suicide, Cicero suffers from a similar fate, and fate is a key concept in this resolution. While the Stoic tendency of Cicero is to allow the fates to play out, and this includes the matter of living and dying, fate may intervene earlier to apply the principle of dying more readily than natural life might dictate. As a result, one may, according to the fates, die an earlier death than traditionally anticipated. On the other hand, Cicero concludes that nature may remain the stronger force in this matter, even more so than the fates.[80] In *De Finibus*, he lays out these two incompatible points of view, "When a man's circumstances contain a preponderance of things in accordance with nature, it is appropriate for him to remain alive; when he possess or sees in prospect a majority of the contrary things, it is appropriate for him to depart from life."[81] In this balancing act is a strange formula whereby the moral agent computes his obligations, his duties, and intended purpose for living, as well as the odds of remaining effective and at a station whereby both the individual and the collective thrive. Romans did not tolerate suicide as a carte blanche practice, but considered it an honorable way to end life when the cards could play no other way or the political reality was easy enough to deduce. Accordingly, an " 'honorable" death by one's own hand was a real possibility.[82] Over time, this conflict between Roman duty and cutting that obligation short was something the Roman world had difficulty reconciling. As the empire Christianized, the value of every life took on new, sanctified dimensions.[83] As with abortion, when compared with Aquinas, Cicero fails to deduce the incompatibility of suicide/euthanasia with natural law reasoning.

Belief in a deity

The idea that belief in a higher power is part of the natural law's essential content would also be completely agreeable to Cicero and Aquinas. Aside from the general transcendence arguments and the providential oversight that weaves its way in each author's work, their texts are replete with references to an eternal, divine, or supreme law. Aquinas clearly constructs a hierarchical system with eternal law towering over the remaining forms. In addition, he advises his readers that the power and play of Salvation History, as set out in the Old and New Testaments, provides direct instruction to the people of God on how to live rightly and justly.[84] Given his time, Cicero's only exposure could have been to the Old Testament but he never shows awareness or knowledge of the Talmudic, Rabbinical, and Jewish philosophical traditions. However, Cicero rarely misses an opportunity to highlight the higher, transcendent, and metaphysical descriptors as to law, once remarking, "But in determining what Justice is, let us begin with that supreme Law which had its origin ages before any written law existed or any State had been established."[85] When commenting on how our makeup must reflect a higher being than our own, Cicero paints a picture of a supreme God that is intimately involved in human engineering: "that animal which we call man, endowed with foresight and quick intelligence, complex, keen, possessing memory, full of reason and prudence."[86] This rational creature mirrors the creative power of a being that does everything, is capable of everything, and yet still shares with the human person a select power and attribute—reason. As a result, humans share a "certain distinguished status by the supreme God who created him; for he is only one amongst so many different kinds of living beings who has a share of reason and thought, while all the rest are deprived of it."[87] Because of this power to reason, only human beings, exercising right reason, are capable of implementing and executing true Law since it too is commonly a characteristic of God. Cicero refers to the "God of transcendent power"[88] who has "begotten and equipped man, desiring him to be the chief of all created beings."[89]

From the Thomist perspective, aside from a more sophisticated theological framework and a Christianized vision of a triune God, St. Thomas concurs on the necessity of a transcendent God and higher being in his natural law theory. His Five Ways proving the existence of God demonstrate the centrality of belief in a deity for St. Thomas.[90] More specifically, when Thomas refers to the Prime Mover, First Cause, Orderliness in the Universe, Gradations and Degrees of Perfection, each of these arguments is discoverable in Cicero's body of work. While the agreement is foundationally obvious, St. Thomas expends more energy compartmentalizing his theory of God as he lays out his natural law jurisprudence. For example, when Thomas queries whether a divine law is necessary, that is the Old and New Testaments, his response emphatically reflects the need for human instruction and "directing" and that man is open to the "law given by God."[91]

Coupled with the divine law, St. Thomas reminds his readers of the eternal law that governs the "whole community of the universe" and that the "world is ruled by Divine Providence."[92] For St. Thomas, everything is ruled by God, subject to God's oversight, created by God's power, and subject to divine reason. God rules in a "Divine Government," which is God himself.[93] Unreserved in his approach, St. Thomas propounds a vision of God as chief ruler and Creator when he remarks:

> Now God, by His Wisdom, is the Creator of all things in relation to which He stands as the artificer to the products of his art … Moreover, He governs all the acts and movements that are to be found in each single creature … Wherefore as the type of the Divine Wisdom, inasmuch as by it all things are created, has the character of art, exemplar or idea; so the type of Divine Wisdom, as moving all things to their due end, bears the character of law.[94]

God's relationship with the human person is grounded in our creator-created status, which results in an undeniable imprint in each person fashioned in his image. Thomas argues that we naturally know of God, for reason has been imprinted with this natural reflection, which is fully shaped and crafted by the Creator. Our inclinations, dispositions, and general predilections reflect the imprinted authorship of God, eventually discoverable in reason itself and manifest in the practical applications of human life. Hence Cicero and Aquinas construct a natural law theory that assumes and depends upon the ultimate end of the human person, namely a supreme being—a God all powerful and ever-present.

Procreation and sexual attraction

The natural law delineates a clear cut sexual ethic for St. Thomas and provides unequivocal advice and conclusions about certain behaviors in a universal context. Sexual behavior, as all other forms of human conduct, must be consistent with proper ends and goods that must include the potential and possibility of the procreative act. Thomas concludes that sexual intercourse concerns itself with the "welfare of the whole human race"[95] and "in keeping with the end of human procreation."[96] This is a metaphysical vision of the human person, not the respect based on secular culture, or the demand for rights in a legal context, but a vision based on God's creative power and a recognition that personhood arises from God. Sexuality plays a vital role in the continuation and growth of the human species, but the framework for sexuality is tied to the marital state and procreation.[97]

For Cicero, the picture is a bit more generalized. In Aquinas all sexual activity, to be in its proper context, must occur in the marital state and remain open to the procreative possibility. In this sense, many sexual acts, according to Aquinas, are in contravention to nature, such as incest, bestiality, homosexuality, and polygamy. All of these activities generate a "sense of shame."[98] These unnatural acts are hidden and concealed as violations of nature, "not before gods or beasts, but before other humans."[99] In incest, Aquinas condemns all forms.[100]

For those who share bonds of blood and emotion, sexual activity is dangerous and harmful for all its participants. These behaviors are ruinous to individuals, destructive to the family unit, and harmful to the community at large.[101] Incest results in shame and disgrace for its victims,[102] and permits the manipulation of those relying upon others and trusting in a subordinate relationship.[103]

Bestiality receives similar treatment since the act is unbecoming, unnatural, and especially offensive. Any type of sexual activity with animals offends our eternal God.[104] Bestiality is a grievous vice against nature that offends God. St. Thomas analyzes unnatural sexual crimes on a continuum of depravity and gravity. Bestiality falls in a most depraved light. St. Thomas relays: "Vices against nature are also against God ... and are so much more grievous than the depravity of sacrilege, as the order impressed on human nature is prior to and more firm than any subsequently established order."[105]

Homosexuality falters on similar grounds. Sodomy, in addition to failing to meet the proper ends of the human species, directly assaults nature and represents a serious disregard for the natural law. St. Thomas states: "Vices against nature are also against God ... and are much more grievous."[106] "Therefore since by the unnatural vices man transgresses which has been determined by nature with regard to the use of venereal actions, it follows that in this matter the sin is gravest of all."[107]

Cicero, as in other portions of his analysis, lacks the specificity of particular sins, offenses, or vices for that matter. Rarely do we hear any commentary on specific sexual practices and instead usually encounter a critique of the slavish Epicurean philosophy. Cicero urges his readers to restraint in sexual activity, exhorting a sort of Aristotelian mode of moderation rather than an unchecked lust.

Thomas's commentary on fornication, once defined as the copulation between unmarried parties, clearly is at odds with contemporary practice which generates minimal condemnation. St. Thomas provides scholarly perception into why fornication is a road to personal and collective destruction. Fornication was once a common practice in much of the world, including the more sophisticated cultures of Rome and Greece. In biblical times, there were a variety of outlooks on sex outside of marriage as is evident in the story of God's chosen people. The moral framework inherent in Jewish theology and philosophy put the question of fornication on a different level. Sexual intercourse between consenting adults was no longer a matter of personal choice once the Old Testament raised the bar in moral terms. St. Thomas spends a great deal of time outlining fornication's moral calculation: "For among the Gentiles, fornication was not deemed unlawful, on account of the corruption of natural reason: whereas the Jews, taught by the Divine law, considered it unlawful. The other things mentioned were loathsome to the Jews through custom introduced into their daily life."[108]

Finally, adultery does not escape the critical eye of St. Thomas, and this practice too contradicts the natural law. For Aquinas, adultery was a most hideous offense because of the resulting destruction on many fronts. Adultery is only a vice of lust, but betrays the promise made in the sacrament of matrimony and therefore breaks a promise made before God. Adultery was much more than a minor indiscretion but is instead an egregious offense against one's spouse. Adultery is a "special deformity" in "contravention of the marriage compact, whether through the impulse of one's own lust, or with the consent of the other party."[109]

The adulterer displays a lack of chastity as well as a failure of integrity—his or her own as well as the integrity of others. The adulterer undermines both the institution of marriage in a civil sense and the sacrament of matrimony in a theological sense. Human procreation without the stability and dependability of the marital state is put at risk as well in light of the possibility of resultant unwanted pregnancies and children in the community. St. Thomas clearly holds, "But adultery is especially opposed to matrimony, in the point of breaking the marriage faith which is due between a husband and wife."[110]

Each of these conducts is in contravention to the goods and ends of human operation, undermine our capacity to become virtuous, and almost guarantee the inability to become a more perfect being. All of these actions directly contradict the fundamental principles of the natural law.

In Cicero's eyes, these sexual acts undermine the nature and order of the human being, appeal to baser instincts, as well as encourage cruder and objectively disordered states. At a minimum, the bulk of these practices conform to the pleasure principle alone and this unbounded hedonism is frequently chided by Cicero. That sexual activity is pleasurable, cannot serve as the sole foundational building block for a sexual ethic because many sexual activities may provide or deliver pleasure, false or otherwise, yet still be lacking the proper end of sexual and conjugal activity. In fact, pleasure often confuses those that follow the sexual attraction theory. Pleasure, Cicero relates, is the "great imitator" of just action. Pleasure, in and of itself, provides no rational basis for its legitimacy and eventually may enslave the human actor.[111] In *De Re Publica*, Cicero graphically describes this false reality.

> For the spirits of those who are given to sensual pleasure and have become their slaves, as it were, and who violate the laws of the gods and men at the instigation of those desires which are subservient to pleasure—their spirits, after leaving their bodies, fly about close to the earth, and do not return to this place except after many ages of torture.[112]

As to homosexuality, Cicero rarely discusses what, in select cultural circles, was once common practice, especially between certain slave states and higher noble classes using youths for homoerotic experiences.[113] The ambiguity of this practice appears partly the result of historic Greek practices that were subsequently either adopted into the Roman moral system or outright rejected.[114] Cicero references these practices in *De Re Publica* when he comments:

> it was {considered} a disgrace to youths if they did not have lovers ... To say nothing of the Eleans and Thebans, among whom lust is actually given free rein in the relations of free men, the Spartans themselves, who give every freedom to love relations with young men except that of actual defilement, protected only by a thin wall this one exception; for, providing only that cloaks be interposed, they allow embraces and sharing of the bed.[115]

Expressly, Cicero never outspokenly condemns homosexuality or its aligned conduct, although he is quick to condemn debauchery and decadent behavior, lust without limitation, irresponsible sexual practices, and obsessive hedonism that blots out rational decision making. In addition, Cicero's commentary on his enemies, such as Mark Antony and others, often contain derogatory remarks as to promiscuity, prostituting oneself and effeminacy. His comments are stinging to say the least:

> You assumed the manly gown, which you soon made a womanly one: at first a public prostitute, with a regular price for your wickedness, and that not a low

> one. But very soon Curio stepped in, who carried you off from your public trade, and, as if he had bestowed a matron's robe upon you, settled you in a steady and durable wedlock. No boy bought for the gratification of passion was ever so wholly in the power of his master as you were in Curio's. How often has his father turned you out of his house? How often has he placed guards to prevent you from entering? While you, with night for your accomplice, lust for your encourager, and wages for your compeller, were let down through the roof. That house could no longer endure your wickedness.[116]

To be sure, Cicero's many observations on the functions and uses of the human body and its particular parts might permit some implicit inferences as to proper usage of sexual organs. This bio-functional analysis has been discussed previously, although a revisit sheds light on this inferential method for reaching conclusions about Cicero and homosexuality. Again, the functionalist perspective simply measures morality by intended, natural usage of an organ or bodily part in question. And if that person uses his parts incorrectly, or attempts to alter a man's demeanor for a woman's, or undergo other intentional alterations to how one should be, that person is acting in contravention to nature. Cicero states in *De Finibus* that if a man were to act in accord with nature (*naturae congruentes*) that person would use their biology correctly.[117] Hence to walk on one's hands or to walk backward, is to reject the natural human usage and hence to display *naturam odisse*—a hatred of nature.[118] The same could be said of the sexual organs. "Implicitly, the nature wills men's bodies to move and to function in certain ways; men who violate these principles of masculine comportment are acting both effeminately and ... unnaturally."[119]

When compared with St. Thomas, Cicero's theory of natural law never generates a list of human activity subject to this sort of moral evaluation as does his counterpart. Thomas poses a systematic delineation of moral quandaries whereby the practical application of the natural law takes on a most meaningful life. In Cicero, the ethical dynamic remains aloof, teleologically defined but incapable of universal application.

Social-familial-communal existence

Cicero holds firm to the Aristotelian notion that man is a social being who cannot live in isolation. Human interaction is part of our natural needs—a tenet of the natural law that inclines us to human association. Human beings have been born and placed into a communal context since "natural fellowship" is the only state of association that comes to us from simple observation.[120] In *De Re Publica* he states:

> Well, then, a commonwealth is the property of a people. But a people is not any collection of human beings brought together in any sort of way, but an assemblage of people in large numbers associated in an agreement with respect to justice and a partnership for the common good. The first cause of such an association is not so much the weakness of the individual as a certain social spirit which nature has implanted in man. For man is not solitary or unsocial creature, but born with a nature that not even under conditions of great prosperity of every sort [is he willing to be isolated from his fellow men.][121]

In Cicero's *On Friendship*, we witness an unending exhortation to the value of a life filled with friends, brothers, and sisters that give meaning and purpose to our lives. Cicero speaks often of the extraordinary sacrifices friends make for one another.

> How many things are there which we would not do for our own sake, but which we are constantly doing for the sake of our friends; asking favors of those beneath us, humbling ourselves before them, making truly violent attacks on others, pursuing them relentlessly. Such things we cannot do on our own behalf without loss of honor, but on behalf of our friends they may be done without the slightest stigma.[122]

In the context of social interaction, where friends and neighbors live in harmony, the human agent has the opportunity to live in accordance with virtue for all virtuous activity is relational. Cicero further remarks:

> This, I declare, is the partnership which contains within itself, everything deemed desirable: honor, glory, peace of mind, and joy. When men have these, life is happy; without them, it cannot be. This is the best and finest thing in life. If we wish to obtain it, we must strive ever for virtue, for without virtue, we cannot gain possession either of friendship or of anything else desirable. If men pass virtue by, they may think they have friends, but in the end they discover their error.[123]

Finally, Cicero fully appreciates the value of the collective in light of individual preferences for a just society cannot be strictly the product of unilateral action, but instead reflects the relational quality inherent in human interaction. It is the commonwealth that enables the society to function and flourish, not the individual preference. The commonwealth, Cicero indicates, is the "property of the people."[124] The collective represents more than the random mingling of people without particular purpose, but rather, an assemblage with common beliefs and goals.[125]

So too does St. Thomas declare that the human person best operates in a social—familial context and as a result, both parties declare that isolation is never preferable to a social content. When discussing the commonwealth, St. Thomas presents a picture that unites the individual citizen with the collective whole, rather than isolated actors existing in space. "The common good of a human society is similarly at the service of the person. The "good" is a communion of life between all the members of society."[126] A community is nothing more than a multitude of individuals simultaneously exercising reason. Any legal system at odds with the idea of communal goods, which emphasizes private gains at the expense of the social order, will be an unjust enterprise. Thomas's *On Kingship* relates: "Moreover, a government becomes unjust by the fact that the ruler, paying no heed to the common good, seeks his own private good. Wherefore the further he departs from the common good the more unjust will his government be."[127]

Being an active, upstanding member of the community is of utmost importance for St. Thomas. Citizens must respect not only legal, political, and spiritual authors, but also "behave well towards those who are his fellows and partners in the community."[128] A communal society "will be the more perfect the more it is sufficient unto itself to procure the necessities of life."[129] Those who show little concern for the community at large are incapable of being good citizens. In many cases this can be the result of corrupted states or nations that in turn generate weak citizens. Both the whole and its parts share a unity of purpose for "the common good of the state cannot flourish, unless the citizens be virtuous, at least those whose business it is to govern."[130] At its heart, the common good depends upon much more than individual development, for "common good is that state of society through which the attainment of the existential ends of its members is made possible."[131]

In this collective framework, "the good of the multitude is greater and more divine than the good of one man."[132] St. Thomas rightly proclaims that laws failing to enhance the common good are "without binding power,"[133] and urges disobedience to such a law when "the observance of that law would be injurious to the general welfare."[134] Human beings naturally form into groups "for the purpose of *living well* together, a thing which the individual man living alone could not attain, and *good life* is virtuous life."[135] The human agent is neither isolated nor communized in Thomistic thinking, but integrated into whole, functioning systems. Individual goods ultimately rely on common goods, which cannot be realized without the assessment of individual goods. St. Thomas's elaborate review of the virtue *justice*, or any of the other virtues, recognizes this fact of interdependency. The "good of a part can be directed to the good of the whole"[136] and the chief end is the individual as well as the collective whole, "so that all acts of virtue can pertain to justice, in so far as it directs man to the common good."[137] Much of contemporary life is fervently dedicated to the separation of individual and community. As a result, the language of personal preferences, rights, privacies, and regulatory protections has replaced the collective mind.[138]

As to the matter of social and communal living, in relation to the natural law, Cicero and Aquinas are in solid agreement.

Conclusion: Implications for natural law reasoning

Many things are assured by this form of research, but it is a certainty that this examination will likely raise more questions than deliver solutions. At the early stages of this analysis a host of matters were posed that needed consideration. First, is it possible that thinkers, from such divergent worlds, could agree on the particular moral and ethical conclusions? More specifically, do Cicero and Aquinas reach similar conclusions about what is good and what is bad? Do their respective theories of nature, of reason, of the natural order, and the natural law easily blend and rest comfortably with one another? In more particular terms, does the natural law theory of Cicero and Aquinas reflect a compatible vision or a horizon of contrast and difference? The answers here will depend on many issues beyond the capacity of this work to fully cover, though a few deductions are permissible. First, their ideas of nature and natural order manifest similar approaches. Second, the role of reason as a focal point for the content and application of the natural law is equally undeniable. That there is a transcendent perspective, an outlook that includes the clear conclusion that human law and promulgation lack the necessary depth and permanency for any such system, that is dependent upon God and some divine component for its overall validity, is undeniable. That a natural law exists cannot be denied in either perspective as well; each thinker resolute that a law of nature, a natural law, exists and is readily discoverable within the rational makeup of the human person.

With these foundational agreements, it seems that debate is minimized due to conceptual concurrence, yet this conclusion may be premature. If anything, Cicero and Aquinas seem to agree on the elementary elements of a natural law system. Even so, an examination of each thinker manifests how natural law is part of an evolutionary history in the development of ideas despite the proclamations of universality, immutability, and unchangeability. While stoical visions of nature, the cosmos, and the natural order are part of the Ciceronian dialogue, in addition to debate about how positive law can never be an adequate system for discovering the right and just, the overall systematic treatment of natural law is apparently still in its infancy. Cicero does not offer an encyclopedic vision of the natural law, but rather imparts pieces of something that Thomas will microscopically scrutinize. Cicero can also be said to talk the talk of the natural law but not be fully capable of walking the walk. When Cicero is pushed into particular determinations that are now commonly associated with the natural law, the text is either silent, the problem is not adequately covered, or its consideration has yet to be connected to the natural law phenomena. Aquinas never misses a trick in any of these discussions. Abortion he covers; he dissects the nature of suicide; homosexuality and sodomy are tackled; adultery and fornication are comprehensively analyzed. Cicero never formally addresses these issues but discusses them under the haze of larger cultural problems. Obsession with pleasure, hedonism, and Epicureanism find their way into the Ciceronian discourse but not the specific natural law problems. Because this skirting coverage differs from Thomas, is it fair to impute differing outlooks and resolutions of moral problems? It may be that Cicero cannot yet appreciate the natural law connection to a specific ethical situation, such as divorce, adultery, or other subjects, but he may easily discern that a life of endless decadence is bound to lead to failure for self and the collective. In his own case, married thrice, never outwardly condemnatory of select behaviors, at odds with the Thomistic natural law regimen such as prostitution, abortion, or homosexuality, and in fact, living in times when these behaviors were even sanctioned and tolerated in select circles, Cicero may possess a vastly more tolerant or undeveloped vision of natural law applications than St. Thomas. It could also be said, that Cicero's paganism and his corresponding lack of an ethical and moral framework rooted in traditional, religious proscriptions, may not generate the level of moral clarity that institutional religion provides. On the other hand, this lack of moral clarity might be read as a more tolerant view of the moral life than Aquinas will ever be capable of. For Cicero, suicide can be an honorable event; sexual activity with slaves acceptable; abortion of female children plausibly defended. Yet when the language of Cicero is evaluated, and compared with the language and meaning posed by Aquinas, how can such a starkly different vision of the natural law be possible?

Aside from his incomplete application of natural law principles to particular facts and circumstances, does the difference in content represent the world as Cicero encountered it rather than the ideal world that the Thomist expects? Argued from another vantage point, does culture impact our understanding of the natural law, or as St. Thomas affirms, can various levels of understanding of the natural law, depending upon person and the sophistication of that person's intellectual ability to discover and apply these principles, exist? Is there, for lack of a better way of arguing it, an unintentional cultural relativity that cannot be avoided fully in natural law analysis? Thomas actually leaves this door open when he discusses addition and subtraction in the natural law, as well as claims of ignorance in the understanding of natural law content. In this scenario, Thomas projects that future human activity may tug at natural law principles not previously thought of or described, such as genetic manipulation of the fetus or an honorable, nonmechanical, or pharmacological end of life choice, or other troublesome moral dilemma. In this way, Thomas says we might add further natural law principles, which preclude particular behaviors, and in all cases, we are dealing with secondary precepts of the natural law not the primary one. Thomas lays this out in the *Summa Theologica* when he notes:

> In this sense, the natural law is altogether unchangeable in its first principles; but in its secondary principles … the natural law is not changed so that what it prescribes be not right in most cases. But it may be changed in some particular cases of rare occurrence, through some special causes hindering the observance of such precepts.[139]

St. Thomas continues this line of reasoning when comparing knowledge of the speculative intellect whereby natural law content is the "same in all men both as to principles and as to the conclusions."[140] Thus what reason naturally knows regarding the natural law is a "common notion" known by all human persons, although this universality of understanding withers a bit when dealing with particular applications of the practical intellect since "matters of action, truth or practical rectitude is not the same for all" nor is it "equally known to all."[141] From another perspective, Cicero may represent a school of the natural law that, aside from its infancy, may possess a more expansive view of nature than the Thomist could ever envision. Nature instructs in many ways and not all of the instructions are fully compatible with the principles that are foundational to natural law reasoning. For example, the argument that human beings naturally care for offspring, which is a generically true statement for most human beings, does not negate the significant minority that could care less because of their obsessions or addictions. Some people act worse than animals in the care and feeding of their own children.

This reality does not make care of offspring a tenet outside of the natural law, but an exception to it. Similarly, nature witnesses a great many sexual behaviors that undercut notions of exclusive heterosexuality with select creatures capable of switching sexual orientation, engaging in bisexual activity, or physiologically mutating to either gender. Nature poses, of course, a base set of rules and operational commands for the average person, and at the same time, manifests a great deal of exceptional differences. In this sense, nature may be more inclusive than Thomas holds and which Cicero may have already understood. The world of genetics, the genome and DNA correlations to physical traits and behaviors may, in the future, cause quakes in the debate that will revolutionize natural law theory. If a behavior, like homosexuality, can be naturally demonstrated by gene or chromosome, what happens to the idea that nature instructs in accordance with what reason knows? These arguments may be strictly academic and speculative but these queries represent another vision of the natural order that may or may not impact the interpretation of natural law. Contrarily, it may not matter for a follower of St. Thomas and his theory of natural law because his vision and panorama regarding sexuality and nature leaps well beyond strict biology, for the human person is neither beast nor inanimate object, but a creature fashioned in the image and likeness of God and redeemed by the salvific history of Christianity. That finding may say more about the evolution of natural law reasoning since the time it was first posed by the pre-Socratics than any other fact in history. For in Christianity, the central figure, the most transformational person the world has ever encountered, in the person of Christ, natural law reaches the fulfillment of its promise. Natural law, despite the well-intended efforts of John Finnis and his followers, can only make as much sense as nature will permit. Biology alone cannot deliver a moral system that lacks dispute, nor will brotherly love, charity toward all, human respect and dignity meet the bill. For these rationales cannot urge its adherents to gaze toward the heavens as Cicero exhorted, or to achieve the Beatific Vision as Thomas says comes only to the blessed. Nature for all its teaching ability, cannot replace a philosophical system resting upon the true Divine element.

Notes

1 Background and Context: Cicero and Aquinas

1 Charles E. Rice, "Some Reasons for a Restoration of Natural Law Jurisprudence," *Wake Forest Law Review* 24 (1989): 539.

2 Richard A. Epstein, "The Utilitarian Foundations of the Natural Law," *Harvard Journal of Law & Public Policy* 12 (1988): 713.

3 For a full and comprehensive analysis of this need for teleology in any ethical framework see Alasdair MacIntyre, *Whose Justice? Whose Rationality?* (South Bend, IN: University of Notre Dame Press, 1988).

4 Alasdair MacIntyre, *After Virtue: A Study in Moral Theory*, 3rd ed. (South Bend, IN: University of Notre Dame Press, 2007).

5 Ibid., 62.

6 Ibid.

7 Ibid., 70.

8 Jeremy Bentham, *An Introduction into the Principles of Morals and Legislation* (New York: Macmillan, 1948).

9 Jean Porter, *Nature as Reason: A Thomistic Theory of the Natural Law* (Grand Rapids, MI: William. B. Eerdmans, 2004), 240.

10 H. L. Hart, "Positivism and the Separation of Law and Morals," *Harvard Law Review* 21 (1958): 593.

11 Heinrich Rommen, *The Natural Law: A Study in Legal and Social History* (St. Louis, MO: B. Herder, 1948), 113.

12 Ibid., 110.

13 The major works of Cicero include *On the Republic, On the Laws, Brutus, Stoic Paradoxes, The Orator, Consolation, Hortensius, Academics, On Ends, Tusculan Disputations, On the Nature of the Gods, On Divination, On Fate, On Old Age, On Friendship, Topics, On Glory*, and *On Duties*.

14 Anton Herman Chroust, "The Philosophy of Law from St. Augustine to St. Thomas Aquinas," *The New Scholasticism* 20 (1946): 26, 71.

15 Thomas N. Mitchell, *Cicero: The Senior Statesman* (New Haven, CT: Yale University Press, 1991), 35.

16 S. Adam Seagrave, "Cicero, Aquinas and Contemporary Issues in Natural Law Theory," *Review of Metaphysics* 62 (2009): 491, 494.

17 Mitchell, *Cicero*, 92.

18 Anthony Everitt, *Cicero: The Life and Times of Rome's Greatest Politician* (New York: Random House, 2001).
19 Some of St. Thomas Aquinas's major works include *On Being and Essence, Commentary on the Sentences of Peter Lombard, Summa contra Gentiles, On Kingship to the King of Cyprus, Commentary on Aristotle's De anima, Commentary on Aristotle's Politics*, and *Summa Theologica.*
20 Rommen, *Natural Law*, 49.
21 John F. Wippel, "Thomas Aquinas and the Condemnation of 1277," *The Modern Schoolman* 72 (January/March 1995): 233–272; Leonardas V. Gerulaitis, "The Canonization of Saint Thomas Aquinas," *Vivarium* 5, no. 1 (1967): 25–46.
22 For all of the enticing similarities, one would think the literature on this proposed study would be in greater numbers but surprisingly, there has never been a comprehensive study as posed here. There have been a few studies but these tend to go in differing directions. See Edward K. Rank, *Cicero in the Courtroom of St. Thomas Aquinas* (Milwaukee, WI: Marquette University Press, 1949); Seagrave, "Cicero, Aquinas and Contemporary Issues," 491.
23 Mitchell, *Cicero*, 10.
24 Ibid., 13.
25 Everitt, *Cicero*, 46.
26 G. K. Chesterton, *St Thomas Aquinas: The Dumb Ox* (New York: Sheed and Ward, 1933), 10.
27 See Daniel Angelo Philip Callus, *The Condemnation of St. Thomas at Oxford*, 2nd ed. (London: Aquin Press, 1955).
28 George N. Shuster, *St Thomas Aquinas* (New York: Heritage Press, 1971), v.
29 Chesterton, *Dumb Ox*, 36.
30 MacIntyre, *Whose Justice.*
31 Ibid., 172.
32 Carol Robinson, *My Life with Thomas Aquinas* (Kansas City, MO: Angelus Press, 1992), 17.
33 Marcus Tullius Cicero, *Cicero: Selected Letters*, trans. D. R. Shackleton Bailey (New York: Penguin Books, 1995), 9.
34 Marcus Tullius Cicero, *Nature of the Gods*, trans. J. M. Ross (New York: Penguin Books, 1972), 9.
35 Marcus Tullius Cicero, *De Inventione* (Whitefish, MT: Kessinger Publishing, 2004).
36 Everitt, *Cicero*, 61.
37 Ibid., 64.
38 Ibid., 68.
39 Mitchell, *Cicero*, 5.
40 Marcus Tullius Cicero, *Select Orations*, trans. Charles Duke Yonge (Philadelphia, PA: David McKay, 1896).

41 Mitchell, *Cicero*, 7.
42 Ibid.
43 Ibid., 64.
44 Cicero, *Selected Letters*, 10–11.
45 Cicero, *Nature of Gods*, 15.
46 Mitchell, *Cicero*, 325.
47 Ibid., 325.
48 Some representative biographies and critiques include but are not limited to James Weisheipl, *Friar Thomas D'Aquino: His Life, Thought, and Work*, 1st ed. (Garden City, NY: Doubleday, 1974); Frederick Copleston, *Aquinas: An Introduction to the Life and Work of the Great Medieval Thinker* (New York: Penguin Books, 1991); Ralph M. McInerny, *St Thomas Aquinas* (Notre Dame: University of Notre Dame Press, 1982).
49 Pope Benedict XV, *Encyclical Fausto appetente die*, AAS 13 (June 29, 1921): 332; Pope Pius XI, *Encyclical Studiorum Ducem*, AAS 15 (June 29, 1923): §11.
50 Chesteron, *Dumb Ox*.
51 Ibid.
52 Eleanor Stump, *Aquinas* (Boston, MA: Routledge Press, 2003), 3.
53 Vernon J. Bourke, *Selections from the Writings of St Thomas: The Pocket Aquinas* (New York: Washington Square Press, 1960), xv–xvi.
54 Anton C. Pegis, *An Introduction to St. Thomas* (New York: The Modern Library, 1948), xii.
55 Anthony Kenny, *Aquinas* (London: Oxford University Press, 1980), 19.
56 I. T. Eschmann, O.P., "A Catalogue of St Thomas' Works: Bibliographical Notes" in Etienne Gilson, *The Christian Philosophy of Saint Thomas Aquinas* (New York: Random House, 1956), 381–439.
57 Thomas Aquinas, *Commentary on the Nicomachean Ethics*, trans. C. I. Litzinger (South Bend, IN: Dumb Ox Books, 1993).
58 Pegis, *Introduction to St Thomas*, xiv.
59 Bourke, *Selections*, xvii.
60 Ibid., xviii.
61 Kenny, *Aquinas*, 25.
62 Ibid., 26.
63 Brian Davies, *The Thought of Thomas Aquinas* (Oxford: Oxford University Press, 1993), 9.
64 Raissa Maritain, *St Thomas Aquinas: Angel of the Schools* (New York: Longmans, Green and Company, 1942), 108.
65 Leonardas V. Gerulaitis, "The Canonization of Saint Thomas Aquinas," *Vivarium* 5, no. 1 (1967): 25–46; *The Catholic Encyclopedia*, vol. 14, (New York: Robert Appleton, 1912) s.v. "St Thomas Aquinas" (by Daniel Kennedy), http://www.newadvent.org/cathen/14663b.htm (accessed March 16, 2015). Nihil Obstat.

66 Bourke, *Selections*, xix.

67 Pegis, *Introduction to St Thomas*, xxx.

2 Nature and the Natural Order in Cicero and Aquinas

1 Jean Porter, *Nature as Reason: A Thomistic Theory of the Natural Law* (Grand Rapids, MI: Erdmann, 2005), 70.

2 John Finnis, *Natural Law and Natural Rights* (Boston, MA: Clarendon Press, 2011), 49.

3 S. Adam Seagrave, "Cicero, Aquinas, and Contemporary Issues in Natural Law Theory," *Review of Metaphysics* 62 (2009): 493.

4 Martin Cook, "Ways of Thinking Naturally," *The Annual of the Society of Christian Ethics* (1988): 163.

5 Aristotle, *The Basic Works of Aristotle: The Physics*, trans. Richard A. McKeon (New York: Random House, 1941), 236–237.

6 John F. McCormick, *Scholastic Metaphysics, Part 2: Natural Theology* (Chicago, IL: Loyola University Press), 12.

7 Aristotle, *The Basic Works*, 340.

8 Thomas Aquinas, *Summa Contra Gentiles, Book II: Creation*, trans. James E. Anderson (South Bend, IN: University of Notre Dame Press, 1975), ch. 3, 33.

9 Jan Aersten, *Nature and Creature: Thomas Aquinas's Way of Thought* (New York: E. J. Brill, 1988).

10 Ibid., 141.

11 Ibid., 146.

12 D. J. B. Hawkins, *Nature as the Ethical Norm* (London: Blackfriars, 1951), 3.

13 Mark D. Jordan, "Cicero, Ambrose and Aquinas 'On Duties' or the Limits of Genre in Morals," *Journal of Religious Ethics* 33 (2005): 485–490.

14 Hawkins, *Ethical Norm*, 18.

15 Elaine Fantham, "The Concept of Nature and Human Nature in Quintilian's Psychology and Theory of Instruction," *Rhetorica* 13 (1995): 136.

16 Cynthia S. W. Crysdale, "Revisioning Natural Law: From the Classicist Paradigm to Emergent Probability," *Theological Studies* 56 (1995): 466.

17 Ibid., 465.

18 Ibid., 484.

19 Cicero's *De Legibus* and *De Re Publica* are filled with such references.

20 At no place is this more obvious than Cicero, *On Academic Scepticism*, trans. Charles Brittain, (Indianapolis, IN: Hackett, 2006).

21 See J. Annas, "Stoic Epistemology," in *Epistemology*, ed. S. Everson (London: Cambridge University Press, 1999), 184–303.

22 Cicero, *Academic Scepticism*, xx.
23 Richard A. Horley, "The Law of Nature in Philo and Cicero," *Harvard Theological Review* 71 (1978): 40.
24 J. F. G. Powell, *Cicero the Philosopher* (London: Clarendon Press, 2002), 24.
25 Cicero, *Academic Scepticism*, xx.
26 Horsley, "Nature in Philo," 57.
27 Cicero, *De Re Publica and De Legibus*, trans. Clinton Walker Keyes (Cambridge, MA: Harvard University Press, 1988), 39.
28 Cicero, *De Re Publica De Legibus*, 349.
29 Ibid.
30 Ibid., 326–327.
31 Germain Grisez, "Natural Law, God, Religion, and Human Fulfillment," *The American Journal of Jurisprudence* 46 (2001): 8–9.
32 Cicero, *The Nature of the Gods*, trans. C. P. McGregor (New York: Penguin Books, 1972), 129.
33 Ibid., 173–177.
34 Ibid., 175–176.
35 Jordan, "Limits of Genre," 489.
36 Cicero, *Nature of Gods*, 181–182.
37 Ibid., 179.
38 Cicero, *On Old Age and Friendship*, trans. Frank O. Copley (Ann Arbor: University of Michigan Press, 1980), 5.
39 Cicero, *Nature of Gods*, 180.
40 Jordan, "Limits of Genre," 490; see also Cicero, *De Officiis*, ed. Michael Winterbottom (Oxford: Clarendon Press, 1994), 5–7.
41 Cicero, *On Old Age*, 19.
42 Ibid., 35.
43 Ibid., 37.
44 Ibid., 36.
45 Ibid.
46 Ibid., 27.
47 Ibid.
48 Alexander Litman, "Cicero's Doctrine of Nature and Man" (PhD diss., Columbia University, 1930), 12.
49 Seth Bernadette, "Cicero's De Legibus I: Its Plan and Intention," *American Journal of Philology* 108 (1987): 305.
50 Cicero, *Nature of Gods*, 172.
51 Ibid., 131.
52 Ibid., 170.
53 Ibid., 140.

54 Ibid., 156.
55 Eli Edward Burriss, "Cicero and the Religion of His Day," *The Classical Journal* 21 (1926): 524.
56 E. K. Rand, *Cicero in the Courtroom of St. Thomas Aquinas* (Milwaukee, WI: Marquette University Press, 1946), 56.
57 Cicero, *Nature of Gods*, 140.
58 Litman, "Cicero's Doctrine," 13.
59 Cicero, *De Re Publica De Legibus*, 211.
60 Ibid.
61 Marcus Tullius Cicero, *Select Orations*, trans. Charles Duke Yonge (New York: The Translation Publishing Company, 1927), 239.
62 Seagrave, "Cicero, Aquinas and Contemporary Issues," 503; see also Andrew R. Dyck, *A Commentary on De Officiis* (Ann Arbor: University of Michigan Press, 1996).
63 Cicero, *Nature of Gods*, 164.
64 Cicero, *De Re Publica De Legibus*, 321.
65 Ibid., 327.
66 Cicero, *De Re Publica De Legibus*, 365.
67 Cicero, *Nature of Gods*, 180.
68 Ibid.
69 H. D. Gardeil, *Introduction to the Philosophy of St. Thomas Aquinas: Book IV: Metaphysics* (St. Louis, MO: Herder, 1967), 42.
70 Ibid.
71 Ibid., 73.
72 St. Thomas Aquinas, *Summa Theologica*, vol. 1, trans. Fathers of the English Dominican Province (New York: Benzinger Brothers, 1947), 11, Bk. I, Q. 2, art. 1, corpus.
73 Ibid., 16, Q. 3, art. 3.
74 Ibid.
75 Ibid.
76 Ibid., 17, art. 4.
77 Ibid.
78 Ibid., 16–19, Bk. I, Q. 3–7.
79 Eventually, St. Thomas posits, that without an unmoved mover the problem of infinite regression will control the debate for "one motion from one mover is, as has been said, either from a moved mover or a non-moved mover. If it is the former, it follows that it is moved by something, as was proved above. But this cannot go on ad infinitum, as was proved above. Therefore, the series of movers and mobiles must stop and a first mobile moved by an immobile mover be reached, which mover does not move of necessity, because it is not moved by another. For

whatever is moved by another, moves of necessity, to the extent that necessity is imposed upon it by its mover." See St. Thomas Aquinas, *Commentary on Aristotle's Physics: Book VII: The Nature of Motion and the First Mover* (New Haven: Yale University Press, 1958–1962), Question 1166.

80 St. Thomas Aquinas, *Commentary on Aristotle's Physics: Book II: Principles of Natural Science, Lectio 1*, trans. Richard J. Blackwell, Richard J. Spath and W. Edmund Thirlkel (New Haven, CT: Yale University Press, 1963).

81 St. Thomas, *Summa*, vol. I, 471–472, Bk. I, Q. 93, art. 4.

82 Ibid., 495, Bk., I, Q. 99, art. 1.

83 St. Thomas Aquinas, *Summa Theologica*, vol. 2, trans. Fathers of the English Dominican Province (New York: Benzinger Brothers, 1947), 2256, Bk. II–III, Q. 44, art. 2.

84 St. Thomas, *Summa*, vol. I, 465, Bk. I, Q. 91, art. 4.

85 Ibid., 465.

86 Ibid., 461–462, art. 1.

87 Ibid., 464.

88 See Fulvio Di Blasi, *God and the Natural Law: A Rereading of Thomas Aquinas* (South Bend, IN: St. Augustine's Press, 2006), 30.

89 St. Thomas, *Summa*, vol. I, 464, Bk. I, Q. 91, art. 3, corpus.

90 Ibid., r.obj. 1.

91 Ibid.

92 Porter, *Nature as Reason*, 93.

93 St. Thomas, *Summa*, vol. I, 495, Bk. I, Q. 99, art. 2.

94 Ibid., 464, Bk. I, Q. 91, art.3.

95 Ibid., r. obj. 1.

96 Ibid., r. obj. 3.

97 Ibid.

98 Porter, *Nature as Reason*, 69.

99 St. Thomas, *Summa*, vol. I, 505–582, Bk. I, Q. 103, art. 1.

100 Ibid., 505.

101 Ibid., 217, Bk. I, Q. 42, art. 3.

102 Ibid., 505, Bk. I, Q. 103, art. 1.

103 Ibid., 507, art.3, r. obj. 3.

104 Ibid., 510, art. 8, corpus.

105 Ibid., 993–1119, Bk. I–II, Q. 90–108; see also Charles P. Nemeth, *Aquinas in the Courtroom* (Westport, CT: Praeger and Greenwood Press, 2001); Charles P. Nemeth, *Aquinas and Martin Luther King: A Discourse on Civil Disobedience* (South Bend, IN: St. Augustine's Press, 2010).

106 St. Thomas, *Summa*, vol. I, 996, Bk. I–II, Q. 91, art. 1.

107 Ibid.

108 Ibid., 1006, Bk. I–II, Q. 93, art. 5, corpus.
109 Ibid., 1007, art. 6.
110 Ibid., art. 1.
111 Ibid., 505, Bk. I, Q. 103, art. 1.
112 Etienne Gilson, *Moral Value and the Moral Life: The System of St. Thomas*, trans. I. R. Ward (New York: Herder, 1931), 197.
113 Jan Aersten, *Nature and Creature: St. Thomas's Way of Thought* (New York: E. J. Brill, 1988), 296.
114 Ibid.
115 St. Thomas, *Summa*, vol. 2, 1295, Bk. II–II, Q. 26, art. 1.
116 Ibid.
117 See Charles P. Nemeth, *Aquinas on Crime* (South Bend, IN: St. Augustine's Press, 2009).
118 St. Thomas, *Summa*, vol. 1, 898, Bk. I–II, Q. 71, art. 2.
119 For a recent law review article providing a series of resources on the challenges, see Eugene Volokh, "Same-Sex Marriage and Slippery Slopes," *Hofstra Law Review* 33 (2006): 101–147, http://www2.law.ucla.edu/volokh/marriage.pdf.
120 St. Thomas, *Summa*, vol. 2, 1825, Bk. II–II, Q. 154, art. 11–12.
121 539 U.S. 558 (2003).
122 St. Thomas, *Summa*, vol. 2, Bk. II–II, Q. 154, art. 12.
123 Ibid., art. 11.
124 Ibid., 1825, art. 12.
125 Ibid., 1826.
126 Ibid., 1824, art. 10.
127 Ibid.
128 Ibid.
129 Ibid.
130 Ibid.
131 Ibid., 1825, art. 11.
132 Ibid., 1826, art. 12.
133 Ibid., 1826–7, r. obj. 4.

3 Cicero and Aquinas: Nature and Reason

1 Jean Porter, "Reason, Nature, Natural Law in Medieval Accounts of the Natural Law," *The Journal of Religious Ethics* 24 (1996): 208.
2 Jean Porter, *Nature as Reason: A Thomistic Theory of the Natural Law* (Grand Rapids, MI: William B. Eerdmans, 2005), 233.

3 Frank J. Yartz, "Order and Right Reason in Aquinas' Ethics," *Medieval Studies* 27 (1975): 407.

4 Anton-Hermann Chroust, "The Fundamental Ideas in St. Augustine's Philosophy of Law," vol. 19, *The American Journal of Jurisprudence* (1973): 59.

5 St. Thomas Aquinas, *Summa Theologica*, vol. 1, trans. Fathers of the English Dominican Province (New York: Benzinger Brothers, 1947), 469–478, Bk. I, Q. 93.

6 Chroust, "Fundamental Ideas," 60.

7 St. Thomas, *Summa*, vol. 1, 471, Bk. I, Q. 93, art. 4.

8 Cicero, *De Re Publica and De Legibus*, trans. Clinton Walker Keyes (Cambridge, MA: Harvard University Press, 1988), 329.

9 Ibid.

10 St. Thomas, *Summa*, vol. 1, 1008, Bk. I–II, Q. 94; see also St. Thomas on the idea of inherent or infused virtue at Ibid., 822, Bk. I–II, Q. 55, art. 4.

11 Ibid., 406, Bk. I, Q. 79, art. 11.

12 Cicero, *De Re Publica De Legibus*, 333.

13 Ibid., 323.

14 Vernon J. Bourke, *St. Thomas and the Greek Moralists* (Milwaukee, WI: Marquette University Press, 1947), 23.

15 St. Thomas, *Summa*, vol. 1, 469, Bk. I, Q. 93, art. 1.

16 Cicero, *De Re Publica De Legibus*, 321.

17 St. Thomas, *Summa*, vol. 1, 1004, Bk. I–II, Q. 93, art. 2, corpus.

18 St. Thomas, *Summa*, vol. 1, 1009, Bk. I–II, Q. 94, art. 2.

19 Marcus Tullius Cicero, *Selected Works of Cicero*, trans. Isabel K. Raubitschek (New York: Walter J. Black, 1948), 228; see also Charles P. Nemeth, *Criminal Law, 2nd* ed. (Boston, MA: Taylor & Francis Group, 2012), 10.

20 Cicero's theory of Law is best discovered in his *De Legibus*, a work that some claim was never fully completed and others indicate purposefully hard to pin down in meaning. See Clinton W. Keyes, "Did Cicero Complete the De Legibus?" *The American Journal of Philology* 58 (1937): 403–417.

21 Cicero, *De Re Publica De Legibus*, 383.

22 Ibid., 211.

23 Ibid., 181.

24 Ibid.

25 Ibid., 213–215.

26 Ibid., 213.

27 Ibid., 211.

28 Ibid., 215.

29 Ibid., 317.

30 Ibid., 317–318.

31 Ibid., 389.

32 Marcus Tullius Cicero, *The Nature of the Gods*, trans. Horace McGregor (London: Penguin Classics, 1978), 155.
33 Cicero, *De Re Publica De Legibus*, 39.
34 Ibid., 279.
35 Ibid., 281.
36 Ibid.
37 Cicero, *Selected Works*, 228.
38 Ibid.
39 Ibid.
40 Cicero, *De Re Publica De Legibus*, 349.
41 Cicero, *Selected Works*, 233.
42 Cicero, *De Re Publica De Legibus*, 321.
43 Ibid., 323–324.
44 Ibid., 365.
45 Ibid., 365–367.
46 Marcus Tullius Cicero, *On the Good Life*, trans. Michael Grant (New York: Penguin Books, 1971), 58–59.
47 Ibid., 63.
48 Ibid.
49 Ibid.
50 Ibid., 76.
51 Cicero, *De Re Publica De Legibus*, 339.
52 Ibid., 351.
53 Ibid.
54 Ibid.
55 Ibid., 389.
56 Ibid., 333.
57 Ibid., 335.
58 Cicero, *Good Life*, 90.
59 Ibid., 329.
60 Ibid., 345.
61 Ibid., 347.
62 Ibid., 349.
63 Ibid., 347.
64 Ibid., 385.
65 John Finnis, *Aquinas: Moral, Political and Legal Theory* (London: Oxford University Press, 1998), 62.
66 Ibid., 62–71.
67 St. Thomas, *Summa*, vol. 1, Bk. I, Q. 78; Paul J. Glenn, *A Tour of the Summa* (Rockford, IL: Tan, 1998), 64.

68 Ibid., 583–589, Q. 1.
69 Porter, *Nature as Reason*, 232.
70 St. Thomas, *Summa*, vol. 1, 403, Bk. I, Q. 79, art. 8.
71 Ibid., 404.
72 Ibid., 403.
73 Porter, *Nature as Reason*, 232.
74 St. Thomas, *Summa*, vol. 1, 404, Bk. I, Q. 79, art. 9.
75 Ibid., 404–405.
76 Glenn, *Tour of the Summa*, 65.
77 Porter, *Nature as Reason*, 249.
78 Finnis, *Aquinas*, 79.
79 Ibid., 81.
80 St. Thomas, *Summa*, vol. 1, 406, Bk. I, Q. 79, art. 11.
81 Ibid.
82 Ibid.
83 Ibid., 415, Q, 82, art. 3.
84 Finnis, *Aquinas*, 315.
85 Ibid.
86 St. Thomas Aquinas, *Summa Contra Gentiles*, trans. Vernon J. Bourke (South Bend, IN: University of Notre Dame Press, 1956), Bk. III, ch. 25.
87 St. Thomas, *Gentiles*, 42, Bk. II, ch. 11.
88 St. Thomas, *Summa*, vol. 1, 469, Bk. I, Q. 93, art. 1.
89 Ibid.
90 Ibid., 469.
91 Ibid., 470, Q. 93, art. 2.
92 Ibid., 471, art. 3.
93 Ibid.
94 Ibid., art. 4.
95 Ibid., 475, art. 8.
96 Ibid., 477, art. 9.
97 Ibid., 993, Bk. I–II, Q. 90, art. 1.
98 Ibid., 996, Q. 91, art. 1.
99 Ibid., 997, art. 2.
100 Ibid.
101 Ibid., 1004, art. 3.
102 Ibid.
103 Ibid., 703–894, Q. 49–70.
104 St. Thomas Aquinas, *On Aristotle's Love and Friendship*, trans. Pierre Conway (Providence, RI: Providence College Press, 1951), IX, ch. 3.
105 Etienne Gilson, *The Christian Philosophy of St. Thomas Aquinas* (New York: Random House, 1956), 260.

106 Vernon J. Bourke, "Right Reason in Contemporary Ethics," *The Thomist* 38 (1974): 108.
107 Ibid., 108.
108 St. Thomas, *Love & Friendship*, IX, Ch. 3.
109 Bourke, "Right Reason," 107.
110 St. Thomas, *Summa*, vol. 1, 823, Bk. I–II, Q. 56, a. 1, corpus.
111 St. Thomas, *Summa Theologica*, vol. 2, trans. Fathers of the English Dominican Province (New York: Benziger Brothers, 1947), Bk. II–II, Q. 109, a. 2, corpus.
112 St. Thomas, *Summa*, vol. 1, 1010, Bk. I–II, Q. 94, a. 3, corpus.
113 Ibid., 820–822, Bk. I–II, Q. 55, art. 3, 4.
114 Alisdair MacIntyre, *After Virtue: A Study in Moral Theory* (South Bend, IN: University of Notre Dame Press, 1981), 59–60.
115 Ibid., 61.
116 John J. Osterle, *St. Thomas Aquinas: Treatise on the Virtues* (South Bend, IN: University of Notre Dame Press, 1984), xiii.
117 Ibid.
118 St. Thomas, *Summa*, vol. 1, 834, Bk. I–II, Q. 58, art. 3.
119 Ibid.
120 Ibid., 820, Bk. I–II, Q. 55, art. 3.
121 Porter, *Nature as Reason*, 182.
122 Finnis, *Aquinas*, 84.
123 St. Thomas, *Summa*, vol. 1, 806–813, Bk. I–II, Q. 52–53.
124 Ibid., 811, Bk. I–II, Q. 53, art. 1.
125 Ibid., 819–822, Bk. I–II, Q. 55, art. 1–4.
126 Ibid., 821, art. 3.
127 Ibid., 826, Bk. I–II, Q. 56, art. 5.
128 Ibid., 860, Bk. I–II, Q. 64, art. 1.
129 Ibid., 858, r. obj. 2.
130 Ibid., 859, art. 3, corpus.
131 Gilson, *Christian Philosophy*, 264.
132 St. Thomas, *Summa*, vol. 1, 815, Bk. I–II, Q.54, art. 3.
133 Charles P. Nemeth, *Aquinas on Crime* (South Bend, IN: St. Augustine's Press, 2008), 5.
134 St. Thomas, *Summa*, vol. 1, 993, Bk. I–II, Q. 90, art. 1.
135 Ibid., 994.
136 Ibid., 1001, Bk. I–II, Q. 92, art. 1.
137 Ibid.
138 Ibid., 997, Bk. I–II, Q. 91, art. 2.
139 Ibid., art. 3.
140 Ibid., 997–998.

141 Ibid., 1010, Bk. I–II, Q. 94, art. 3.
142 Ibid., 1019, Bk. I–II, Q. 96, art. 3.
143 Ibid., 1018, art. 2.
144 Ibid.; see Finnis, *Aquinas*, 222.
145 Charles P. Nemeth, *Aquinas in the Courtroom* (Westport, CT: Praeger Press, 2001), 58; see also Bourke, "Right Reason," 113; Brian T. Mullady, "The Meaning of the Term 'Moral' in St. Thomas Aquinas," in *Studi Thomistica*, vol. 27 (Vatican City: Libreria Editric Vaticana, 1986), 90; Robert J. Kreyche, "Virtue and Law in Aquinas: Some Modern Implications," *Southwest Journal of Philosophy* 5 (1974): 130.
146 Porter, *Nature as Reason*, 230.
147 St. Thomas, *Summa*, vol. 1, 996, Bk. I–II, Q. 91, art. 2.

4 Cicero and Aquinas on the Natural Law

1 St. Thomas Aquinas, *Summa Theologica, vol. 1*, trans. Fathers of the English Dominican Province (New York: Benzinger Brothers, 1947), 1014–1015, Bk. I–II, Q. 95, art. 2.
2 Alisdair MacIntrye, *Whose Justice? Whose Rationality?* (South Bend, IN: University of Notre Dame Press, 1988), 180–181.
3 S. J. Wilson, *The Thought of Cicero* (London: G. Bell, 1964), 13.
4 Ibid., 12.
5 Marcus Tullius Cicero, *On Old Age and Friendship*, trans. Frank O. Copely (Ann Arbor: University of Michigan Press, 1980), ix.
6 Marcus Tullius Cicero, *On the Good Life*, trans. Michael Grant (New York: Penguin Books, 1971), 20–21.
7 Ibid., 33.
8 Plato, *The Laws of Plato*, ed. Thomas L. Pangle (New York: Basic Books, 1980); Aristotle, *Nicomachean Ethics*, trans. Martin Ostwald (New York: Bobbs-Merrill, 1962); Aristotle, "Politics," in *The Basic Works of Aristotle*, ed. Richard McKeon (New York: Random House, 1941).
9 Marcus Tullius Cicero, *Verres in Sicily: Selections from Cicero's Verrine Orations*, trans. and comp. H. Grouse-Hodge and E. W. Davies (Cambridge, MA: Cambridge University Press, 1964), 28.
10 L. P. Wilkinson, *Letters of Cicero: A Selection in Translation* (New York: W. W. Norton, 1968), 20.
11 Cicero, *De Re Publica and De Legibus*, trans. Clinton Walker Keyes (Cambridge, MA: Harvard University Press, 1988), 379.
12 Ibid., 343.

13 Ibid., 381.
14 Ibid., 211.
15 Marcus Tullius Cicero, *The Nature of the Gods*, trans. C. P. McGregor (New York: Penguin Books, 1972), 158.
16 Ibid.
17 Cicero, *De Re Publica De Legibus*, 315.
18 Ibid., 49.
19 Ibid.
20 Ibid., 316.
21 Ibid., 139.
22 Ibid.
23 Cicero, *Nature of Gods*, 175–176.
24 Cicero, *De Re Publica De Legibus*, 325–327.
25 Cicero, *Nature of Gods*, 178.
26 Ibid.
27 Ibid., 178–180.
28 Ibid., 180.
29 Ibid., 181.
30 Ibid.
31 St. Thomas, *Summa*, vol. 1, 13–14, Bk. I, Q. 2, art. 3.
32 Cicero, *Nature of Gods*, 243.
33 Richard P. Francis, "Natural Law as Essentially Definitive of Human Nature," *Vera Lex* 14 (1994): 65–88.
34 Cicero, *Nature of Gods*, 272.
35 Cicero, *On Old Age*, 5.
36 Ibid.
37 Ibid., 36.
38 Cicero, *Nature of Gods*, 158.
39 Ibid., 164.
40 Cicero, *On the Good Life*, 72.
41 Cicero, *Nature of Gods*, 34.
42 Cicero, *De Re Publica De Legibus*, 461.
43 St. Augustine, *On Free Choice of the Will*, trans. Anna S. Benjamin and L. H. Hackstaff (New York: Macmillan, 1964).
44 Cicero, *Nature of Gods*, 130.
45 Cicero, *De Re Publica De Legibus*, 381.
46 Ibid., 383.
47 Wilson, *Thought of Cicero*, 47.
48 Cicero, *De Re Publica De Legibus*, 349.
49 Ibid., 343.

50 Ibid.
51 Ibid., 345.
52 Ibid., 349.
53 Cicero, *De Re Publica De Legibus*, 211; see Cicero, *Nature of the Gods*, 158.
54 Ibid.
55 Ibid.
56 Cicero, *On Old Age*, 21.
57 Cicero, *De Re Publica De Legibus*, 321.
58 Cicero, *Nature of Gods*, 128.
59 St. Thomas, *Summa*, vol. 1, Bk. I–II, Q. 90.
60 See by way of example Ernest J. Fortin, "The New Rights Theory and the Natural Law," *Review of Politics* 44 (1982): 610; see also Christopher Wolfe, *Natural Law Liberalism* (Cambridge, MA: Cambridge University Press, 2006).
61 Cicero, *De Re Publica De Legibus*, 312.
62 John Finnis, *Natural Law and Natural Rights* (Oxford: Oxford University Press, 1980), 49.
63 S. Adam Seagrave, "Cicero, Aquinas and Natural Law Theory," *Review of Metaphysics* 62 (March, 2009): 491.
64 Maryanne C. Horowitz, "The Stoic Synthesis of the Idea of Natural Law in Man: Four Themes," *Journal in the History of Ideas* 35 (1974): 3–15.
65 Seagrave, "Natural Law Theory," 493–495.
66 St. Thomas, *Summa*, vol. 1, 1009–1010, Bk. I–II, Q. 94, art. 2.
67 Ibid., art. 1–2.
68 Ibid., 1003–1008, Bk. I–II, Q. 93.
69 Cicero, *De Re Publica De Legibus*, 47.
70 Ibid., 49.
71 Ibid., 251.
72 Ibid.
73 Ibid., 339.
74 Cicero, *Nature of Gods*, 115.
75 Cicero, *De Re Publica De Legibus*, 345.
76 Ibid.
77 Ibid., 347.
78 Ibid.
79 Ibid., 365–367.
80 Ibid., 361.
81 Cicero, *De Re Publica De Legibus*, 269.
82 Ibid., 347.
83 Ibid., 267–269.
84 Jo-Ann Shelton, *As the Romans Did: A Sourcebook in Roman Social History*, 2nd ed, (New York: Oxford University Press, 1998), 356.

85 Cicero, *De Re Publica De Legibus*, 341.
86 Cicero, *Nature of Gods*, 175–176.
87 Cicero, *De Re Publica De Legibus*, 213.
88 Cicero, *On Old Age*, 21.
89 Cicero, *De Re Publica De Legibus*, 365.
90 Ibid., 283.
91 Cicero, *On Old Age*, 88–89.
92 Cicero, *De Re Publica De Legibus*, 349.
93 Ibid., 355.
94 Cicero, *On the Good Life*, 101.
95 Cicero, *De Re Publica De Legibus*, 207.
96 Cicero, *On the Good Life*, 75.
97 Shelton, *As the Romans Did.*
98 E. K. Rand, *Cicero in the Courtroom of St. Thomas Aquinas* (Milwaukee, WI: Marquette University Press, 1945), 38.
99 See Shelton, *What the Romans Did*, 16–66, Cicero's grieving Letter to Atticus 12:46 on the loss of his daughter.
100 K. R. Bradley, *Discovering the Roman Family* (New York: Oxford University Press, 1991).
101 Cicero, *De Re Publica De Legibus*, 251.
102 Ibid.
103 Cicero, *Nature of Gods*, 176.
104 Cicero, *On Old Age*, 18.
105 Ibid., 83.
106 Ibid., 82.
107 Cicero, *De Re Publica De Legibus*, 345.
108 Ibid., 353.
109 Ibid., 333.
110 Ibid., 65.
111 Ibid., 281.
112 Ibid., 323–325.
113 Ibid., 211.
114 Ibid.
115 Ibid., 213.
116 Ibid., 319.
117 Ibid., 323.
118 Ibid., 281.
119 Ibid.
120 St. Thomas, Summa, vol. 1, 1034, Bk. I–II, Q. 99, art. 4, r. obj. 1.
121 For some well-grounded discussion of positive law in Thomistic jurisprudence see Vincent McNabb, *St. Thomas Aquinas and Law* (Blackfriars, 1955) and Barry F.

Smith, "Of Truth and Certainty in the Law: Reflections on the Legal Method," *The American Journal of Jurisprudence* 30 (1985): 119.

122 St. Thomas, *Summa*, vol. 1, 854, 1010, 1013, Bk. I–II, Q. 63, art. 1; Q. 94, art. 3; Q. 95, art. 1, corpus.

123 Ibid., 1013, Bk. I–II, Q. 95, art. 1, corpus.

124 Charles Skok portrays Thomas' vision as realistic rather than pessimistic. "St. Thomas often made reference to men in their present condition. Not many men are truly virtuous or highly virtuous. Laws have to be made for the general run of the people in the state in which they are found. This is not pessimism but realism." Charles D. Skok, A. B., Ed.B., S. T. L., *Prudent Civil Legislation According to St. Thomas and Some Controversial American Law* (Rome: Catholic Book Agency, 1967), 119.

125 St. Thomas, *Summa*, vol. 1, Bk. I–II, Q. 95, art. 1, r. obj. 1.

126 Ibid., art. 3.

127 Ibid., art. 4, corpus.

128 St. Thomas Aquinas, *The Treatise on Law: Summa Theologiae, I–II; qq. 90–97*, ed. R. J. Henle (Notre Dame, IN: University of Notre Dame Press, 1993), 335.

129 St. Thomas, *Summa*, vol. 1, 1020, Bk. I–II, Q. 96, art. 5, corpus.

130 Ibid., 1093, Bk. I–II, Q. 105, art. 1, r. obj. 5.

131 Ibid., 1036, Bk. I–II, Q. 99, art. 6, r. obj. 2.

132 Ibid., 1014, Bk. I–II, Q. 95, art. 2, corpus.

133 Etienne Gilson, *Law on The Human Level: Moral Values and Moral life The System of St. Thomas*, trans. L. Ward (St. Louis, MO: B. Herder,1931), 204.

134 St. Thomas, *Summa*, vol. 1, 1005, Bk. I–II, Q. 93, art. 3, r. obj. 2.

135 Ibid., 1004–1005.

136 Ibid., r. obj. 1.

137 Ibid., r. obj. 2.

138 Raymond Dennehy addresses the law's ultimate aim in "The Ontological Basis of Human Rights." "For, as a rational being, man attains his self-perfection by transcending the limitations of his finite, temporal self. Through the immanence of knowing, he achieves ever higher levels of reality as he identifies himself ontologically with Being and its facets. Truth, Goodness, Beauty, and ultimately with the fullness of Being, God; and all the while he retains his own unique selfhood." *The Thomist* 42 (1978): 455.

139 Heinrich A. Rommen, *The Natural Law*, trans. T. Hanley (St. Louis, MO: B. Herder, 1948), 54–55.

140 St. Thomas, *Summa*, vol. 1, 1018, Bk. I–II, Q. 96, art. 2.

141 Daniel Nelson, *The Priority of Prudence*, (University Park: Pennsylvania State University Press, 1992), 107. See also Daniel J. Sullivan, *An Introduction to Philosophy: The Perennial Principles of Classical Realist Tradition* (Rockford, IL: Jan Books, 1992); Bernard Beodder, *Natural Theology* (New York: Longmans, Green.

1927); Etienne Gilson, *The Christian Philosophy of St. Thomas Aquinas*, trans. L. K. Shook, (New York: Random House, 1956), 266; Thomas E. Davitt, *The Nature of Law* (St. Louis, MO: Herder, 1951), 39–54.

142 Thomas Aquinas, *Summa Contra Gentiles*, trans. Vernon J. Bourke, vol. 4 (Notre Dame: University of Notre Dame Press, 1975), III–II, 114.

143 St. Thomas, *Gentiles*, III–II, 115.

144 Ibid., III–II, 114.

145 Ibid.

146 St. Thomas, *Summa*, vol. 1, 993, Bk. I–II, Q. 90, art. 1, sed contra.

147 Ibid., corpus.

148 Walter Farrell, "The Natural Moral Law According to St. Thomas and Suarez" (PhD diss., University of Fribourg, Switzerland, 1930), 10. See also Davitt, *The Nature of Law*, 39–54; Robert J. Henle, "St. Thomas Aquinas and American Law," *Thomistic Papers II*, eds. Leonard A. Kennedy and Jack C Marler (Houston: Center for Thomistic Studies, 1986), 67.

149 St. Thomas Aquinas, *Summa Contra Gentiles*, trans., Vernon J. Bourke, vol. 3 (Notre Dame: University of Notre Dame Press, 1975), III–I, 2.

150 St. Thomas Aquinas, *Commentary on the Sentences*, 4 vols., ed. P. Mandonnet and M. F. Moos (Paris: P. Lethielleus, 1929, 1933, 1947), Suppl., Q. 65, art. 1.

151 St. Thomas, *Gentiles*, ch. 129, 4.

152 St. Thomas, *Summa*, vol. 1, 1039, Bk. I–II, Q. 100, art. 3.

153 Ibid., 1099, Bk. I–II, Q. 94, art. 2, corpus.

154 Ralph McInerny correctly cautions interpreters not to equate natural law reasoning with the physical laws or imperatives. "Natural law is not simply the rational recognition of physical imperatives, nor is it a judgment of how we should act which ignores the given teleology of the physical. Natural law relates to inclinations other than reason, which have their own ends, by prescribing how we should humanly pursue them. For Thomas, natural law is a dictate of reason, not a physical law." *Ethica Thomistica: The Moral Philosophy of Thomas Aquinas* (Washington, DC: Catholic University of American Press, 1982), 46.

155 St. Thomas, *Summa*, vol. 1, 1009, 1011, Bk. I–II, Q. 94, art. 2, 4; R. A. Armstrong, *Primary and Secondary Precepts in Thomistic Natural Law Teaching* (The Hague: Martinus Nijhoff, 1966), 125.

156 C. S. Lewis, *Studies in Words* (Cambridge: Cambridge University Press, 1960), 43.

157 Anton-Hermann Chroust, "The Philosophy of Law of St. Thomas Aquinas: His Fundamental Ideas and Some of His Historical Precursors," *The American Journal of Jurisprudence* 19 (1974): 24.

158 Gilson, *Law on the Human Level*, 266.

159 Lewis, *Studies in Words*, 37.

160 Ibid., 24.

161 St. Thomas Aquinas, *On Kingship*, trans. Gerald B. Phelan (Toronto: Pontifical Institute of Mediaeval Studies, 1982), ch. II, 19.

162 Bernard Boedder, *Natural Theology* (New York: Longmans, Green, 1927), 46.

163 Gilson, *Law on the Human Level*, 266.

164 Alasdair MacIntyre's often cited work, *Whose Justice? Which Rationality?* (Notre Dame: University of Notre Dame Press, 1988), 194, warns the critic and ally alike that the natural law is not merely a registry of pre- and proscriptions. "Obeying the precepts of the natural law is more than simply refraining from doing what those precepts prohibit and doing what they enjoin. The precepts become effectively operative only as and when we find ourselves with motivating reasons for performing actions inconsistent with those precepts; what the precepts can then provide us with is a reason which can outweigh the motivating reasons for disobeying them, that is, they point us to a more perfect good than do the latter."

165 St. Thomas, *Summa*, vol. 1, 1008, Bk. I–II, Q. 94, art. 1.

166 Ibid., 997, Bk. I–II, Q. 91, art. 2, corpus.

167 Ibid.

168 Ignatius T. Eschmann, *The Ethics of St. Thomas Aquinas* (Toronto: Pontifical Institute of Mediaeval Studies, 1997), 187.

169 Ibid., 166–167.

170 St. Thomas, *Summa*, vol. 1, 1013, Bk. I–II, Q. 94, art. 6.

171 Ibid., 1009, art. 2, corpus.

172 St. Thomas, *Gentiles*, III–I, ch. 4, 2.

173 Ibid., ch 6, 5.

174 St. Thomas, *Summa*, vol. 1, 1010, Bk. I–II, Q. 94, art. 2, r. obj. 2.

175 See Brian Tierney, *The Idea of Natural Rights: Studies on Natural Rights, Natural Law and Church Law* (Atlanta, GA: Scholars Press, 1998), 1150–1625.

176 St. Thomas, *Summa*, vol. 1, 1011, Bk. I–II, Q. 94, art. 4, corpus.

177 Ibid., r. obj. 3.

178 Gratian, *The Treatise on Law (Decretum DD. 1–20)*, trans. James Gordley (Washington, DC: Catholic University Press of America, 1993), I, v, prol. (I,7); St. Thomas, *Summa*, vol. 1, 1012, Bk. I–II, Q. 94, art. 5, sed contra.

179 Gilson, *Law on the Human Level*, 266.

180 Chroust, "The Philosophy of St. Thomas," 25.

181 St. Thomas, *Summa*, vol. 1, 1003, Bk. I–II, Q. 93, art. 1.

182 Ibid., 234, Bk. I, Q. 45, art. 3.

183 Ibid., 1003, Bk. I–II Q. 93, art. 1, corpus.

184 Ibid.

185 Henle, *Treatise on Law*, 149.

186 St. Thomas, *Summa*, vol. 1, 1005, Bk. I–II, Q. 93, art. 3, sed contra.

187 Ibid.

188 Ibid., 993, Q. 90, art. 1, r. obj. 1.

189 Ibid., 996, Q. 91, art. 1.

190 Ibid., 1004, Q. 93, art. 2, r. obj. 1.

191 Ibid., 1005, art. 4, corpus.

192 Ibid., 996, Q. 91, art. 1, corpus.

193 Ibid.

194 Ibid., 1008, Q. 93, art. 6, r. obj. 3.

195 Ibid., 1007, r. obj. 2.

196 Ibid.

197 Ibid., 1004, art. 1, r. obj. 3.

198 Ibid., 1049, Q. 100, art. 11, corpus.

199 See Henle, *Treatise on Law*.

200 St. Thomas, *Summa*, vol. 1, 1011, Bk. I–II, Q. 94, art. 4, corpus.

201 Ibid., 1012, art. 5, corpus.

202 Armstrong, *Primary and Secondary Precepts*, 134.

203 St. Thomas, *Summa*, vol. 1, 1012, Q. 94, art. 5, corpus.

204 St. Thomas, *Gentiles* III–II, Ch. 122, 4.

205 Jeremy Bentham, *The Principles of Morals and Legislation* (New York: Hafner, 1948).

206 J. V. Dolan, "Natural Law & Modern Jurisprudence," *Laval Theologique et Philosophique* 16 (1990): 40.

207 Ibid., 40.

208 Anton-Hermann Chroust, "The Fundamental Ideas in St. Augustine's Philosophy of Law," *The American Journal of Jurisprudence* 18 (1973): 67.

209 Daniel Nelson appreciates this comprehensive view of law when he states, "Law in all of its manifestations derives from God's reason." *Priority of Prudence*, 107. See also Chroust, "Fundamental Ideas," 67.

210 St. Thomas, *Gentiles*, III–II, Ch. 112, 3.

211 St. Thomas, *Summa*, vol. 1, 1009, Bk. I–II, Q. 94, art. 2, corpus.

212 Gilson, *Law on the Human Level*, 266.

213 Nelson, *Priority of Prudence*, 107.

214 Even the appetitive process exhibits a certain inclination. "This certitude is based on the nature of the being. Things are constituted in a determined way, and their inclination follows and is one with their determination, so that, even without knowledge of what is and what is not appetible, a natural inclination will seek the appetible." Gustaf J. Gustafson, "The Theory of Natural Appetency in the Philosophy of St. Thomas" (PhD diss., The Catholic University of America, 1944), 71.

215 St. Thomas, *Summa*, vol. 1, 997, Bk. I–II, Q. 91, art. 3.

216 Ibid., 1011, Q. 94, art. 4, corpus.

217 Eschmann, *Ethics of St. Thomas*, 188.
218 Ibid.
219 St. Thomas, *Summa*, vol. 1, 1037, Bk. I–II, Q. 100, art. 1, corpus.
220 Ibid., 1010, Q. 94, art. 3, r. obj. 2.
221 Ibid.
222 St. Thomas Aquinas, *Summa Theologica*, vol. 2, trans. Fathers of the English Dominican Province (New York: Benzinger Brothers, 1947), 1471, Bk. II–II, Q. 64, art. 7, corpus.
223 Ibid., sed contra.
224 Ibid., corpus.
225 Joseph Rickaby, *Aquinas Ethicus: The Moral Teaching of St. Thomas* (London: Burnes and Oates, 1892), 47.
226 St. Thomas, *Summa*, vol. 2, 1471, Bk. II–II, Q. 64, art. 7, corpus; see Rickaby, *Aquinas Ethicus*, 47–48.
227 Ibid., 1469, art. 5, corpus.
228 Ibid., 1467, art. 2, r. obj. 3.
229 Charles P. Nemeth, *Aquinas on Crime* (South Bend, IN: St. Augustine's Press, 2009), 58–59.
230 St. Thomas, *Gentiles*, 88–89.
231 St. Thomas, *Summa*, vol. 1, 574, Bk. I, Q. 118, art. 2.
232 Ibid.
233 See Daniel A. Dambrowski, "Rachels, Abortion and the Seventeenth Century," *International Journal of Applied Philosophy* 9 (1998): 38.
234 St. Thomas, *Summa*, vol. 2, 1811, Bk. II–II, Q. 153, art. 2.
235 Ibid.
236 Ibid.
237 Ibid., 1810.
238 Ibid., 1813, art. 5.
239 Ibid., 1826, Q. 154, art. 12.
240 Ibid., 1825, art. 11.
241 Ibid.
242 Ibid., 1825, art. 12.
243 Ibid., 1826.
244 Ibid.
245 Ibid., 1824, art. 10.
246 Ibid.
247 Ibid.
248 Ibid.
249 St. Thomas, *Gentiles*, III–II, Ch. 122, 4.
250 Ibid., ch. 124, 1.

251 Ibid., ch. 125, 7.

252 Ibid., ch. 127.

253 Ibid., 7.

254 St. Thomas, *Summa*, vol. 2, 1816, Bk. II–II, Q. 154, art. 2.

255 Ibid.

256 Ibid., 2722–2723, Bk. III, Q. 44, art. 1.

257 Ibid., 2724, art. 3.

258 Ibid., 2814, Q. 66, art. 1.

259 Ibid.

260 Ibid.

261 Ibid.

262 Ibid., 2807, Q. 65, art. 1.

263 John F. Dedek, "Intrinsically Evil Acts: An Historical Study of the Mind of St. Thomas," *The Thomist* 43 (1979): 392.

264 Ibid., 2808, Q. 65, art. 1.

265 Ibid.

266 Ibid., 2809.

267 St. Thomas, *Summa*, vol. 1, 1017, Bk. I–II, Q. 96, art. 1, corpus.

268 Ibid., 1018, r. obj. 2.

269 Ibid., art. 2, corpus.

270 Ibid., 994, Q. 90, art. 2, corpus.

271 Ibid., 1026, Q. 98, art. 1, corpus.

272 Noel Dermot O'Donoghue, "The Law Beyond the Law," *The American Journal of Jurisprudence* 18 (1973): 158.

273 St. Thomas, *Summa*, vol. 1, 998, Bk. I–II, Q. 91, art. 4, corpus.

274 Ibid.

275 Patrick M. J. Clancy, "St. Thomas on Law," in St. Thomas Aquinas, *The Summa Theologica*, vol. 3, trans. Fathers of the English Dominican Province (New York: Benziger Brothers, 1947), 3275.

276 St. Thomas, *Summa*, vol. 1, 1029, Bk. I–II, Q. 98, art. 4, r. obj. 3.

277 Ibid.; Clancy, "St. Thomas on Law," 3275.

278 St. Thomas, *Summa*, vol. 1, 1030, Bk. I–II, Q. 98, art. 5, corpus.

279 Ibid., 999, Q. 91, art. 4, r. obj. 1.

280 Ibid., 998, corpus.

281 Ibid.

282 Gilson artistically blends this divine law and human agent into a *union*, a *unity*, a bridge spanning the chasm of the temporal and the eternal, attaching him to God by means of his love. *Law on the Human Level*, 333.

283 Ibid., 1038, Q. 100, art. 2, corpus.

284 St. Thomas, *Gentiles*, III–II, ch. 128, 2.

285 St. Thomas, *Summa*, vol. 1, 1037, Bk. I–II, Q. 100, art. 1.
286 Ibid., 1045, art. 8, corpus.
287 Ibid., 1032, Q. 99, art. 2, r. obj. 2.
288 Ibid.
289 Ibid., 999–1000, Q. 91, art. 5, r. obj. 1.
290 Henry Mather, "Natural Law and Right Answers," *The American Journal of Jurisprudence* 38 (1993): 334; see also Skok, *Prudent Civil Legislation*, 22.

5 Cicero and Aquinas: Compatibility and Contrast

1 Cicero, *De Re Publica and De Legibus*, trans. Clinton Walker Keyes (Cambridge, MA: Harvard University Press, 1988).
2 St. Thomas Aquinas, *Summa Theologica, vols. 1* and 2, trans. Fathers of the English Dominican Province (New York: Benzinger Brothers, 1947).
3 Ibid.
4 Ibid.
5 St. Thomas, *Summa*, vol. 1, 1014, Bk. I–II, Q. 95, art. 2.
6 Cicero, *De Re Publica De Legibus*, 349.
7 St. Thomas, *Summa*, vol. 2, 1477, Bk. II–II, Q. 66, art. 2.
8 Alisdair MacIntyre, *After Virtue: A Study in Moral Theory* (South Bend, IN: University of Notre Dame Press, 1981); Jean Porter, *Nature as Reason: A Thomistic Theory of the Natural Law* (Grand Rapids, MI: William B. Eerdmans, 2005).
9 Cicero, *De Re Publica De Legibus*, 365.
10 Ibid., 347.
11 Ibid., 279.
12 St. Thomas, *Summa*, vol. 1, 996, Bk. I–II, Q. 91, art. 1.
13 Ibid., 1010, Bk. I–II, Q. 94, art. 3, r. obj. 2.
14 Ibid., 1011, art. 4, corpus.
15 Ibid.
16 Marcus Tullius Cicero, *The Nature of the Gods*, trans. C. P. McGregor (New York: Penguin Books, 1972), 129, 176–182.
17 St. Thomas, *Summa*, vol. 2, Bk. II–II, 1825, Q. 154, art. 12.
18 Ibid., art. 11.
19 Ibid., art. 12.
20 Ibid., 1800, Bk. II–II, Q. 150, art. 2.
21 Cicero, *De Re Publica De Legibus*, 349.
22 Charles P. Nemeth, *Aquinas in the Courtroom* (Westport, CT: Praeger Press, 2001), 58.

23 Porter, *Nature as Reason*, 230.
24 St. Thomas, *Summa*, vol. 1, 996, Bk. I–II, Q. 91, art. 2.
25 Cicero, *De Re Publica De Legibus*, 321.
26 Ibid., 383.
27 St. Thomas, *Summa*, vol. 1, 997, Bk. I–II, Q.91, art. 2.
28 Ibid.
29 Cicero, *De Re Publica De Legibus*, 211.
30 Ibid., 333.
31 St. Thomas, *Summa*, vol. 1, 997, Bk. I–II, Q.91, art. 2.
32 Ibid., 993, Bk. I–II, Q. 90, art. 1.
33 Ibid.
34 Ibid., Bk. I–II, Q. 94.
35 Cicero, *De Re Publica De Legibus*, 321.
36 St. Thomas, *Summa*, vol. 1, 1011, Bk. I–II, Q. 94, art. 4.
37 Cicero, *De Re Publica De Legibus*, 339.
38 St. Thomas, *Summa*, vol. 1, Bk. I–II, Q. 94, art. 4.
39 Ibid., 1013, Bk. I–II, Q. 94, art. 6.
40 Cicero, *De Re Publica De Legibus*, 345.
41 St. Thomas, *Summa*, vol. 1, 1005, Bk. I–II, Q. 93, art. 3.
42 Ibid., 1012, Bk. I–II, Q. 94, art. 5.
43 Cicero, *De Re Publica De Legibus*, 211.
44 Ibid., 347.
45 St. Thomas, *Summa*, vol. 1, 1014, Bk. I–II, Q. 95, art. 3.
46 Ibid., I–II, 1013–1014, art. 5 & 6.
47 Ibid., 1012, Bk. I–II, Q. 94, art. 5.
48 Ibid., art. 6.
49 Ibid.
50 Ibid., 997, Bk. I–II, Q. 91, art. 2.
51 Cicero, *De Re Publica De Legibus*, 321.
52 S. Adam Seagrave, "Cicero, Aquinas and Contemporary Issues in Natural Law Theory," *Review of Metaphysics* 62 (2009): 492–493.
53 Ibid., 494.
54 Cicero, *De Re Publica De Legibus*, 51.
55 Ibid., 213.
56 Ibid., 317–319.
57 Alexander Litman, "Cicero's Doctrine of Nature and Man" (PhD diss., Columbia University, 1930), 7.
58 Thomas G. West, "Cicero's Teaching on Natural Law," *St. John's Review* 32 (1981): 76.
59 Seth Bernadette, "De Legibus I: Its Plan and Intention," *The American Journal of Philology* 108 (1987): 305.

60 St. Thomas, *Summa*, vol. 1, 1009, Bk. I–II, Q. 94, art. 2.

61 Ibid.

62 Even this broad way of thinking about natural law does not always readily fit as neatly as one might think. See Martin Cook, "Ways of Thinking Naturally," *The Annual of the Society of Christian Ethics* (1988): 161–178.

63 St. Thomas, *Summa*, vol. 2, 1472, Bk. II–II, Q. 65, art. 8.

64 St. Thomas, *Summa*, vol. 1, 575–578, Bk. I, Q. 118–119.

65 Francisco de Vitoria, *On Homicide and Commentary on Summa Theologiae Q. 64*, trans. John P. Doyle (Milwaukee, WI: Marquette University Press, 1997), 48n120.

66 St. Thomas Aquinas, *Summa Contra Gentiles, vol. 2*, trans. Vernon Bourke (South Bend, IN: University of Notre Dame Press, 1975), 88–89.

67 St. Thomas, *Summa*, vol. 1, 574, Bk. I, Q. 118, art. 2.

68 Ibid.

69 See Daniel A. Dambrowski, "Rachels, Abortion and the Seventeenth Century," *International Journal of Applied Philosophy* 9 (Winter/Spring 1998): 38.

70 John Finnis, *Natural Law and Natural Rights* (Boston, MA: Clarendon Press, 2011), 186.

71 St. Thomas, *Summa*, vol. 1, Q. 90.

72 St. Thomas, *Summa*, vol. 2, 1470, Bk. II–II, Q. 64, art. 6.

73 Ibid., 1468–1469, art. 5.

74 Ibid.

75 Ibid.

76 Ibid.

77 Helen Philos Ravid, "The Pro-Life/Pro-Choice Argument as Sociocultural Symbolism: A Sociology of Knowledge Study" (PhD diss., Wayne State University 2008), 133.

78 John Kiddle, *Contraception and Abortion from the Ancient World* (Boston, MA: Harvard University Press, 1992), 63.

79 Cicero, *De Re Publica De Legibus*, 481.

80 D. M. Shaw, "Euthanasia and Eudaimonia," *Journal of Medical Ethics* 35 (2009): 530–533.

81 Marcus Tullius Cicero, *De Finibus Bonorum Et Malorum*, trans. H. Rackham (London: William Heinemann, 1914), Book III at 60–1.

82 Edwin Rubin, "Assisted Suicide, Morality, and Law: Why Prohibiting Assisted Suicide Violates the Establishment Clause," *Vanderbilt Law Review* 63 (2010): 772; see also David W. Louisell, "Euthanasia and Biathanasia: On Dying and Killing," *Catholic University Law Review* 22 (1973): 725.

83 Anton J. L. Van Hooff, "Ancient Euthanasia: 'Good Death' and the Doctor in the Graeco-Roman World," *Social Science and Medicine* 58 (2004): 982.

84 St. Thomas, *Summa*, vol. 1, 998, Bk. I–II, Q. 91, art. 4.

85 Cicero, *De Re Publica De Legibus*, 319.
86 Ibid., 321.
87 Ibid.
88 Ibid., 323.
89 Ibid., 327.
90 St. Thomas, *Summa*, vol. 1, 13–14, Bk. I, Q. 2, art. 3.
91 Ibid., 998, Bk. I–II. Q. 91, art. 4.
92 Ibid., 996, art. 1.
93 Ibid., art. 2.
94 Ibid., 1003, Bk. I–II, Q. 93, art. 1.
95 St. Thomas, *Summa*, vol. 2, 1811, Bk. II–II, Q. 153, art. 2.
96 Ibid.
97 Ibid., 1810, art. 2.
98 Mark D. Jordan, "Cicero, Ambrose and Aquinas: On Duties or the Limits of Genre in Morals," *Journal of Religious Ethics* 33 (2005): 490.
99 Ibid., 490.
100 St. Thomas, *Summa*, vol. 2, 1824, Bk. II–II, Q. 154, art. 10.
101 Charles P. Nemeth, *Aquinas on Crime* (South Bend, IN: St. Augustine's Press, 2008), 67–88.
102 Ibid.
103 Ibid.
104 St. Thomas, *Summa*, vol. 2, Bk. II–II, 1825, Q. 154, art. 11.
105 Ibid., art. 12.
106 Ibid., 1826.
107 Ibid.
108 Ibid., 1816, art. 2.
109 Ibid., 1822, art. 8.
110 Ibid.
111 For an excellent analysis of how pleasure will never be a suitable measure for the good of sexual activity, see Marcus Tullius Cicero, *Discussions at Tusculum*, ed. Michael Grant (New York: Penguin Books, 1971), 102.
112 Cicero, *De Re Publica De Legibus*, 283.
113 F. X. Ryan, "The Lex Scantinia and the Prosecution of Censors and Aediles," *Classical Philology* 89 (April 1994): 159, where the distinction between older men having sexual relations with freeborn youth versus slaves is discussed.
114 See Craig A. Williams, "Greek Love at Rome," *The Classical Quarterly* 45 (1995): 517–539; Thomas K. Hubbard, "The Varieties of Greek Love," *Gay and Lesbian Review*, May–June 2004, 11.
115 Cicero, *De Re Publica De Legibus*, 233–235.
116 Marcus Tullius Cicero, *Select Orations*, trans. Charles Duke Yonge (New York: Translation Publishing Company, 1927), Cic. Phil. 2.18
117 Cicero, *de Finibus*, 5.35

118 Ibid.

119 Craig A. Williams, *Roman Homosexuality: Ideologies of Masculinity in Classical Antiquity* (Oxford: Oxford University Press, 1999), 235; see also Nancy Myers, "Cicero's Trumpet: Roman Women and the Second Phillipic," *Rhetoric Review* 22 (2003): 347.

120 Cicero, *De Re Publica De Legibus*, 315.

121 Ibid., 65.

122 Marcus Tullius Cicero, *On Old Age and Friendship*, trans. Frank O. Copley (Ann Arbor, MI: University of Michigan Press, 1980), 71.

123 Ibid., 81.

124 Cicero, *De Re Publica De Legibus*, 65.

125 Ibid.

126 Cornelius F. Murphy, "Distributive Justice, Modern Significance," *American Journal of Jurisprudence* 17 (1972): 157.

127 St. Thomas Aquinas, *On Kingship*, trans. Gerald B. Phelan (Toronto: Pontifical Institute of Mediaeval Studies, 1982) I, ch. III, 24; J. Messner's *Social Ethics: Natural Law in the Modern World* describes the common good as "intrinsically a dynamic process … neither at any moment finished and completed nor ever ceasing to assimilate fresh driving forces from the perpetual development of the human mind, human interests and technical means." trans. J. J. Doherty (St. Louis, MO: B. Herder, 1952), 130.

128 St. Thomas, *Summa, vol. 1*, 1041, Bk. I–II, Q. 100, art. 5, corpus.

129 St. Thomas, *Kingship*, I, ch. I, 14.

130 St. Thomas, *Summa, vol. 1*, 1001, Bk. I–II, Q. 92, art. 1, ad 3.

131 Messner, *Social Ethics*, 137.

132 St. Thomas, *Kingship*, I, ch. IV, 70.

133 St. Thomas, *Summa, vol. 1*, 1021–1022, Bk. I–II, Q. 96, art. 6.

134 Ibid.,

135 St. Thomas, *Kingship*, II, Chap III (I, 14), 106.

136 St. Thomas, *Summa, vol. 2*, 1438, Bk. II–II, Q. 58, art. 5, corpus.

137 Ibid.

138 James V. Schall warns the legal thinker that the substitution of a communal jurisprudence with an individual one has adverse consequences. "There should be no doubt, then, that natural law and civilization are intimately related. To the degree that they are not, right order of soul as well as of the city collapse. When the collapse does occur, we can only begin to think about the disorder and wonder how it occurred." "The Natural Law Bibliography," *American Journal of Jurisprudence* 40 (1995): 168.

139 St. Thomas, *Summa*, vol. 1, 1012, Bk. I–II, Q. 94, art. 5.

140 Ibid., 1011, art. 4.

141 Ibid.

Bibliography

Aersten, Jan. *Nature and Creature: Thomas Aquinas's Way of Thought* (New York: E. J. Brill, 1988).

Annas, J. "Stoic Epistemology," in *Epistemology*, edited by S. Everson (London: Cambridge University Press, 1999).

Aquinas, Thomas. *Commentary on Aristotle's Physics, Book II: Principles of Natural Science, Lectio 1*, translated by Richard J. Blackwell, Richard J. Spath, and W. Edmund Thirlkel (New Haven, CT: Yale University Press, 1963).

Aristotle. *The Basic Works of Aristotle: The Physics*, translated by Richard A. McKeon (New York: Random House, 1941), 236–237.

Aristotle. *Nicomachean Ethics*, translated by Martin Ostwald (New York: Bobbs-Merrill, 1962).

Aristotle. "Politics," in *The Basic Works of Aristotle*, edited by Richard McKeon (New York: Random House, 1941).

Armstrong, R. A. *Primary and Secondary Precepts in Thomistic Natural Law Teaching* (The Hague: Martinus Nijhoff, 1966).

Armstrong, R. A. *Commentary on Aristotle's Physics, Book VII: The Nature of Motion and the First Mover* (New Haven, CT: Yale University Press, 1958–1962).

Armstrong, R. A. *Commentary on the Nicomachean Ethics*, translated by C. I. Litzinger (South Bend, IN: Dumb Ox Books, 1993).

Armstrong, R. A. *Commentary on the Sentences*, 4 vols., edited by P. Mandonnet and M. F. Moos (Paris: P. Lethielleus, 1929, 1933, 1947).

Armstrong, R. A. *On Aristotle's Love and Friendship*, translated by Pierre Conway (Providence, RI: Providence College Press, 1951).

Armstrong, R. A. *On Kingship*, translated by Gerald B. Phelan (Toronto: Pontifical Institute of Mediaeval Studies, 1982).

Armstrong, R. A. *Summa Contra Gentiles*, translated by Vernon J. Bourke (South Bend, IN: University of Notre Dame Press, 1956).

Armstrong, R. A. *Summa Contra Gentiles, Book II: Creation*, translated by James E. Anderson (South Bend, IN: University of Notre Dame Press, 1975).

Armstrong, R. A. *Summa Theologica*, vol. 1, translated by *Fathers of the English Dominican Province* (New York: Benzinger Brothers, 1947).

Armstrong, R. A. *Summa Theologica*, vol. 2, translated by *Fathers of the English Dominican Province* (New York: Benzinger Brothers, 1947).

Armstrong, R. A. *The Treatise on Law: Summa Theologiae*, I–II; qq. 90–97, edited by R. J. Henle (Notre Dame, IN: University of Notre Dame Press, 1993).

Augustine. *On Free Choice of the Will*, translated by Anna S. Benjamin and L. H. Hackstaff (New York: Macmillan, 1964).

Bentham, Jeremy. *An Introduction into the Principles of Morals and Legislation* (New York: Macmillan, 1948).

Bernadette, Seth. "Cicero's De Legibus I: Its Plan and Intention," *American Journal of Philology* 108 (1987): 305.

Boedder, Bernard. *Natural Theology* (New York: Longmans, Green, 1927).

Bourke, Vernon J. "Right Reason in Contemporary Ethics," *The Thomist* 38 (1974): 108.

Bourke, Vernon J. *Selections from the Writings of St Thomas: The Pocket Aquinas* (New York: Washington Square Press, 1960).

Bourke, Vernon J. *St. Thomas and the Greek Moralists* (Milwaukee, WI: Marquette University Press, 1947).

Bradley, K. R. *Discovering the Roman Family* (New York: Oxford University Press, 1991).

Burriss, Eli Edward. "Cicero and the Religion of His Day," *The Classical Journal* 21 (1926): 524.

Callus, Daniel Angelo Philip. *The Condemnation of St. Thomas at Oxford*, 2nd ed. (London: Aquin Press, 1955).

Catholic Encyclopedia, vol. 14 (New York: Robert Appleton Company, 1912) s.v. "St Thomas Aquinas" (by Daniel Kennedy), http://www.newadvent.org/cathen/14663b.htm (accessed March 16, 2015). Nihil Obstat.

Chesterton, G. K. *St Thomas Aquinas: The Dumb Ox* (New York: Sheed and Ward, 1933).

Chroust, Anton Herman. "The Fundamental Ideas in St. Augustine's Philosophy of Law," *The American Journal of Jurisprudence* 19 (1973): 59.

Chroust, Anton Herman. "The Philosophy of Law from St. Augustine to St. Thomas Aquinas," *The New Scholasticism* 20 (1946): 26.

Chroust, Anton Herman. "The Philosophy of Law of St. Thomas Aquinas: His Fundamental Ideas and Some of His Historical Precursors," *The American Journal of Jurisprudence* 19 (1974): 24.

Cicero, Marcus Tullius. *Cicero: Selected Letters*, translated by D. R. Shackleton Bailey (New York: Penguin Books, 1995).

Cicero, Marcus Tullius. *De Inventione* (Whitefish, MT: Kessinger, 2004).

Cicero, Marcus Tullius. *De Officiis*, edited by *Michael Winterbottom* (Oxford: Clarendon Press, 1994).

Cicero, Marcus Tullius. *De Re Publica and De Legibus*, translated by *Clinton Walker Keyes* (Cambridge, MA: Harvard University Press, 1988), 39.

Cicero, Marcus Tullius. *Discussions at Tusculum*, edited by Michael Grant (New York: Penguin Books, 1971).

Cicero, Marcus Tullius. *Nature of the Gods*, translated by J. M. Ross (New York: Penguin Books, 1972).

Cicero, Marcus Tullius. *The Nature of the Gods*, translated by Horace McGregor (London: Penguin Classics, 1978).

Cicero, Marcus Tullius. *On Academic Scepticism*, translated by Charles Brittain (Indianapolis, IN: Hackett, 2006).

Cicero, Marcus Tullius. *On Old Age and Friendship*, translated by Frank O. Copley (Ann Arbor, MI: University of Michigan Press, 1980).

Cicero, Marcus Tullius. *On the Good Life*, translated by Michael Grant (New York: Penguin Books, 1971), 58–59.

Cicero, Marcus Tullius. *Select Orations*, translated by Charles Duke Yonge (Philadelphia, PA: David McKay, 1896).

Cicero, Marcus Tullius. *Selected Works of Cicero*, translated by Isabel K. Raubitschek (New York: Walter J. Black, 1948).

Cicero, Marcus Tullius. *Verres in Sicily: Selections from Cicero's Verrine Orations*, translated and compiled by H. Grouse-Hodge and E. W. Davies (Cambridge, MA: Cambridge University Press, 1964).

Clancy, Patrick M. J. "St. Thomas on Law," in *St. Thomas Aquinas, The Summa Theologica*, vol. 3, translated by *Fathers of the English Dominican Province* (New York: Benziger Brothers, 1947).

Cook, Martin. "Ways of Thinking Naturally," *The Annual of the Society of Christian Ethics* (1988): 163.

Copleston, Frederick. *Aquinas: An Introduction to the Life and Work of the Great Medieval Thinker* (New York: Penguin Books, 1991).

Crysdale, Cynthia S. W. "Revisioning Natural Law: From the Classicist Paradigm to Emergent Probability," *Theological Studies* 56 (1995): 466.

Dambrowski, Daniel A. "Rachels, Abortion and the Seventeenth Century," *International Journal of Applied Philosophy* 9 (1998): 38.

Davies, Brian. *The Thought of Thomas Aquinas* (Oxford: Oxford University Press, 1993).

Davitt, Thomas E. *The Nature of Law* (St. Louis, MO: B. Herder, 1951).

Dedek, John F. "Intrinsically Evil Acts: An Historical Study of the Mind of St. Thomas," *The Thomist* 43 (1979): 392.

Dennehy, Raymond. "The Ontological Basis of Human Rights," *The Thomist* 42 (1978): 455.

Di Blasi, Fulvio. *God and the Natural Law: A Rereading of Thomas Aquinas* (South Bend, IN: St. Augustine's Press, 2006), 30.

Dolan, J. V. "Natural Law & Modern Jurisprudence," *Laval Theologique et Philosophique* 16 (1990): 40.

Dyck, Andrew R. *A Commentary on De Officiis* (Ann Arbor, MI: University of Michigan Press, 1996).

Epstein, Richard A. "The Utilitarian Foundations of the Natural Law," *Harvard Journal of Law & Public Policy* 12 (1988): 713.

Eschmann, Ignatius T. "A Catalogue of St Thomas' Works: Bibliographical Notes," in *The Christian Philosophy of Saint Thomas Aquinas*, edited by *Etienne Gilson* (New York: Random House, 1956).

Eschmann, Ignatius T. *The Ethics of St. Thomas Aquinas* (Toronto: Pontifical Institute of Mediaeval Studies, 1997).

Everitt, Anthony. *Cicero: The Life and Times of Rome's Greatest Politician* (New York: Random House, 2001).

Fantham, Elaine. "The Concept of Nature and Human Nature in Quintilian's Psychology and Theory of Instruction," *Rhetorica* 13 (1995): 136.

Farrell, Walter. "The Natural Moral Law According to St. Thomas and Suarez" (PhD diss., University of Fribourg, Switzerland, 1930).

Finnis, John. *Aquinas: Moral, Political and Legal Theory* (London: Oxford University Press, 1998).

Finnis, John. *Natural Law and Natural Rights* (Boston, MA: Clarendon Press, 2011).

Fortin, Ernest J. "The New Rights Theory and the Natural Law," *Review of Politics* 44 (1982): 610.

Francis, Richard P. "Natural Law as Essentially Definitive of Human Nature," *Vera Lex* 14 (1994): 65–88.

Gardeil, H. D. *Introduction to the Philosophy of St. Thomas Aquinas, Book IV: Metaphysics* (St. Louis, MO: B. Herder, 1967).

Gerulaitis, Leonardas V. "The Canonization of Saint Thomas Aquinas," *Vivarium* 5, no. 1 (1967): 25–46.

Gilson, Etienne. *The Christian Philosophy of St. Thomas Aquinas* (New York: Random House, 1956), 260.

Gilson, Etienne. *Law on the Human Level: Moral Values and Moral Life: The System of St. Thomas*, translated by L. R. Ward (St. Louis, MO: B. Herder, 1931), 204.

Gilson, Etienne. *Moral Value and the Moral Life: The System of St. Thomas*, translated by L. R. Ward (St, Louis, MO: B. Herder, 1931).

Glenn, Paul J. *A Tour of the Summa* (Rockford, IL: Tan, 1998).

Gratian. *The Treatise on Law* (Decretum DD. 1–20), translated by James Gordley (Washington, DC: Catholic University Press of America, 1993).

Grisez, Germain. "Natural Law, God, Religion, and Human Fulfillment," *The American Journal of Jurisprudence* 46 (2001): 8.

Gustafson, Gustaf J. "The Theory of Natural Appetency in the Philosophy of St. Thomas" (PhD diss., The Catholic University of America, 1944).

Hart, H. L. "Positivism and the Separation of Law and Morals," *Harvard Law Review* 21 (1958): 593.

Hawkins, D. J. B. *Nature as the Ethical Norm* (London: Blackfriars, 1951).

Henle, Robert J. "St. Thomas Aquinas and American Law," *Thomistic Papers II*, edited by Leonard A. Kennedy and Jack C. Marler (Houston, TX: Center for Thomistic Studies, 1986).

Horley, Richard A. "The Law of Nature in Philo and Cicero," *Harvard Theological Review* 71 (1978): 40.

Horowitz, Maryanne C. "The Stoic Synthesis of the Idea of Natural Law in Man: Four Themes," *Journal in the History of Ideas* 35 (1974): 3–15.

Hubbard, Thomas K. "The Varieties of Greek Love," *Gay and Lesbian Review* (May–June 2004): 11.

Jordan, Mark D. "Cicero, Ambrose and Aquinas 'On Duties' or the Limits of Genre in Morals," *Journal of Religious Ethics* 33 (2005): 485–490.

Kenny, Anthony. *Aquinas* (London: Oxford University Press, 1980).

Keyes, Clinton W. "Did Cicero Complete the De Legibus?" *The American Journal of Philology* 58 (1937): 403–417.

Kiddle, John. *Contraception and Abortion from the Ancient World* (Boston, MA: Harvard University Press, 1992).

Kreyche, Robert J. "Virtue and Law in Aquinas: Some Modern Implications," *Southwest Journal of Philosophy* 5 (1974): 130.

Lewis, C. S. *Studies in Words* (Cambridge, MA: Cambridge University Press, 1960).

Litman, Alexander. "Cicero's Doctrine of Nature and Man" (PhD diss., Columbia University, 1930).

Louisell, David W. "Euthanasia and Biathanasia: On Dying and Killing," *Catholic University Law Review* 22 (1973): 725.

MacIntyre, Alasdair. *After Virtue: A Study in Moral Theory*, 3rd ed. (South Bend, IN: University of Notre Dame Press, 2007).

MacIntyre, Alasdair. *Whose Justice? Whose Rationality?* (South Bend, IN: University of Notre Dame Press, 1988).

Maritain, Raissa. *St Thomas Aquinas: Angel of the Schools* (New York: Longmans, Green, 1942).

Mather, Henry. "Natural Law and Right Answers," *The American Journal of Jurisprudence* 38 (1993): 334.

McCormick, John F. *Scholastic Metaphysics, Part 2: Natural Theology* (Chicago, IL: Loyola University Press).

McInerny, Ralph M. *Ethica Thomistica: The Moral Philosophy of Thomas Aquinas* (Washington, DC: Catholic University of American Press, 1982).

McInerny, Ralph M. *St. Thomas Aquinas* (Notre Dame: University of Notre Dame Press, 1982).

McNabb, Vincent. *St. Thomas Aquinas and Law* (London: Blackfriars, 1955).

Messner, J. *Social Ethics: Natural Law in the Modern World*, translated by J. J. Doherty (St. Louis, MO: B. Herder, 1952).

Mitchell, Thomas N. *Cicero: The Senior Statesman* (New Haven, CT: Yale University Press, 1991).

Mullady, Brian T. "The Meaning of the Term 'Moral' in St. Thomas Aquinas," in *Studi Thomistica*, vol. 27 (Vatican City: Libreria Editric Vaticana, 1986).

Murphy, Cornelius F. "Distributive Justice, Modern Significance," *American Journal of Jurisprudence* 17 (1972): 157.

Myers, Nancy. "Cicero's Trumpet: Roman Women and the Second Phillipic," *Rhetoric Review* 22 (2003): 347.

Nelson, Daniel. *The Priority of Prudence* (University Park, PA: Pennsylvania State University Press, 1992).

Nemeth, Charles P. *Aquinas and Martin Luther King: A Discourse on Civil Disobedience* (South Bend, IN: St. Augustine's Press, 2010).

Nemeth, Charles P. *Aquinas in the Courtroom* (Westport, CT: Praeger and Greenwood Press, 2001).

Nemeth, Charles P. *Aquinas on Crime* (South Bend, IN: St. Augustine's Press, 2009).

Nemeth, Charles P. *Criminal Law*, 2nd ed. (Boston, MA: Taylor and Francis, 2012).

O'Donoghue, Noel Dermot. "The Law Beyond the Law," *The American Journal of Jurisprudence* 18 (1973): 158.

Osterle, John J. *St. Thomas Aquinas: Treatise on the Virtues* (South Bend, IN: University of Notre Dame Press, 1984).

Pegis, Anton C. *An Introduction to St. Thomas* (New York: The Modern Library, 1948).

Plato. *The Laws of Plato*, edited by Thomas L. Pangle (New York: Basic Books, 1980).

Pope Benedict XV. *Encyclical Fausto appetente die*, AAS 13 (June 29, 1921): 332.

Pope Pius XI. *Encyclical Studiorum Ducem*, AAS 15 (June 29, 1923): §11.

Porter, Jean. *Nature as Reason: A Thomistic Theory of the Natural Law* (Grand Rapids, MI: William B. Eerdmans, 2004).

Porter, Jean. "Reason, Nature, Natural Law in Medieval Accounts of the Natural Law," *The Journal of Religious Ethics* 24 (1996): 208.

Rand, E. K. *Cicero in the Courtroom of St. Thomas Aquinas* (Milwaukee, WI: Marquette University Press, 1946).

Ravid, Helen Philos. "The Pro-Life/Pro-Choice Argument as Sociocultural Symbolism: A Sociology of Knowledge Study" (PhD diss., Wayne State University, 2008).

Rice, Charles E. "Some Reasons for a Restoration of Natural Law Jurisprudence," *Wake Forest Law Review* 24 (1989): 539.

Rickaby, Joseph. *Aquinas Ethicus: The Moral Teaching of St. Thomas* (London: Burnes and Oates, 1892).

Robinson, Carol. *My Life with Thomas Aquinas* (Kansas City, MO: Angelus Press, 1992).

Rommen, Heinrich. *The Natural Law: A Study in Legal and Social History*, translated by T. Hanley (St. Louis, MO: B. Herder, 1948).

Rubin, Edwin. "Assisted Suicide, Morality, and Law: Why Prohibiting Assisted Suicide Violates the Establishment Clause," *Vanderbilt Law Review* 63 (2010): 772.

Ryan, F. X. "The Lex Scantinia and the Prosecution of Censors and Aediles," *Classical Philology* 89 (April, 1994): 159.

Schall, James V. "The Natural Law Bibliography," *American Journal of Jurisprudence* 40 (1995): 168.

Seagrave, S. Adam. "Cicero, Aquinas and Contemporary Issues in Natural Law Theory," *Review of Metaphysics* 62 (2009): 491.

Shaw, D. M. "Euthanasia and Eudaimonia," *Journal of Medical Ethics* 35 (2009): 530–533.

Shelton, Jo-Ann. *As the Romans Did: A Sourcebook in Roman Social History*, 2nd ed. (New York: Oxford University Press, 1998).

Shuster, George N. *St Thomas Aquinas* (New York: Heritage Press, 1971).

Skok, Charles D. *Prudent Civil Legislation According to St. Thomas and Some Controversial American Law* (Rome: Catholic Book Agency, 1967).

Smith, Barry F. "Of Truth and Certainty in the Law: Reflections on the Legal Method," *The American Journal of Jurisprudence* 30 (1985): 119.

Stump, Eleanor. *Aquinas* (Boston, MA: Routledge Press, 2003).

Sullivan, Daniel J. *An Introduction to Philosophy: The Perennial Principles of Classical Realist Tradition* (Rockford, IL: Jan Books, 1992).

Tierney, Brian. *The Idea of Natural Rights: Studies on Natural Rights, Natural Law and Church Law* (Atlanta, GA: Scholars Press, 1998).

Van Hooff, Anton J. L. "Ancient Euthanasia: 'Good Death' and the Doctor in the Graeco-Roman World," *Social Science and Medicine* 58 (2004): 982.

de Vitoria, Francisco. *On Homicide and Commentary on Summa Theologiae Q.* 64, translated by John P. Doyle (Milwaukee, WI: Marquette University Press, 1997).

Volokh, Eugene. "Same-Sex Marriage and Slippery Slopes," *Hofstra Law Review* 33 (2006): 101–147, http://www2.law.ucla.edu/volokh/marriage.pdf.

Weisheipl, James. *Friar Thomas D'Aquino: His Life, Thought, and Work*, 1st ed. (Garden City, NY: Doubleday, 1974).

West, Thomas G. "Cicero's Teaching on Natural Law," *St. John's Review* 32 (1981): 76.

Wilkinson, L. P. *Letters of Cicero: A Selection in Translation* (New York: W. W. Norton, 1968).

Williams, Craig A. "Greek Love at Rome," *The Classical Quarterly* 45 (1995): 517–539.

Williams, Craig A. *Roman Homosexuality: Ideologies of Masculinity in Classical Antiquity* (Oxford: Oxford University Press, 1999).

Wilson, S. J. *The Thought of Cicero* (London: G. Bell, 1964).

Wippel, John F. "Thomas Aquinas and the Condemnation of 1277," *The Modern Schoolman* 72 (January/March 1995): 233–272.

Wolfe, Christopher. *Natural Law Liberalism* (Cambridge, MA: Cambridge University Press, 2006).

Yartz, Frank J. "Order and Right Reason in Aquinas' Ethics," *Medieval Studies* 27 (1975): 407.

Index